BIBLIOGRAP
CLASSIFICATION

CW01619775

History and Foundations of Information Science

Edited by Michael Buckland, Jonathan Furner, and Markus Krajewski

Human Information Retrieval by Julian Warner

Good Faith Collaboration: The Culture of Wikipedia by Joseph Michael Reagle Jr.

Paper Machines: About Cards & Catalogs, 1548–1929 by Markus Krajewski, translated by Peter Krapp

Information and Intrigue: From Index Cards to Dewey Decimals to Alger Hiss by Colin B. Burke

Indexing It All: The Subject in the Age of Documentation, Information, and Data by Ronald E. Day

Bibliometrics and Research Evaluation: The Good, the Bad, and the Ugly by Yves Gingras

Search Foundations: Toward a Science of Technology-Mediated Experience by Sachi Arafat and Elham Ashoori

The Information Manifold: Why Computers Can't Solve Algorithmic Bias and Fake News by Antonio Badia

Documentarity: Evidence, Ontology, and Inscription by Ronald E. Day

The Infographic: A History of Data Graphics in News and Communications by Murray Dick

The Typographic Medium by Kate Brideau

Power of Position: Classification and the Biodiversity Sciences by Robert D. Montoya

Picture-Work: How Libraries, Museums, and Stock Agencies Launched a New Image Economy by Diana Kamin

Cats, Carpenters, and Accountants: Bibliographical Foundations of Information Science by Wayne de Fremery

Interception: State Surveillance from Postal Systems to Global Networks by Bernard Keenan

Bibliographic Classification: From Mimetic Representation to Isomorphic Documentality by Joacim Hansson

BIBLIOGRAPHIC CLASSIFICATION

FROM MIMETIC REPRESENTATION TO ISOMORPHIC DOCUMENTALITY

JOACIM HANSSON

THE MIT PRESS CAMBRIDGE, MASSACHUSETTS LONDON, ENGLAND

The MIT Press
Massachusetts Institute of Technology
77 Massachusetts Avenue, Cambridge, MA 02139
mitpress.mit.edu

© 2025 Massachusetts Institute of Technology

This work is subject to a Creative Commons CC-BY-NC-ND license.

This license applies only to the work in full and not to any components included with permission. Subject to such license, all rights are reserved. No part of this book may be used to train artificial intelligence systems without permission in writing from the MIT Press.

BY-NC-ND

The MIT Press would like to thank the anonymous peer reviewers who provided comments on drafts of this book. The generous work of academic experts is essential for establishing the authority and quality of our publications. We acknowledge with gratitude the contributions of these otherwise uncredited readers.

This book was set in Stone Sans and Stone Serif by Westchester Publishing Services. Printed and bound in the United States of America.

Library of Congress Cataloging-in-Publication Data

Names: Hansson, Joacim, 1966– author
Title: Bibliographic classification : from mimetic representation to
isomorphic documentality / Joacim Hansson.
Description: Cambridge, Massachusetts : The MIT Press, 2025. |
Series: History and foundations of information science | Includes
bibliographical references and index.
Identifiers: LCCN 2025000332 (print) | LCCN 2025000333 (ebook) |
ISBN 9780262553490 paperback | ISBN 9780262384865 epub |
ISBN 9780262384872 pdf
Subjects: LCSH: Classification—Books—Social aspects | Libraries and society
Classification: LCC Z696.A4 H37 2025 (print) | LCC Z696.A4 (ebook) |
DDC 025.4/2—dc23/eng/20250512
LC record available at https://lccn.loc.gov/2025000332
LC ebook record available at https://lccn.loc.gov/2025000333

EU Authorised Representative: Easy Access System Europe, Mustamäe tee 50, 10621 Tallinn, Estonia | Email: gpsr.requests@easproject.com

For Lotta,
with deep love and gratitude

CONTENTS

ACKNOWLEDGMENTS ix

1 AN INTRODUCTION IN TWO PARTS 1
2 CLASSIFICATION SYSTEMS AS (SOCIAL) DOCUMENTS 21
3 QUESTIONING REPRESENTATION: A BRIEF NOTE ON METHODOLOGY 43
4 UNIVERSAL KNOWLEDGE, UNIVERSAL LANGUAGE: PAUL OTLET AND THE UNIVERSAL DECIMAL CLASSIFICATION FOR ESPERANTO 61
5 NATIONALISM AND DEMOCRACY: PUBLIC LIBRARIES AND BIBLIOGRAPHIC CLASSIFICATION IN EARLY TWENTIETH-CENTURY SWEDEN 87
6 BIBLIOGRAPHIC CLASSIFICATION IN JEWISH CULTURE AND THE PROBLEM OF THE HOLOCAUST 123
7 THE MIMETIC AND THE ISOMORPHIC 151

NOTES 163
BIBLIOGRAPHY, INCLUDING ANALYZED CLASSIFICATION SYSTEMS 185
INDEX 201

ACKNOWLEDGMENTS

I have visited and revisited the themes and problems addressed in this book on and off over many years. During this time, I have been allowed to call upon the attention of esteemed colleagues around the world in talks, seminars, and conference presentations. Some of these have provided me with insights so important and well formulated that I can easily say that without them, this book would not be able to exist.

I would especially like to thank the entire Document Academy (DOCAM) community for its continuous discussions on document theory. I have attended the DOCAM annual meetings on a regular basis for more than twenty years, and I consider this to be my intellectual home. I cannot mention everyone, but my encounters there with Niels Windfeld Lund, Michael Buckland, Kiersten Latham, Roswitha Skare, Geir Grenersen, Ronald Day, Carol Choksy, Tim Gorichanaz, Jodi Kearns, Marc Kosciejew, and Brian O'Connor have extended discussions way beyond the academic into the realms of life itself.

I am grateful to spend my working weeks within the fruitful academic environment of the Department of Cultural Sciences at Linnaeus University in Växjö, Sweden. The exchange of ideas, and the daily struggles of academia, with my Library and Information Science colleagues has meant a great deal to me, and still does.

I am deeply grateful to Ronald Day, Koraljka Golub, Mats Dahlström, and Christa Shusko who all took time from their intense schedules to read, correct, and comment on the manuscript of this book. Their accomplished insights helped improve the text immensely. Benjamin Felon has provided valuable advice on my translations from French to English in chapters 3 and 4.

Michael Buckland, Jonathan Furner, and Markus Krajewski have, in their roles as series editors, been encouraging ever since the first proposal was submitted to the History and Foundation of Information Science imprint a few years back. It has been important to feel their trust in this project. I am also grateful to my editor at the MIT Press, Gita Manaktala, for her continuous instruction and support throughout the process of creating this book.

And finally, my family, for giving me a reason to get out of bed each morning.

Uråsa, February 2025,
Joacim Hansson

1

AN INTRODUCTION IN TWO PARTS

PART ONE: WHAT THIS BOOK IS ABOUT

This book is about documents. More precisely, it is about a very specific kind of document, bibliographic classification systems. As bibliographic classification systems are at the core of libraries, it also a book about libraries. Libraries are parts of the institutional fabric of society. Thus, it is a book about society, and even the dream of a different society. Most of all, it is a book about how all these things connect to each other. A bibliographic classification system is a tool for organizing documents by means of their content in library catalogs or bibliographies. In some libraries, classification systems do not organize their holdings in accordance with content, but with size, color, type of binding, or thickness of the books in specific collections. I will not concern myself with those kinds of classifications. Instead, I am interested in classification systems meant to organize not particular collections but general knowledge categories transformed into subject divisions for library use. However, it is not the transformation as such that takes center stage, interesting as it is. There is a vast literature on classification systems and their role in the information or knowledge retrieval process, and indeed some of it will occur throughout the pages of this book. What instead interests me here, however, is something more elusive—the relation between how knowledge is transformed into subject divisions as part of the wider development of society. I will consider the formulation of the social dimension of classification in that the basic proposition of this book is that there does exist a connection between the classification system as a document, its institutional context, and the progress of distinct social processes that provides documentary agency to the classification system that reaches beyond pure knowledge representation and acquires social significance to these systems *as documents*. This is what will be talked about as the *documentality* of classification systems. I will engage in debate with previous scholarly attempts to capture these relations, not least from a methodological perspective, with the conviction that, thus far, something has been lacking in the overall understanding of the complexity in the relation between classification and its social environments. One basic question will guide this study:

How do bibliographic classification systems, seen as autonomous documents, (re)present social and cultural norms, values and processes beyond their immediate use as information retrieval tools?

This book is an attempt to further a cross-disciplinary discussion at the intersection between information science, document studies, sociology, and cultural studies because the more perspectives we may take on these complex relations and processes, the better prepared we become in the construction and development of new knowledge organization systems governed by today's social, cultural, and technological conditions.[1] Contemporary bibliographic development favors indexing systems, automated classification, and full text retrieval, and now increasingly artificial intelligence solutions. Still, problems of bias and the reverberation of current norms and values within the hierarchies and relations between index terms and word captures remain more or less the same; what has changed is basically form and retrieval technology.

The analysis will cover classification systems constructed during a limited period of time, approximately between 1870 and 1960. On occasion I will allow myself to go outside of this period, but not for long. The reason is that during this period we find specific kinds of classification systems that, due to the unprecedented increase of scientific documentation from the late eighteenth century and on, cover more subjects combined in more structural detail than in any period before in history. These systems are part of the modern project, sharing the ambition of so many institutions, bureaucracies, and industries to renew, rationalize, and adhere to an idea of social progress. Also, in their attempt to cover "everything," established ideals, values, and collective identities are reproduced in order to make the systems comprehensible in their practical bibliographic applications. For them to function, librarians and, eventually, library users must recognize and accept their underlying logic. This lends them a certain kind of conservatism, usually aligned with institutional norms and practices in professional librarianship. Herein lies a conflict, for modernity is all about change, professionalization, and creating new standards against which progress can be measured. This conflict between structural conservatism and content-oriented progression is never far away in classification practice. I will point to several such examples throughout this book.

Even if the construction of modern universal classification systems is more or less limited to the period covered in this study, libraries have had their shelves and catalogs arranged by subject divisions for as long as we have had them—about five thousand years.[2] For most of this time, however, divisions were rudimentary and generic, depending on individual collections of books and other documents, frequently left to the interests of individual librarians or archivists. More often than not, they were difficult to use, both as systems for knowledge representation and as practical tools for librarians. Sometimes, classification systems were based on premises that made sense as philosophical divisions of knowledge. However, most of them eventually proved poorly suited for bibliographical practice. One such example is the Aristotelian division of pure and applied sciences that was widely used as a basis for libraries in European Christian monasteries and Jewish yeshivot through the medieval period up until the seventeenth century.[3] In libraries and bibliographies, the Aristotelian division over time developed into locally adapted constructions of a philosophically comprehensible system, albeit ill-suited for library practice.

Ever since antiquity, library catalogs and bibliographies have been organized into a brief number of wide areas of knowledge wherein titles are arranged in alphabetical lists either by title or, as conventions altered, author. These main subject fields correspond, for the most part, to contemporary main divisions in higher educational institutions. It is not until the scientific revolution, gradually developing during the sixteenth and seventeenth centuries, that we see a change also in classificatory practice. From a bibliographical point of view, what influences this development is a complex fabric of:

1. the rapid emergence of print culture and with that, new conventions for structural elements in documents such as title pages, indexes, and colophons;
2. the unprecedented expansion of scholarly disciplines, due in part to new ways of thinking about scientific method with the emergence of new tools such as telescopes and microscopes, and not least, the scientific article as the privileged way of reporting results; and
3. the ability for researchers to travel on empirical quests in colonial territories taken by European régimes, often romantically contextualizing the scholar as explorer, accountant, describer, and classifier of natural phenomena, plants, and animals.[4]

In 1545, Swiss polymath Konrad Gesner published the *Bibliotheca Universalis*, arguably the first "universal" bibliography of modernity. This was followed in 1548 by *Pandectae*, an addendum with a systematized index of the entries in *Bibliotheca*, containing a classification system that came to both gain contemporary recognition and exert a widespread influence on bibliographic practice for decades to come.[5] Gesner differed from his contemporaries—there were quite a few ambulating bibliographers recording the holdings of libraries in central Europe at this time—in his ambition to cover "everything" without regard to the inherent quality of individual works. He had no moral or otherwise content-related interest. Instead, he was purely bibliographical in his approach, describing books and other documents, giving indication of their placement in different libraries, and making the entries in his vast bibliography of some three thousand authors and ten thousand works searchable through the systematic index of the *Pandectae*, divided into twenty-one main subjects[6]:

1. Grammatica
2. Dialectica
3. Rhetorica
4. Poetica

12. Divinatio et Magica
13. Artes Literates
14. Physica
15. Metaphysica

5. Arithmetica
6. Geometrica
7. Musica
8. Astronomica
9. Astrologica
10. Historica
11. Geographia
16. Ethica
17. Oeconomia
18. Politica
19. Juriprudentia
20. Medicina
21. Theologica

Gesner's division brought with it two elements from older established classifications: (1) the first eight categories reflect the interpretation of the Aristoteleian *Trivium et Quadrivium*, prevalent in medieval monastery libraries (poetica is, however, an exception that is inserted as a kind of early humanist marker), and (2) the last three categories, law, medicine, and theology, were kept separate in the system as being regarded as more basic and undividable than the rest. The fact that *Bibliotheca Universalis* described books without any other discrimination than language—the ambition was to cover all existing books in Latin, Greek, and Hebrew—gave reason to formulate for instance astrology beside astronomy, and to include a category on magic and divination, all popular subjects on which numerous books were produced. Here we are thus not dealing with a scientific division, but one that relates to actual existing books written about issues that concerned the contemporary erudite reader.

During the decades after *Bibliotheca Universalis*, there was an increase in the number of bibliographies, and eventually, as printshops and publishers were established in the wake of the new print-based book culture, new forms and uses appeared. One of the most important forms was the sales catalog that in the late sixteenth and early seventeenth centuries developed its own conventions, partly based on Gesner's bibliographical principles and the practice it postulated.[7] As time passed, the divisions in sales catalogs and bookshop organization made their way into librarianship and library classification as well. One such example is found in the manifest *Advis pour dresser une bibliothèque* by Gabriel Naudé, published in Paris in two editions: 1627 and 1644. *Advis* is perhaps not mainly reputed for its argumentation concerning classification systems and bibliographical practices. Instead, it is famous for its formulation of the librarian as a professional, for the principle of arms-length distance from the patronage (i.e., the librarian decides what is best for the library, while the role of the owner is to provide space and funding), for its advice on how to create functional rooms for reading, and for its opposition to the vanity of contemporary Baroque libraries. In Naudé's library, content was more important than form, and cheap books and pamphlets from the streets of Paris had their place beside lavish bindings and exclusive editions.[8] His suggestion on how to order the books in a library did not in itself make any claim to originality, but instead pragmatic simplicity: "Le meilleur est tousjours celuy qui est le plus facile, le moins intrigué, le plus naturel, usité."[9] Naudé compared a library classification that cannot be easily used to an author who does not want to be read and who does not interest his practical senses. Therefore, he advocated a classification that has its value not in its philosophical capacity but in its request-oriented representational ability—this is a classification that left the scholastic and the Aristotelian era behind and aligned itself to the capitalist principles of Paris booksellers[10]:

Theology,
Medicine,
Law,
History,
Philosophy,
Mathematics,
Humanities,
Miscellaneous.

It is, however, not the pragmatism of this simple order that in itself is interesting, but rather that Naudé made three maneuvers that together represented advanced classificatory development:

1. Putting the scholastic era behind, theology is treated as any other subject and not, as in Gesner's system, set apart from secular subjects.
2. By proposing the idea of having just a few main categories that open up for locally adapted subdivisions, he created a useful classification suited for individual libraries and yet connected to an intuitive common order. The best example of this is perhaps the *humanities* [*humanitez*] section, which at the time was a new subject category with a possibly large variety of content.

3. He dismissed philosophical orders while instead introducing a user perspective. In this, he emphasized the prerogative of the professional librarian and even suggested the modern idea of open shelves in public libraries, which would place the system in the pragmatic genealogy of Dewey's library system 250 years later, in 1876.

Dewey's pragmatism is, however, of a somewhat different sort, as I will return to later. Still, there was little development in Western library classification in the long period between Naudé and Dewey. That is not to say that there was any shortage of classification systems, but rather there was not much essential progress, and what did change during that time was connected to specific libraries and collections, without claims to any general applicability. The advent of Melvil Dewey brings me to the period that will form the background of the empirical analysis in this book. Therefore, this is a good place to briefly go through the structure and content of its chapters.

THE STRUCTURE OF THIS BOOK

I will address my basic question by looking at three classificatory environments that will complement each other by highlighting a variety of aspects of social significances displayed in the bibliographic classification systems discussed. As already mentioned, all three analyses begin in the second half of the nineteenth century. As time moves into the twentieth, the world of bibliography and librarianship is brimming with life. Much of what happens is brought on by changes in social organization, visions of social and national development, and revision of cultural self-understanding among both nations and groups of people. Libraries and librarianship are also in many ways parts of these processes and contribute actively by creating access to information and culture in local public libraries, and to the world of science in university libraries. Librarianship is subjected to a process of professionalization that develops in two directions: (1) the implementation of new professional standards in both public and academic librarianship, and (2) the creation of information retrieval systems for the storage and dissemination of masses of research documentation in university libraries. Both these avenues of practice lead to new thinking about classification. The ground note is the will to connect users with ever-growing numbers of documents paired with often very specific social visions. The case studies will be preceded by two chapters outlining the theoretical and methodological frameworks used for the analysis.

Chapter 2 discusses classification systems as documents with a thorough discussion on concepts such as document, documentary agency, and documentality and combines these with classification theory relevant for an advanced understanding of the social and cultural dimensions of classification systems.

Chapter 3 proceeds with a brief discussion on methodology, arguing for the value of a hermeneutic approach dealing with the tension between mimetic representation and isomorphic change. In this discussion, I initiate a conversation between, on the one hand, a discussion on hermeneutics both as research and knowledge organization practice in information science, and on the other hand, the formulation of institutional isomorphic change processes within the New Institutionalist School in organizational studies.

Chapter 4, the first case study, situates us in 1905 as Paul Otlet publishes the *Manuel abrégé du répertoire bibligraphique universel*[11] in Brussels as part of an internationalist vision that comprised, among other things, plans for a World City and a standardized information landscape that should be universally available through effective means of information retrieval. Today, this vision is hailed as being one of the first precursors of what eventually became the internet, at least in its original form embodying the ideals of free, universal, and intelligent exchange of information. The *Manuel* stood out as a singular contribution to this vision taking on a life of its own, rapidly growing into an elaborate analytic-synthetic classification system, the *Universal Decimal Classification* (UDC). Today the UDC is translated into more than forty languages and used to organize millions of physical and digital documents in libraries and special collections all over the world.

In chapter 5, the second case takes place in nationalist currents of the early twentieth century, in many ways the opposite of the progressive internationalist environment that gave us the UDC; in 1911, Swedish public library pioneer Valfrid Palmgren presented a government report mapping a vision of a unified Swedish library system, with publicly funded local libraries forming part of the bedrock for a development toward what would eventually become a democratic system of governance and the Swedish welfare state.[12] The report was only partly accepted, but state funding for a national library infrastructure was initiated. As part of this institutionalization, a librarian at Malmö Workers' Library, Frithiof Berlin, suggested in a formal request to the Swedish Library Association at its annual meeting in 1917 that there was a need for a unified national classification system, connecting libraries across the country and facilitating bibliographic development and collaboration. The request resulted in the 1921 publication of the *Klassifikationssystem för svenska bibliotek* (the SAB system)[13] and its immediate implementation, organizing subjects in line with new institutional and administrative structures and political priorities of the emerging Swedish democracy. The system eventually became a cherished part of the Swedish library system, with schoolchildren as well as senior library users knowing it almost by heart. It was in use until 2011, when the National Library of Sweden replaced it with the Dewey decimal system. Times had changed. Technology, globalization, new terms and conditions for the publication industry, and diversified user patterns required different kinds of legitimacy for library services and bibliographical tools.

Chapter 6 presents the third case study. This one differs from the first two in that it covers a significantly wider and more complex set of classifications, both in terms of cultural context, social progress, time span, and geographical distribution. At the center of interest is the development of Jewish library classification systems as they gradually became tools for ethnic identification through new ways of organizing Judaica on terms set by *Jewish* librarians and bibliographers. After a brief historical exposition, the chapter lands in 1906, as Abraham Solomon Freidus publishes a classification system for the expanding Judaica collection at New York Public Library.[14] Previous subject divisions concerning Judaism were deemed insufficient in their ability to cover the complexities of Jewish culture and literature production at the verge of the twentieth century. Based on a cultural self-understanding that grew out of the European Wissenschaft des judentums movement during the previous century,[15] Freidus created a structure of a world of knowledge, connecting Jewish identity, heritage, remembrance, and practice to a non-Jewish library environment of increasing complexity and diversity. His system was followed by several others such as that of Gershom Scholem, a famous German intellectual and friend of Walter Benjamin. The Scholem system was created for the University Library of Jerusalem in the 1920s and bore significant traces of Scholem's own view of Jewish history, colored by his deep knowledge of Jewish mysticism. After World War II, the Jewish experience of the Holocaust necessarily shaped Jewish experience and thus Jewish classification. The heritage from Freidus was picked up by Judaica librarianship in the form of Mae Weine's classification, aimed for primarily Jewish school and yeshiva libraries built as an explicit expansion of the Dewey decimal classification, and in the controversial classification system by brothers David and Daniel Elazar. The Elazar system proposed a completely alternative nonhierarchical way of structuring Jewish identity as a cut path from the Torah to the modern state of Israel, relating it to the American Zionist movement that took shape during the 1950s. All of these efforts not only sought new ways of creating full bibliographic access to the growing body of Judaica but also formulate a common Jewish experience that could hold new cultural conditions where, at least in the western hemisphere, Jews were more and more integrated into modern society while at the same time subjected to an annihilating assault on a scale that redefined the very foundation of international Jewry's place in the world.

Chapter 7 brings all previous chapters together in a discussion that aims to advance our understanding of bibliographic classification systems as autonomous social documents and their relation to overarching social and cultural change processes.

PART TWO: WARRANTS AND CULTURE: PERSPECTIVES ON CLASSIFICATION

In addressing bibliographic classification, I will not so much focus on the classificatory process as such. Nor is it the librarians or scholars making use of a specific classification scheme for the benefit of information retrieval that is at the center of interest. Instead, what interest me are the systems themselves, seen and defined as documents both in the sense of individual documents (*The* classification system) and as parts of a larger documentary collectives (i.e., classification systems based on decimal divisions) wherein the individual documents share certain syntactical and semantical elements, principles of synthesis, and other properties that relate them to each other and shape them into a certain category.

As a category, or genre, classification systems reflect various contextual processes and movements of which they are parts, but, and that is a key point in this book, not only that. They contribute and rewrite these processes and movements. They are not only a result of change and development; they are part of the documentary structure making change possible. To formulate how this contribution is manifested, we need to find new ways of addressing classification systems as socially defined documents. In a famous paper titled "Classifications as Cultural Artefacts," French classification theorist Eric de Grolier sketches a development of bibliographic classification systems, showing how they first and foremost relate to the development of knowledge in the form of written texts. Systems relate directly to the emergence of new subjects in literature over time. This is what is called *literary warrant*. However, as de Grolier concludes his article, he states the following: "There is a kind of hysteresis effect: most classifications reflect an anterior pattern of publications; some of them, on the contrary, appear to be in advance, anticipating future trends."[16] He does not continue to analyze the properties of the classification systems that contribute to this presumed ability, and, to be fair, it is not the intention of his paper. It is, however, this ability to anticipate, to function actively and not just reactively—the hysteresis effect on one or several defined external factors—that is at the core of this book: that is, to find and suggest one such alternative route to the understanding of the role and function of bibliographic classification systems.

The relation between a document and the social and cultural environment in which it is to carry meaning is complex. To find a way to describe and analyze this relation, there are several things that need to be considered. One question of concern is what a document actually is. Another is: What property of a document should be given priority—form or content? One also needs to ask about the context: Does the document relate to specific practices or institutional settings, and is it possible to identify what might be called *cultural elements*, placing a document or a certain type of document in a delimited temporal period or geographic area? A third issue that need to be considered is the arguably more complicated question of whether a document in a certain context is a passive, or reactive, representation of its surrounding conditions or whether it instead has a presentational ability to influence its social and cultural environment in ways that would not have occurred if that very document or type of document would not have existed. The answers to these questions will unavoidably vary depending on what kind of document and documentary processes we are looking at, and what kind of contexts we find them in.

A bibliographic classification system is not just any classification system. Its purpose is to facilitate information or knowledge retrieval from collections of documents based on content analysis of each individual document in the collection. The most famous version of this is the library classification system, which forms the basis for organizing books and other materials by content in any given kind of library so that librarians and users may find what they are looking for. These systems may be general, covering all kinds of subjects, and they may be highly specialized, relating to specific contents within the collections of a special library. Another kind of bibliographic classification system is that which forms the principle of organization by subject in a bibliography—that is, a list of document representations relating to certain properties such as, for instance, ownership (private collections, public libraries), language, institutional category (books in monastery libraries), or period of time (books on the French Revolution from the 1790s). The common denominator of all bibliographic classification systems is the organization of documents or document representations through the *subject description of content* intended for direct or indirect retrieval or allocation. The retrieval aspect is crucial to understand when discussing the relation between these systems and their social and cultural environments. It is important not to read them as philosophical systems organizing human knowledge for its own sake. Such classifications exist in great numbers and have played a huge role in our understanding of the world around us, and a few have exerted influence on the construction of bibliographic systems as well. The two perhaps most important in this context are the tripartite classification of knowledge by Aristotle in *Episteme*, *Techné*, and *Phronesis*, and the equally tripartite division of knowledge by Francis Bacon, developed in the early seventeenth century, correlating knowledge to the mental categories *Reason*, *Imagination*, and *Memory*.[17] These will prove important as connections between the retrieval function and a more general consciousness about knowledge in the development of bibliographical classifications. In this present book, the term *classification system* will be used to denote bibliographical systems, and I will make no distinction between those used for libraries and bibliographies, except when noted.

Classification systems are only rarely seen and treated as autonomous documents with inherent value. Instead, they are regarded as the result of the need to organize and retrieve individual documents or sets of documents in larger collections. Still, while maintaining this primary function, they are developed in accordance with one or several principles, labeled *warrants*. Claire Beghtol distinguishes five such warrants for bibliographic systems[18]:

- literary warrant;
- scientific/philosophical warrant;
- educational warrant;
- institutional warrant; and
- cultural warrant.

I will return to several of these later, but I want to comment on them already at this early stage, as they are important for my ability to answer the basic question of this book. Indeed, they are vital for the entire understanding of current knowledge of classification, both in terms of practice and in terms of the structural elements that give classification systems their highly specialized syntactical character as documents. The warrants identified by Beghtol represent points of departure relevant for the construction of a classification system. In literary warrant, the production of literature and the emergence of new subjects provide guiding principles for, not least, the possibilities to expand the classification systems.[19] Scientific, philosophical, and educational warrants all relate to knowledge development not directly in terms of literature production, but through the organization of disciplines in higher educational institutions. As the division in faculties, departments, and subjects that is still with us today was established in European universities in the aftermath of the Enlightenment movement during the early nineteenth century, it is possible to argue that the most intuitive subject division in university libraries is that of the faculties, and the literature used within their educational programs. The widest warrant is cultural, where the social, cultural, and political environment of the classification system is allowed to influence the structure of hierarchies and options for synthesis within various subjects.[20]

Regardless of preferred warrant, the role of documents in classification theory is that of objects for classification practice, meaning that which is to be classified. Elaine Svenonius has defined documents in this role as "information-bearing messages in recorded form."[21] A document in this sense is either individual or part of a larger set (for example, an article in a journal). Such sets are of importance in constructing or understanding a classification relating to a specific collection or library. Documents that are parts of sets need to have the possibility of being colocated, if not physically then at least in catalogs. Svenonius gives priority to five such document sets as being particularly important for classification as a tool for document and knowledge retrieval[22]:

- all documents sharing essentially the same information (work)
- all documents sharing the same information (edition)
- all documents descended from a common origin (superwork)
- all documents by a given author
- all documents on a given subject

All these sets of documents are crucial for bibliographic analysis and organization, and Svenonius's sophisticated discussion proves that the correspondence between the structural elements in a classification system and the bibliographic organization, both in terms of representation and physical arrangements, is highly complex.[23] The choice of warrant is therefore crucial.

The warrants identified by Begthol are not mutually exclusive. Placing them on a scale from the most specific (literary) to the most general (cultural), there is a gradually increased distance between the classified collection, or set of documents, and the classification system itself. In its most ideal sense, the system built on literary warrant provides an overview of the classified collection that is an exact representation of its contents. It is a situation close to the relational organization of a thesaurus, structuring indexing terms. This does not, however, guarantee "correct" subject descriptions or that the structure of the system does not represent biased choices of terminology or placements of subjects within its hierarchical structure. The only thing it signals is that whatever subject is represented in the system is also represented in the collection on which the system is built. With literary warrant, the classification system is a vessel connecting the interiors of the collection to the information needs of the user. Moving through the other kinds of warrant, the role of the classification system becomes gradually different and other kinds of complexities occur. The status of the system and the principles for classification it carries become more important as the connection to the individual collection or sets of documents becomes less pronounced. It is difficult to uphold boundaries between scientific, educational, and institutional warrants, as they all tend to combine with literary warrant—for instance in a university library, where an organization combining the actual holdings with the institutional structure becomes quite intuitive and easy to grasp for both students and researchers using the library for their designated purposes. Perhaps the most obvious example of this is the student course reference library, organized immediately after courses given on different levels by defined departments and schools. Still, the organization of a classification system based on the organization of the sciences reaches for something wider and more abstract, relating to the very ideas on how to organize knowledge, regardless of the ability to facilitate retrieval. There are ideas that influence classification that may not necessarily be represented in the holdings of a collection or the division of departments and schools in an individual university, but instead relate to more general categories of knowledge. Such categories are necessarily fluid and complex, and with the current development of cross-disciplinary subjects, they are increasingly prevalent. One such example is the emergence of the field of digital humanities, where numerous attempts have been made to place its practice at the crossroads of technology, social sciences, and the humanities in a more traditional understanding of disciplinary division. Does digital humanities constitute a new subject of its own, or should it be regarded as just a methodological development within the humanities, gradually implementing technological tools designed for digitally sustained analysis, for instance, in archaeology or linguistics? Whatever way we look at it, it has bearing on the construction of bibliographic classification that, depending on how digital humanities is treated, represents different ways of approaching the field and makes research within possible for retrieval. When rewriting and restructuring such a complex field into a bibliographic classification system, literary warrant is not enough, but ideas of how to treat academic tradition, new epistemology, and transdisciplinary development are important for providing stability and transparency to the system.[24]

The most general and complex warrant is the cultural. In an analysis of the relation between structure and meaning, Beghtol deepens our understanding, emphasizing that a classification system needs to be in line with a specific cultural identity, defined geopolitically, institutionally, or temporally in order to simply be useful and possible to implement in library practice.[25] Fairthorne speaks of this as a "classificatory landscape" that needs to be jointly recognizable by both the classifier and the user.[26] The metaphor of a landscape appears frequently in information science, most recently perhaps in Annemaree Lloyd's analyses of "information landscapes": the combination of tools (technical devices, information structures) and practices used by refugees to navigate their vulnerable and unpredictable present.[27] The structure of information needs to be recognizable, possible to understand, and able to be acted on in order to be meaningful. The same goes for classification systems—they need to fit expectations and they need to be perceived by users as structurally intuitive, with semantic relations between subjects and aspects of subjects conceived of as, at least, reasonable. The image of a classificatory landscape is appealing in many ways. It invites discovery, interpretation, and knowing that the classification system, just as a map, not only represents but *presents* an understanding of the topography, of the landscape, sufficient for its usability. The relation between the map and the territory further provides an incentive to move forward toward what Beghtol defines as one of the major areas still left to address: "Methods of detecting and comparing the overall cultural warrant of systems to each other."[28]

It has proven difficult to define just in what way cultural warrant presents itself within a classification system, and here the issue of methodology is crucial. The analysis of warrants and their impacts on various systems so far have implied that the relation between the systems and their environments is in one way or another mimetic, and this leaves cases of cultural warrant open for wide readings. In order not to devolve into a rhetoric of representation, where, for instance, ideology and bias are instrumentally reproduced in classificatory structures and terminological choice, there is a need to develop a discourse that takes aim at the agency of classification. The idea of cultural warrant provides opportunities for such a discourse through its seemingly unlimited scope. It also allows for a distancing from the pragmatic dimension of bibliographic classification. While literary and to a certain extent institutional and scientific warrants reduce the classification system to a tool in library practice, with its capacity to effectively document retrieval as the only important evaluation criteria, cultural warrant highlights the system as an autonomous entity, with syntactic solutions and semantic layers understood as wider than its (intended) use. The classification system emerges as a document with inherent social significance and value. Information science research that looks beyond the purely pragmatic and representational in bibliographic classification and directs its analytical powers to the system as a document is scarce. To understand what kind of document a classification system is, and how it relates to other forms of linguistic representation and agency, we need to look elsewhere. Concluding this introductory chapter, I will briefly point to one such theoretical environment that can help to not only create an understanding of what role classification may have but also formulate an absence that helps further the theoretical framework for classification systems as cultural artefacts. It creates an alternative reading on the documentality of classification systems that will prove valuable in the continued discussion.

In his famous study *The Domestication of the Savage Mind*,[29] social anthropologist Jack Goody addresses the much-discussed triad of *Langue* (rule-based, written language), *Parole* (spoken, natural language), and *Écriture* (writings without necessary inherent connection to spoken language), developed within French linguistics.[30] Goody's argument is that written language is best treated as a specific entity that may or may not function separately from the assumed relation between natural language—speech—and its more codified versions in formalized language, most of which are developed *a posteriori* to natural language use and development. Such an assumption is in many ways like those seen in contemporary information science concerning the intricate relation between standardization and natural language in automated classification.[31] Goody argues that written, or formalized, language is merely a representation of natural language (*parole*) and limits our understanding of the role and function of written and formalized linguistic constructs in social development (his focus being a largely historical perspective with exemplification from the development of the Sumerian cuneiform system of writing). Instead, he proposes a triangular model that distinguishes written and formal expressions (*écriture*) from standardized language in general (*langue*). Apart from the traditionally assumed relation between written and spoken language, he further assumes that "the re-ordering and refining of not only sentences, but of individual words. Morphemes can be removed from the body of the sentence, the flow of oral discourse, and set aside as isolated units capable of not simply being ordered within a sentence, but of being ordered outside this frame, where they appear in a very different and highly 'abstract' context."[32]

This "de-contextualization," as Goody calls it, can occur in many forms. For example, in Classical Chinese, the written form is almost completely separated from the language use of ordinary people.[33] It can also appear in the more immediately recognizable forms of lists and, as a development of such, classification systems.

Connecting the analysis of bibliographical classification systems to language construction and discourse development not taken from a primarily semiotic point of view, but an ethnographic and anthropological one, emphasizes them as cultural artefacts in a more pervasive way than that which is covered by cultural warrant. They are not only the results of cultural factors and influences but they are also active parts of a social and cultural reordering and contribute to social reproduction as well as to progress. This has important theoretical and methodological implications.[34]

The need for a developed methodology, as pointed out by Beghtol, can be met by applying modes of analysis from a range of perspectives within the humanities. Among these, hermeneutics is perhaps the most prominent. Adopting a more expansive view on the cultural identity of the classification system, both in terms of structural abstraction and semantic layers, it is possible to disconnect the system from its pragmatic aims, finding legitimacy through context, and then readdress the elements of pragmatism such as sufficient recognizability and the problem of bias. They may, in a third step, converge through a synthesis of social, cultural, and institutional perspectives defining the role of the classification. In that way it is possible to consider the tradition of bibliographic convention as an overall cultural agency.

Goody's work helps us to understand the cultural implications of defining lists and classification systems as examples of *écriture* to various degrees, separated from the flow of discourses in ordinary language. He points to them as constructed entities; they are arguably culturally significant. However, the almost archetypical character of the syntactical composition of a list is unaffected by its immediate context, and so this makes it difficult to ascribe a cultural value to them, at least in regard to popular literacy. And so, he addresses potential, not actual, agency. To address actual agency, one must add to this another discussion that in some cases verges on the French school of linguistics, but mostly finds its nourishment in completely different and often much more practical realms: the study of documents and documentation. Where ethnography, social anthropology, and linguistics can discuss classification systems, lists and other constructions outside of the representative relation between written and spoken language, we may come to a more complete cultural and institutional understanding of their agency by considering them as documents. There is of course a problem here: there is no complete agreement on what a document is.

In the next chapter I will discuss documents and how to understand classification systems as documents. Document theory is an emerging research field, and with its heritage building on the works of European documentation pioneers such as Paul Otlet and Suzanne Briet, contemporary documentation research will be used to gain a perspective not previously used in classification studies. The next chapter will also present brief examples of how bibliographic classification systems have been discussed as documents in early twentieth-century classification theory in an attempt to bring our understanding of documents and classification systems together into a discourse on which to further advance the basic argument of the book.

2

CLASSIFICATION SYSTEMS AS (SOCIAL) DOCUMENTS

Bibliographic classification systems are rarely seen as individual culturally significant entities outside of their use as retrieval tools for the subject-based identification, allocation, and retrieval of documents in libraries or bibliographies. To capture the ability to move beyond the presumed mimetic relation between context and system, it is essential to distance the system from its immediate use, only to later reinsert it in its functional context with a redefined documentary integrity. This is by no means an easy task, as the construction of a library classification system is, on the one hand, tightly connected to an institution or collection, but, on the other, constructed without a direct relation between form and content that could perhaps be expected given the well-defined processes against which its value is measured. In this chapter I will discuss established conceptions of classification, both as systems and practices, and place them in relation to theories on documents and documentation. The purpose of this is twofold: (1) to establish a working definition of a document designed to work as a basis for a developed understanding of classification systems as documents, and (2) to develop this understanding of classification systems as *social* documents, where the concept *documentality* is at the center of interest.

CLASSIFICATION SYSTEMS AND INFORMATION RETRIEVAL: A TOOL-ORIENTED PERSPECTIVE

Considering how classification systems are treated in current research literature as well as in classificatory practice, information science perspectives tend to converge into three main perspectives[1]:

1. A practical perspective, implying an abolition of documentary autonomy, as classification systems are seen to have no intrinsic value of their own, instead being in their entirety connected to, and depending on, their pragmatic information retrieval functionality.
2. A universalist perspective, where classification systems are deprived of extra-institutional contexts yet claiming, in one way or another, the ability to universally represent all subjects and disciplines.
3. A communication perspective, treating classification systems as horizons of interpretation or boundary objects between various poles of a communication process with, most commonly, the document collection on the one side of the specter, and the information user on the other. In this perspective, classification systems become vehicles for communication between classifier and user, and the system is seen as an intermediary tool in the process of individual information retrieval.

These perspectives are brought together in the functional definition of a "quality information retrieval system" provided by Koraljka Golub in her book *Subject Access to Information: An Interdisciplinary Approach*. A quality information retrieval system should, according to Golub, be able to "provide enough information about a resource in the form of a metadata record for the user to be able to decide whether to pursue it."[2] It is an intuitive definition, and it includes classification systems as parts of the retrieval process on either social or cognitive levels, depending on who the user or user group is. Golub distinguishes two major aspects of the process: formal (document description, cataloging, defining metadata) and subject-based (indexing, classification)—both being necessary for the ability to meet the definition. Classification or cataloging systems provide materiality to the retrieval process and are thus not defined as autonomous forms of documents or documentary constructs, but rather as processual particulars depending completely on the documents that are subjected to formal description, for instance, with library catalogs or bibliographic databases. As documents, classification systems are "invisible," and their inherent materiality is, if not denied, at least not prioritized. This does not hinder advanced formulations of classificatory structures or principles for subject definition and analysis, but the system's existence apart from its instrumental functionality is simply not considered particularly interesting. This matters. This lack of autonomy is of crucial interest in relation to the dependency on warrants that I discussed in the previous chapter, but it is also important in another way: it troubles the ability for us to understand the relation between the syntactic (structural) aspects and the semantic (meaning-oriented) aspects on which the cultural significance of classification systems are built.

Of course, this generic and instrumental view on bibliographic classification systems as well as other forms of knowledge organization has been contested. One issue of debate has been that of the dependence of classification systems on scientific disciplines as the basis for the division and hierarchization of subjects. Such dependency is problematic, as disciplines have different traditions concerning, for instance, the use of exact terminology, definitions, sensitizing concepts, and structural relations between them. For example, traditional disciplines within the humanities, such as history, literary studies, and the study of religions all not only show internal variations within the disciplines but as a group display stark differences in publication patterns and indexing conventions, from one another and from those found in the natural sciences.[3] For decades these differences were accepted but not taken into consideration in the construction of classification and indexing systems, usually steeped in a hard science one-size-fits-all form. Nowhere is this more visible than in universal classification systems aiming toward organizing a "totality" of human knowledge within a single structural frame. The perhaps most immediate example is the decimal syntax of the Dewey decimal classification, upheld with no apparent regard for the need of variation between different fields of knowledge. A structural frame, such as the decimal, influences the definition of, and relation between, subjects and subject areas that make up the classificatory hierarchies. How to define "subject" as the entity to be classified has been the object of considerable epistemological analysis in the writings of Birger Hjørland, who has suggested a way forward by defining subjects as the "informative potentials" of documents.[4] For example, the informative potential of a book on uranium can be geology (uranium as element), energy supply (enrichment of uranium for nuclear power plants), warfare (the role of enriched uranium in weapons of mass destruction), or energy policy (the political problem of final disposal for radioactive waste). Which of these subjects are chosen as subjects describing what the book is about depends both on the actual content of the book and its intended use. This is an interesting idea, relevant here as it not only provides a way to explain the problem of bias and trust in classification systems[5] but also understands systems as being, if not autonomous, then at least in part separated from that which is classified. Thus, it acknowledges classification systems as constituting a genre, or a type, of document *sui generis*.

The cognitive perspective in knowledge organization research was concisely pronounced and challenged by Jonathan Furner in a speech given in Toronto at the annual conference of the International Society of Knowledge Organization (ISKO) in August 2008. In this important talk, he proposes a communication perspective on knowledge organization, stating that: "The aim of KO (Knowledge organization) in general is to achieve consistency, to produce identity between the KO systems designer's representation of reality, which basically amounts to the aggregate of the extensions of all subject classes and the relation between them, and the KO system user's model of image of the world."[6]

This perspective is not unique. It builds on a solid theoretical strain within the information science user-centered perspective on the organization of knowledge. This merger between cognitive and more socially defined communication aspects of information behaviors of users and the development of systems intended for information retrieval is perhaps most poignantly formulated by Peter Ingwersen and Kalervo Järvelin in *The Turn: Integration of Information Seeking and Retrieval in Context*, forging a theoretical argument for bringing together research paradigms that since the 1950s have developed in parallel with little connection. The basic idea is that information behavior research and knowledge organization can be said to address the same process, but from two different ends—from the user's perspective and from the perspective of the collection of documents or even the individual document.[7]

The problem with the idea that it is possible to construct a retrieval system, for instance in the form of a library classification system, that merges the worldview of the system designer with that of the user is of course, as

Furner acknowledges, that there are so many views of the world. The conduit metaphor that has been so prevalent in information science, with its aggregate level of communication units and ends, is not embraced here. Instead, Furner opens the door for other relation types that form the basis of the organization of bibliographic indexing and classification systems, two of which are aboutness and relevance. Aboutness is a concept that refers to the relation between the content of a document and the subject description of that document—simply put, the formulation of what the document is about.[8] Relevance is the perceived usability of the document or information resource in a collection—in other words what, in the best of worlds, should be captured by the indexing or classification system consulted by the user.[9]

On the issue of knowledge organization and identity, Furner presents his audience with some challenging questions concerning (1) how well knowledge organization systems represent relationships of identity between classes of documents; (2) how well they help indexers, classifiers, and catalogers organize knowledge about the personal or social identities of members of social groups; and (3) how well classification systems assist people in finding the right labels for classes of documents that are about those identities, in the end allowing them to find the right documents.[10] Questions such as these are important for this present book as well. Not only do they indicate a social value of classification systems as such but they recognize a certain kind of *agency* that originates from the systems as documentary units—as documents and not only defined by the collections or institutions that they represent. The ability of a bibliographic classification system to connect on the levels of individual and social identity is recognized by Furner as a token of quality. To carve out a definition of a bibliographic classification system as a socially significant type of document, I take up these questions while shifting the focus toward documents as objects in the world and as subjects of research.

DOCUMENTS: WHAT THEY ARE AND WHAT THEY DO

For at least a century, the bibliographic community has discussed the problem of what a document is. Both Paul Otlet, founder of the Institut International de Bibliographie in Brussels at the turn of the last century, and later Suzanne Briet, librarian at the Bibliothèque National in Paris, accepted that a document could be more than a text-bearing physical information resource connected with libraries and archives. Objects could also qualify as documents, given that certain criteria of representation were met. Briet's most famous example is that of an antelope that while free is simply an antelope among others in its natural habitat. However, if the antelope is caught and transported to a zoo—in the case of her example, to the Jardin des Plantes in Paris—where it has been described, measured, and classified for scholarly purposes, then it is suddenly transformed into a specimen, an example, a representation of its kind, in this case, a species. It becomes a scholarly object, and as such, a document. Earlier, Otlet's conception of documents included objects outside of intentional institutional objectives. He claimed, for instance, that a statue can be described as a three-dimensional document on par with an artistic painting or a textual work of art. He argued that bibliographical objects—that is, objects that can be cataloged and organized in a classificatory structure—do not necessarily need to have a life outside of description, such as the free antelope, but rather, like books in a library, get their meaning from the analysis of their formal properties. On the one hand, he emphasized documents as tools: "Les choses crées, modéles et mécanismes pour démonstration scientific, éducative, et signalization,"[11] and on the other the possible representation of abstract ideas: "Les constructions, stéréogrammes à trois dimsensions, coordonnent strictement les idées."[12] He also proposed the perhaps most daring kind of document, one that takes Briet's antelope argument to lengths she seems to have had a hard time accepting: the properties of free plants and animals that signify their taxonomical identity, claiming documentary status by means of "les marques de toute nature portées sur les objets et qui serves à leur identification et signalisation."[13] The reason why Briet's argument does not encompass this is that her position is one where documents and documentation processes are intentional constructions, suggesting documentary status to physical information resources such as books, manuscripts, notes, and sheet music, along with collected objects subjected to bibliographical treatment through both formal description and cataloging as well as classification. After all, she was a trained librarian. The fundamental definition of a document provided by Briet is, and I quote from the English translation of *Qu'est-ce que la documentation?*: "Any concrete or symbolic indexical sign [indice], preserved or recorded towards the end of representation, or reconstituting, or of proving a physical or intellectual phenomenon."[14] From this definition, there are primarily two criteria mentioned that have been dealt with in documentation research: the representative and the evidentiary function of documents.

Briet makes an important distinction between the initial document as that which is being represented and the secondary, or derived, document, which consists of the tools and standards that are used to provide the representative and evidentiary function. Among the secondary forms of secondary documents are counted scientific articles, exhibitions, and news on the (antelope as) document. Reconnecting to Golub's distinction between formal and subject-based analysis of an information resource, we find here the basic function of any bibliographic tool, establishing links in two directions: (1) the standards of describing or representing the object, the primary document, that are developed within the scientific field of knowledge that relates to the document—zoology, for instance, in the cases of the antelope or a blue-winged butterfly—and (2) conventions and standards for secondary documentation, as manifested in cataloging rules, classification, and indexing systems. This latter is what I will refer to as the bibliographical tradition, providing rules and tool kits for establishing pertinent information retrieval, whether in a library, archive, or museum setting.

For Briet, connecting the scientific and bibliographic links that establish conventions for description and analysis of collected objects with "documentary fertility"[15] is relatively uncomplicated. She regards documentation as an institutional practice, defined by her place in a transitional period for French scientific libraries in general, and the Bibliothèque National in particular.[16] Documentation is seen as an enhancement of scholarly practice, a refinement of scientific knowledge, connecting the dots of various knowledge fields through documentary practices. Her ideas are those of a movement adapting the role of documentation in a time when new technologies for bibliographical treatment appeared and, as a consequence, redefined the role of documentation practices in the research process.[17] It is important to be aware of these situational conditions in the understanding of her theorizing about documentation as "cultural technique," a term that Ronald Day in his essay complementing the English translation of *Qu'est-ce que la documentation?* points to, which in French incorporates both English terms "technique" and "technology." Day finds it a fruitful ambiguity: "The cultural conditions that Briet sees documentation being born within are those of industrial modernity and its means of production through techniques, tools and various combinations of these."[18] It is the same modernity that Otlet responds to, and they both claim that the ideal way to address it is through (1) intellectual standardization (technique) in the connection between documentation and scholarly practice by providing transparency and establishing a common language of knowledge and its representation, and (2) the development of tools (technology) that correspond not only to the language of knowledge but to the conventions of documentation, catalog rules, and content analysis—scientific practice and results redefined as bibliographic Subjects—in text-bearing information resources as well as objects. With this, the connection between the primary document and its secondary document is established by means of representation as follows from Briet's definition.

Buckland describes the term evidence as something primarily passive: "Evidence, as information-as-thing, does not do anything actively. Human beings do things with it or to it."[19] What is done with or to the evidence is also, however, related to understanding, and may lead to active shifts in knowledge or beliefs. The antelope placed in the Jardin des Plantes does not have to do anything but may still lead to developed knowledge about the species or its taxonomical status. The document thus triggers activity without being formulated as active in itself. What then singles out a document from any other inanimate object? From his reading of Briet, Buckland claims that for an object to be perceived as a document—because at some point, it must be perceived as such—it needs materiality and intentionality, and it must be processed. It must be *made* into a document. In this making, certain characteristics are defined as documentary. While Otlet goes to the extreme, defining more or less anything as a potential document, the ability to inform is the perhaps most important criteria that makes it so. He acknowledges that, to formulate this ability, one needs to define what properties of, for instance, a flower are significant enough to place it in a taxonomical structure. When we pick up a flower on our morning walk, what do we look at to determine its name? The process of documentation is thereby defined by intention and that which Day calls "indexicality."[20] Indexicality implies that there are certain properties in an object or a document that lend themselves to description and adaptation into a syntactical convention such as a taxonomy or a classification system.

The passiveness of documents that Buckland points to in Briet's discussions is a problem. Firstly, it confines documentation to a bibliographical paradigm, inspired by the science of bibliography, traditionally concerned with the formal aspects of the book, seen as an archetypical document.[21] That this paradigm of understanding documents has continued up until the current day even though we deal with non-book objects as documents is not surprising, as the theories of information science pioneers such as Otlet and Briet emerged out of bibliographic practice. A second problem is of a more theoretical nature and relates to the connection between information and documentation in information science. In fruitful attempts to epistemologically distinguish documents and documentation from information and information behavior, several scholars, such as Jonathan Furner, Bernd Frohmann, and Ronald Day, have engaged in critiques of the relation of documentation and information and the communicational model operating in studies of documentation and information (e.g., the conduit metaphor).[22] I will therefore not expand on this discussion here, but instead simply conclude that the problems pointed out by Buckland are interesting and challenging in this present study as well, as classifications themselves develop out of the bibliographical paradigm.

The critique of the bibliographical paradigm in documentation does not direct itself to the intended use and function of bibliographic classification systems, such as for instance the Dewey decimal classification; they are constructed to work in document retrieval. Instead, it is directed toward the intended understanding of these classification systems as documents on the same premises that can be applied to any other document. To understand documents and their abilities, however, we need to move toward a position that does not necessarily discard the evidentiary role of documents—I see that as epistemologically uncontroversial—but that adds to it a layer formulating such in social terms.[23] What is called for is nothing less than a transformation of classification systems from secondary documentation to the status of the primary document. Furthermore, there is a need to develop an understanding beyond instrumental evidentiality, thus establishing a sociologically informed relevance for both documents and documentation as a process or cultural technique.

But is Briet's definition of a document really that passive? If we accept the range of intentionality (catching the antelope), documentary practices (cataloging the antelope), and communicative aspects (exhibiting the antelope) that together make documents out of objects, there seems to be an inherent agency working here. The first step in the processes of revealing this agency is to define the indexicality of the object perceived as having documentary status.

Then I will propose a way to expand the function of the document from being evidence to a more socially defined agency of representation. But one step at a time.

To distance the analysis from the bibliographical paradigm and establish a more sociologically informed understanding of a document, it is necessary to define the properties of indexicality. The document is always about something. It holds some kind of narrative. This may be relatively uncomplicated, relating to simple facts as evidence. The representational and evidentiary formulation of an antelope or the number of known variations of the blue-winged butterfly is relatively straightforward. However, if we instead consider a more complicated document, such as a classification system, the question of what it is about becomes more opaque. Day defines indexical signs, "*indices*," as "sociotechnical devices that have technological and social logics enfolded within them as meaningful functions for information organization and use and they give rise to and mediate the social positioning and information and knowledge values of texts and person and documents, information, and data."[24] Indexicality is closely connected to conventionality and the social agreement of the value of the index as carrying authoritative meaning, defining the "about" or in information science terminology "aboutness" of the document. Accepting this definition of indexical signs leads to a more active documentary function than that of "proof in support of a fact," as Briet formulates it in her introduction to *Qu'est-ce que un document?*[25]

DOCUMENTARY AGENCY AND DOCUMENTALITY

The attribution of agency to documents is usually termed *documentality*. In a discussion of Briet's definition and use of the term document, Frohmann defines documentality as "a thing's agency, power or force," exercised by the complex arrangements in which things are placed in order to perform documentary agency.[26] In an apparent attempt to avoid the somewhat circular character of this definition, Frohmann breaks down the concept of documentality into four features: functionality, historicity, social complexity, and agency. Documentality is a function defined by historical contingency, subjected to various complexities of social and technological development, group dynamics, and institutional settings, all enabling some kind of power or force to emanate from the document. It is a comprehensible definition that, applied to bibliographical classification systems, could work something like this: the documentality of a classification system is its ability to function in accordance with its specific arrangements or conventions, for instance within a specific type of library (e.g., public or academic library). The character of these arrangements and conventions is determined by historical contingency. This could, for instance, relate to the "golden age" of universal classification systems, between, roughly, 1870 to 1940, when several systems were constructed with information retrieval, or bibliographical, functionality in mind. Such systems had a syntactic-semantic construction that often went far beyond what was necessary, first and foremost seen by their levels of abstraction (Dewey's decimal structure of knowledge), or defined worldview (S. R. Ranganathan's combined influences from Vedic philosophy and Western mathematics as the basis for his *Colon Classification*). Formulating an adequate level of abstraction as the intellectual foundation for bibliographic classification systems was important in the modernization and professionalization of libraries and librarianship, thus meeting the criteria for documentary complexity relating to institutional connections and group dynamics. In this light, the agency of a bibliographic classification system should be characterized in relation to their ability to function as Golub's "quality information retrieval systems." Documentality in this sense becomes instrumental. Using Frohmann's understanding of documentality, we can investigate the documentality of classifications. Here, we can apply analyses such as Wittgenstein's emphasis of meaning through language use, Peirce's semiotics, and, as also referred to by Frohmann, Latour's insistence that tools give material meaning to processes also non-afflicted by human intentionality.[27]

I will return to the discussion on classification systems as documents shortly, but first I would like to dwell on the idea of documentality, the power or force of documents, in order to move beyond the traditional passive understanding of documents. To do so, I take a first step out of the discussion as it has taken shape in information science and address similar arguments made by the Italian philosopher Maurizio Ferraris. In his book *Documentality: Why It Is Necessary to Leave Traces*,[28] Ferraris provides not only an alternative definition of documents but also, which is more interesting and relevant here, a deepened understanding of the concept of documentary agency and documentality. This understanding comes from a fundamentally realist critique of conceptions of social processes as defined primarily by Jacques Derrida, Ferraris's late friend and coauthor.

In his book *Documentality*, Ferraris makes the simple claim that there is such a thing as a reality against which our understanding of the world must be measured. In this critique of the postmodern, documents and documentality become ontologically interesting, insofar as he is interested in social objects, and so, social reality in this book. He provides two definitions of a document that work on different premises than those discussed thus far. The first sees a document as "any inscription with institutional value."[29] This definition does not in itself contradict the evidentiary definitions. Instead, it aligns well with the historical, informative, and juridical aspects of established definitions of a document. The second definition takes a somewhat different direction: "A document should be understood rather as something that is given once and for all and as making up a class of stable objects, as the reification of social acts which, in turn, change over time and space."[30] While the first definition refers to the traditional evidentiary function in a relatively intuitive sense, this second one gives us something else, more complex, to work with in forging a view on documents that may enhance our understanding of bibliographic classification systems.

Considering documents as reifications of social acts places the document, or that which we perceive as a document, in a developed capacity transgressing the mimetic representation of a fact—it provides to the document signifying and legitimating powers to social and cultural processes. Adding to such powers an emphasis on institutional value, we see an understanding of documents that may be useful in the present context. Combining Ferraris's two definitions into one provides the following:

A document is an inscribed reification of social acts with an informative potential of institutional value.

I will use this as a working definition that can help us understand classification as socially powerful documents. Such a definition is beneficial in several ways:

- It puts decisive emphasis on materiality and fixity. A document may be subjected to contextual changes, but if so, there will be versions or editions of the document that may be related to its specific historicity and social complexity.
- The notion of a document being a reification of a social act offers a more socially engaged understanding of documentary function than mere representation. It does so in at least two ways: the fixation of past acts and the standardization of current acts and practices of institutional value.
- Inscription presupposes indexicality in that there must exist an agreement of what properties constitute the institutional value of a document.
- The informative potential, a term taken from Hjørland as discussed above, indicates that a document consists of a creative tension between form and content for which it is possible to, within limits, interpret differently in each given situation.
- The need for institutional value promotes a documentary agency that places the document in a context that not only makes sense but can explain the range of its stability—for example, in terms of versions, multiple samples, or editions, over time.
- The stability of a document, understood as the reification of a social act placed in ever-changing institutional contexts, provides for an understanding of documentality that transgresses the notion of passivity. Documents can now be understood as active entities in the maintenance and development of social institutions, whether defined in sociological or organizational terms.

Not only does this definition help the transition from the bibliographical to a more sociologically informed comprehension of documents and documentality but it makes it possible to begin a discussion on how this active and institutionally integrated documentality takes shape in concrete institutional settings. In the next chapter I will return to this question in more detail when I place it in a context informed by organizational theory on isomorphic cultural change and development in social institutions.

One could, and should always, ask why it is necessary to dwell on definitions. In a discussion of Buckland's understanding of Briet's definition of a document, Frohmann criticizes the very need for a stable definition of documents, based on a Wittgensteinian understanding of language as something that gets its meaning only through actual use. He provides a healthy critique of the desire for essentials and absolutes in documentation theory, claiming that documentation is primarily a hands-on activity related to certain institutional processes. Instead of through definition, the meaning of a term can be inferred through our use of it. We speak of documents and documentation processes in a way we assume everyone can agree on. In such a situation, we would most likely end up thinking of documents through the examples of passports or marriage licenses—common valid documents with well-defined functions within the realm of "evidence."[31] I agree with Frohmann's critique of defined absolutes outside of linguistic practice. However, my working definition above should be considered, more than anything else, a pragmatic way of establishing a common understanding of what I will be talking about in the case studies later in this book. A working definition allows me to make the necessary distinctions that prevent possible mix-ups between the intended use of classification systems and the systems themselves. And, as I further venture into several discussions of both theoretical and methodological character in the following chapter as well, my definition will ensure a safe return to the central theme of this book: bibliographic classification systems as inscribed reifications of social acts of institutional value.

But how does all this work in relation to the discussion on what classification systems are, when formulated by classification theorists? As the cases in chapters four to six will all fall within the social and institutional developments of the twentieth century, with an emphasis on its first half, I will here only refer to a few classic examples that capture the discussion relevant for the formation of the studied environments and systems: *Classification, Theoretical and Practical* from 1901 by Ernest Cushing Richardson,[32] *The Organization of Knowledge in Libraries* from 1933 by Henry Evelyn Bliss,[33] and the French treatise *Theorie et pratique des classifications documentaires* from 1956 by Eric de Grolier.[34] What I will examine is the way in which these books define any kind of social documentality in bibliographic classification systems and how they relate to social development and change.

PERSPECTIVES FROM EARLY CLASSIFICATION THEORY

It is in no way given that it is meaningful to disconnect a classification system from that which it classifies and its intended use, whether defined in terms of institutional processes or ability to meet the demands of a user. And indeed, it is not necessary to make a *total* disconnection, just as it would be no point in making a total disconnection between the manual to a new car and the car itself. However, as suggested in the previous chapter, there have been several shifts in the forms and intentions of bibliographic classification systems due to other factors than that which is being classified, whether we look at library use of the Aristotelian ideals of *Trivium et Quadrivium*, the generic broad subject divisions of Konrad Gesner in *Bibliotheca Universalis*, or the seventeenth century bookstore-based classification by Gabriel Naudé. Here, I am mostly concerned with the very specific form of universal classification systems that was developed as part of the Western project of modernization and that became increasingly common in the mid-nineteenth century only to decrease, in terms of new systems, with the advent of new knowledge organization technologies about a hundred years later. After all, the fundamental legitimacy of a bibliographic classification system is its usability, its ability to guide users to documents whose content is relevant to their requests. This is the one most important thing that sets them apart from philosophical divisions of knowledge, even when the claim of universality sometimes makes them resemble each other either by reference, as in Melvil Dewey's formulation of his system as "inverted Baconian,"[35] or implicitly in the classificatory work of Ranganathan. What characterizes these systems is on the one hand to strive for stability in their schedules, and on the other hand, mnemonics and efficiency in use. In his introduction to the fourth edition of his decimal classification system, dated at the New York Public Library on Christmas Day 1890, Melvil Dewey defends the "procrustean 10" by comparing his system's efficiency with that of a train:

A railroad also has the fault that it is procrustean in its path and in its time. It cannot come to your door nor wait your convenience, as did the stage-coach or carriage; it cannot go to the fields for its loads of produce; it cannot turn out for obstacles; and it is simply because it is procrustean that it can do its work so much better and quicker and cheaper.[36]

While Richardson stressed the need for rational and logical progress and relations between classes in a system, he was even more concerned with how to relate the stability of the system to an order of *true subject division* existing outside of the system. He sought the same kind of logic and rationality that Dewey defended, but his means were different. The way in which a classification system emerges as a document with documentality is directly linked to its ability to replicate the true order of the sciences. In the introduction to *Classification, Theoretical and Practical,* he states: "The true classification of the idea of things that have been, in short, the classification of the sciences, is simply the order of nature paralleled. The classification of new ideas or art is by this same token not an imitation of nature and is endless in possible variety."[37]

Richardson, a librarian at Princeton, creator of the so-called Princeton System,[38] and president of American Library Association in 1904 and 1905, was concerned about the stability of classification systems, and was relying heavily on the stability of both the order of the sciences ("nature paralleled") and of the content of the collections themselves. The process of subject analysis depends on the same kind of stability, and he finds books to be "intellectual petrification," or "planets in an advanced stage of evolutions, where the mass of ideas has passed out of the fluid into a solid unchanging state."[39] Classificatory practice is, however, considered not a science, but an art. It relies also on conditions somewhat beside this true order, and the systems need to adjust to "delicate common sense"[40] to work as tools in practical librarianship. Once common sense is included in the argument, the mimetic order of "nature paralleled" is loosened upon, and the classifier is able to provide for the classification system a specific kind of institutionally defined documentality:

The general order in which the main classes [of the classification system] are to be placed with reference to one another in a library may not be so much determined by their natural relation as by the shape of the library building and by the rule that the most used books are to be placed nearest the delivery desk."[41]

It is worth noting how this kind of pragmatism is combined with the idea of classificatory stability, and that the order of classification sometimes must make way for more professionally legitimized consideration such as labor division and economy. It not only places the classification systems in a situation where it is broken up by material circumstances but also manifests documentality in the system's ability to interact. Principles of intended use become tokens of quality.

By the time Henry Evelyn Bliss published his in many ways comparable treatise three decades after Richardson's, the experiences of World War I had thrown the bourgeoise stability of Europe overboard. The idea of clinging to the order of science had shifted from being transcendental to being practical to scholarly practice. Nothing is fixed anymore, the idea of "intellectual petrification" as a classificatory value is gone. The 1920s and 30s were also a period of intense professionalization in libraries, and as Bliss stressed throughout his book, subject analysis and classification systems are at the center of the librarian's professional identity. In his *The Organization of Knowledge in Libraries*, a follow-up to his book, *The Organization of Knowledge and the System of the Sciences*, published in 1929,[42] the main problem is basically how to maintain the balance between functionality and stability—that is, how to construct a classification system that can work as an integrated part in a developed institutionalized context searching for new professional roles in technological, scientific, and educational practices. The construction and availability of functional classification systems was seen as crucial for establishing both scientific and public libraries as places of social and intellectual significance: "There must be organization of knowledge, thought and purpose. It [the classification system] must be functional, but it must first be structural. It should be as free as possible, as plastic and adaptive; but it must not the less be coherent and stable; else our whole scientific and educational undertaking crumble in confusion."[43] Bibliographic classification is, as is the library, firmly placed within the scientific and educational sphere providing prerequisites for defining the relation between flexibility and function, and stability. As in so many other areas in the 1930s, old truths are challenged and new solutions sought. The conflict is real: "The established systems are maintained by professional conservatism in the midst of professional progress."[44] He describes the library situation and the need for new ideals and systems of classification.

This need "has now become a social and intellectual one,"[45] suggesting a solution based on "centralized coöperative classifying."[46] The process is one of detachment, similar to that in many other areas of librarianship at the time.[47] The classification system as a document has a fully integrated position contributing to the definition of institutional context of which it is part, and as such it is important to social and intellectual development. It is a highly particular documentality, independent of the person who designs the system or adapts it to institutional conditions, such as spatial and functional situations in individual libraries. The bibliographic classification system becomes a cogwheel in the social machinery, a cultural technique. With Bliss, the classification system begins a journey from being seen as purely mimetic to being treated as a document type with a designated social and institutional documentality in harmony with libraries as "virtual and influential centers of . . . intellectual communities."[48]

This movement in the discourse proposing bibliographic classification systems as parts of an intellectual community that connects societal development with the dynamics of research and higher education is further formulated in the quite singular environment that is found in France and particularly Paris in the early 1950s, two decades after the contributions from Bliss. This is the place and time of Suzanne Briet's *Qu'est-ce que la Documentation?* (*What Is Documentation?*) It is the place and time also of the perhaps most ambitious book on classification systems until then, *Théorie et pratique des classifications documentaires* by linguist and classification theorist Eric de Grolier.[49] This book was published in 1956 by the Union Française des Organismes de Documentation (UFOD), an organization founded in 1931 by Jean Gérard and Suzanne Briet.[50] De Grolier took, alongside for instance Robert Pagès,[51] a degree in documentation at the Institut National des Sciences et Techniques de la Documentation (INTD) in the early 1950s, with courses being taught by Briet with ideas that would later appear in her book. Later in life, de Grolier would himself return to INTD as an instructor. De Grolier is among the few French documentalists from this period who would exert influence on his contemporary international research scene, not least through his engagement in the International Society for Knowledge Organization (ISKO). His claim that a bibliographic classification system is a "cultural artefact" is based on the substantial research that underpins his book.[52]

Théorie et pratique des classifications documentaires has built its reputation on three pillars: (1) the excavation of hidden and forgotten classification systems; (2) the idea that it is possible to create one truly universal classification system that has the ability to not only present a coherent overview of all human knowledge but also break it down into consistent subject developments for use in special libraries; and (3) the understanding of classification systems as search systems rather than document organization tools. They all inform each other. For instance, the proposal of a universal classificatory foundation, developed as the "Projet de symbolisation alphabétique internationale"[53] in the treatise, stems from the assumption that such a structure could be accomplished through a synthesis of past and present special classification systems. The ability to facilitate future specializations thus emerges as a kind of feedback loop, continuously developed by culturally informed changes in the search practices of users. The systems themselves are thus seen as documentary structures, and indeed de Grolier commences with a brief discussion of Ferdinand de Saussure's langue/parole distinction that I discussed in the previous chapter in the form developed by anthropologist Jack Goody in his analysis of the social significance of lists and object classification.[54] By arguing for a socially informed retrieval perspective, never falling into the trap of cognition, rather than a mimetic reproduction of the "true" structure of the sciences, de Grolier contributes to our understanding of the classification system as a socially significant document type by ascribing documentality to the system as a document. He does so while distancing bibliographic systems from philosophical systems, and by treating institutional context as the defining warrant against which the system must be evaluated. He calls this contextual process "le cycle documentaire," within which the classification system creates a synthesis of the author/document perspective and the user perspective through an "organisme de documentation." This "organisme" defines the institutional limitation put on documentation as a communicative process, both in terms of reach and social significance. This is in many ways consistent with the document theory of both Suzanne Briet and later Michael Buckland and Maurizio Ferraris. This theoretical conformity also places de Grolier's work as a bridge between a sociological view of the roles of documents, and contemporary critical classification research addressing issues such as bias and value conservatism in systems still widely used today.

Taken together, these three important books on bibliographic classification show a progression from first, the idea of a division of subjects reflecting a true and given order of sciences to second, practical document organization devices depending on institutional and professional preconditions to third, documentation processes with synthesizing agencies acting as boundary objects between document collections and user needs. From an information science perspective, this last may seem almost like truism. However, during the decades that these texts were published, and the periods of the subsequent cases de Grolier's book, it was still all new. By returning to works of this period, we can find the origins of later ideas.

CONCLUDING REMARKS

Over these first two chapters I have pointed to a couple of problems concerning how to discuss bibliographic classification systems as documents. In the first chapter, I reiterated the placement of social classification systems made by Jack Goody. Here, classification systems are defined as something outside of the instrumental relation between written and spoken language, forming a separate category of linguistic constructs aiming not at being read (in the everyday sense of the term), but instead used to fulfill a need of documentary representation, for instance in trade or legislation. Still, the way in which this order is carried out, how classes are constructed, placed, and divided by content, is socially constructed and culturally dependent and, according to Goody, can provide important knowledge about the societies using a classification system. This corresponds well to discussions within contemporary document studies. I have found the arguments of Maurizio Ferraris, that documents can be seen as inscribed social acts, as a fruitful way into the sociological understanding of the classification systems. A working definition of a document as an inscribed reification of social acts with informative potential of institutional value was developed to indicate a point of reference from which it is possible to advance the discussion on classification systems both in a direction toward their position in the "documentary cycle," in the words of de Grolier, and toward a broader discussion that eventually may take us back to the view on classification systems as socially integrated forms of documents, which may help us to see their role and function in a wider sociocultural development.

I will in the next chapter expand upon these sociological and institutional discussions to provide a framework for an interpretative process that may fill the proposed definition with both content and direction. I will start this discussion in a by now familiar context, the French documentation movement in late 1940s and early 1950s Paris, but with a somewhat alternative perspective—that of Robert Pagès and his theory of social documentation. From there, I will proceed to suggest a hermeneutic framework for the case analysis—one that places the concept of mimetic reflection in the light of institutionally isomorphic change.

3

QUESTIONING REPRESENTATION: A BRIEF NOTE ON METHODOLOGY

A recurring problem in every bibliographic classification system is how to treat the relation between context, time, and representation. A fixed structure needs to be flexible enough to develop over time in order to maintain its legitimacy. The definition of a document presented in the previous chapter displays a similar kind of tension between fixity and progress, between the halting of social fluidity and, at the same time, being part of it. One of the most urgent challenges in classification practice is to maintain a comprehensible contemporaneity in a system while creating a stability necessary for its predictability and utility in information retrieval situations. Changes and updates cannot be made randomly but need to follow one or several principles tied to the dominant warrants that set the requirements for the basic structural-semantic relation in the individual system. In documents understood as contextually dependent singular units, and classification systems understood as types of documents with specific properties, their social legitimacy, by means of their documentality, is dependent on the ability to transgress fixity and embrace change in the environment of which they are to be part.

So, in this chapter, I will discuss bibliographic classification systems as documents in relation to contextual change. I will discuss Robert Pagès and his concept of *isomorphism* to characterize how contextual relations change over time and can be perceived from within a documentation context.

I will then develop this further into a more general introduction to *institutional isomorphism* as an analytical concept, serving as a foundation upon which the case studies in the three succeeding chapters can be built. I will advance my argument by pointing out specific kinds of contextual change processes, both in terms of concrete impetuses on the classification systems and what these, as documents, have to offer contextual progression. It is important to emphasize these temporal aspects as they not only map the geographical and cultural situations of the individual classification systems in the analysis but furthermore present an overarching panorama of different contextual requirements, ranging from the progressive to an understanding of time as something that has, in a certain way, come to an end.

While throughout most of the bibliographical and institutional history of library environments subject divisions have been local and adapted to concrete collections in need of order by subject entries, a new kind of systems emerged in the early nineteenth century. There are several reasons for this, and, although it is tempting to define a specific point in time when these new systems emerged, such would be an arbitrary choice. We often speak of collection-bound classification systems in the 1850s, taking the US as a point of departure with the Dewey decimal classification, and from then on others that organize collections beyond a single institution. However, Ann Blair counts, as I wrote about in the introductory chapter, general bibliographical systems that date back to the *Bibliotheca Universalis*, Konrad Gesner's bibliography from 1545, consisting of ten thousand entries with an elaborate classification built from twenty-one main categories.[1] Gesner's work was part of a bibliographic movement experimenting with document representation across central Europe in the sixteenth and seventeenth centuries as part of the emerging *Nuova Scienza*. And although the *Bibliotheca Universalis* counts as the perhaps first manifestation of modern bibliographic practice, we can trace its roots all the way back through the medieval period and into Roman antiquity.[2] It is important to recognize the premodern heritage of universal classification within bibliography and librarianship not only because such creates a hereditary lineage of practice but because such systems bear witness to a way of addressing the idea of knowledge organization distinct from metaphysics and more rooted in serving industry. None of the protagonists of the major classification systems that have exerted influence on bibliographic practice have been philosophers or, indeed, held any deeper philosophical claims for their systems. Instead, they were, like Paul Otlet or Melvil Dewey, driven by different kinds of entrepreneurial and reformist ambitions. Still, regardless of the level of idealism or philosophical claims that goes into the construction of a classification system, not only is it necessary to find a legitimate and intuitive systematization of relating subjects to each other, but it is as important to find a way in which this systematization can evolve to represent prioritized warrants whether literary, scientific, institutional, or cultural.

On a technical level, there are two main ways of solving the problem of time and change in bibliographic classification systems: incremental change or editorial distinction. Incremental change means that changes are made currently as needed within the individual classes of the system. In such systems, whereof the Universal Decimal Classification is the perhaps most prominent, structural elements are designed to accommodate the addition of individual subjects, or aspects of subjects, through for instance auxiliary tables listing temporal, formal, geographical, and other aspects connected to the classified documents. The structure of the system can also be used, as I will show in the next chapter, to construct special classification systems, addressing specific knowledge areas or institutional needs in ways consistent with the overall main system. Editorial distinction means that the same version of the system is used in different libraries and bibliographical contexts until a new version is fully available and published, whereafter necessary changes can be made accordingly. This is how the Dewey decimal system has been designed to develop, giving priority to changes within the main tables through additions of new subjects to existing hierarchies.[3]

However, in addressing bibliographic classification systems as autonomous, socially defined documents, these comparably straightforward technical solutions need to be complemented with a more complex discussion that focuses on the seemingly contradictory properties of fixity and documentality, the mimetic function of any document and its change-inducing or active role in a wider social progression of occurrences. I will in the coming three chapters consider a variety of classification systems that all, in different ways, correspond to certain defined social and cultural change processes. Suzanne Briet's definition of documentation as a cultural technique will be given both content and direction through the system-context relations that are given at each point in time and place of occurrence. Such contextual dependency is also possible to define in a more general sense, in relation to large all-permeating cultural changes due to political and technological developments alike.

I have already introduced the three cases studies of this book, but would like just to mention them again here, with the problem of time and change in focus. Each of them covers a certain period. The first is the so-called *Belle Époque* or *Fin de Siècle*, with its apex around the turn of the nineteenth century, characterized by a firm belief in social, cultural, and entrepreneurial progress based on ideas of universal enlightenment. I focus primarily on the European version (not the American), broadly characterized by social, technological, and scientific progress while simultaneously hosting fervent social, economic, nationalistic, and colonial tensions. Paul Otlet and Henri La Fontaine's development of the Universal Decimal Classification system in Belgium during the last decade of the nineteenth century is symptomatic of a bourgeoise faith in knowledge-based progress and collaborative international avenues to social progress. In such a worldview, universal access to scientific knowledge becomes crucial, and thus there is a need for a bibliographic infrastructure to support this access. The Universal Decimal Classification can thus be seen as an example of how certain ideas and cultural preferences are manifested in documentary practices, forming the basis not only of a general access to knowledge but, more concretely, the ability for progressive social movements to interact, exchange information, and provide documentation of the progress in their designated areas, be it the suffrage movement, the artificial language movement, first-wave feminism, or, in the personal cases of Henri La Fontaine and Paul Otlet, the peace movement.

That which eventually came to break the expansionist spirit of the *Belle Époque* culture was the outbreak of World War I in 1914. With this, any idea of internationalist endeavor came to an end, instead being replaced by protectionist nationalist sentiments and the perceived need to define culturally homogenous units based on the idea of national heritage and character of the people. It is as a part of such a definitional phase of nationalist expressions that we will examine in the next case the Swedish SAB-system, published in 1921. It is a classification system that was effectively constructed to promote a general sense of national uniqueness, as seen by the denouncement of the then internationally recognized Dewey decimal classification System, and instead claiming a specific Swedish bibliographic "tradition" legitimizing the use of an alphabetic notation. With the SAB-system, we can perceive a development where nationalistic cultural expressions across Europe led to the idea that the division of knowledge finds its foundational legitimacy by explicitly representing administrative structures, religious beliefs, and the cultural expressions of a nation in need of unification. This perceived need must also be understood in the context of the dissolution of the Norwegian-Swedish Union in 1905, which resulted in a strong Swedish national identity movement. Simultaneously, Norwegian libraries went in the opposite direction, finding their national identity, in bibliographic terms, as part of a larger international community with the introduction of the Dewey decimal classification System across Norway's publicly funded library system in 1905.

The final case we will examine, on Jewish classification, presents a considerably longer historical perspective as it builds on the relation between cultural identity and bibliographic expression. The impetus for change and temporal influences are traced through Jewish classification from the seventeenth century, as the first Judaica bibliographies constructed *by Jews* and not Christians appear, to the twentieth and the experiential redefinition succeeding the Holocaust, which forced bibliographers to find ways to incorporate a new kind of cultural trauma into the general Jewish experience. Although primarily situated in Europe, and later in the US as well, the various iterations of Judaism and the Jewish bibliographic tradition gradually developed a balancing act between an exclusively Jewish cultural identification on the one hand and, on the other, a bibliographic context correlating to the wider, non-Jewish, societal fabric of which Jews also were a part. During most of the twentieth century, this balancing act plays out as a continuous trial of the usability of the Dewey decimal classification system, which comes to function either as a point of departure for singular cultural expressions or as a system adapted to the practical needs of Jewish libraries. In both cases, the interpretation of the geographically scattered Jewish cultural experience becomes pronounced and situated in classificatory structures when translated into library practice. This leaves the question of "which Jewry" should be represented in the mimetic struggle of classificatory structuring, and not the least, how to deal with change over time.

Approaching the cases from a document theory perspective, it becomes clear that the reification of social acts is complicated and that the idea of documentality—that is, the ability of documents to contribute to the constitution of external conditions within which they can find legitimacy and functionality—is more complex than simply expressing a mimetic relationship between classificatory structures and their institutional or sociocultural surroundings. All systems analyzed in the case studies are parts of wider processes of social change and progression, whether defined as cultural in a wide anthropological sense or political in the sense that bibliographic expressions are part of a national or cultural identity project. This complexity forces a need to find another way to conceptualize the documentality of bibliographic classification systems.

BREAKING FREE FROM THE MIMETIC

In a paper presented at the 2021 Annual Meeting of the Document Academy, Ronald Day addressed the problem of representation by elaborating on two kinds of bibliographic understanding of books and other forms of documents: one traditional mimetic, considering documents as containers of reference and meaning, and one materialist and performative, where reference and meaning are provided through documents' relation to cultural expressions and social circulation.[4] The former is found in the writings, for instance, of Paul Otlet and Suzanne Briet, and was historically recovered and commented on in the early neo-documentalist analyses of the 1990s. The latter has been more recently analyzed and expressed in current research efforts and practices in alignment with concepts such as agency and documentality. Here, an alternative to the mimetic function of document needs to be defined: "The first step away from the mimetic tradition is to understand that what counts as documents vary, there is no documentary or 'informational' epistemic content per se, and so, correspondingly, there are different types of 'document acts.'"[5]

This is an important point that also relates to understanding of classification systems as documents. While understanding classification systems mimetically may be intuitive within traditional bibliography and documentation, the analysis in this book stresses the functions of classification systems between structure and actual use, both from an information seeker's point of view and, crucially for our analysis, from a societal or cultural point of view. Such an analysis views normative expressions within a semantic-structural dialectic through choices of subjects and divisions of individual knowledge fields. Day builds his argument on, among others, the theoretical contribution on documentality by Bernd Frohmann that I discussed previously,[6] but also on influences from the 1990s regarding alternative ways of addressing information retrieval and knowledge organization. During this period, stretching into the new millennium, the epistemic perspective shifts from representation to presentation, taking bibliographic classification systems into a realm of hermeneutic interpretation, both as objects of study and classificatory practice. This route avoids "postmodern" epistemic relativism, based on the reduction of reality to language alone. It is important here to remember that hermeneutics *as such* has nothing to do with the postmodern construct. Influential contributions to this discussion, such as Ian Cornelius's 1996 book *Meaning and Method in Information Studies* and Hope Olson's *The Power to Name: Locating the Limits of Subject Representation in Libraries* from 2002, provide tools and entries for the understanding of classification systems as documents with the ability to challenge the idea of a fixed warrant-based relation between semantic-structural properties of the systems and their institutional, social, and cultural significance.[7]

Tracing Day's argument back to discussions on hermeneutics around the turn of the twenty-first century is still not enough. Although methodologically oriented, this discussion still leaves us with a need to more robustly articulate the type of "document act" or acts performed by classification systems. One indication that points toward a path of increased conceptualization and understanding is provided at the intersection of classification research and documentation studies within the fertile intellectual context of the French Documentation movement of the late 1940s, which indeed takes us back to the influence of Briet (that Day wants to let go of). This time, however, not in a direct sense through her own texts but indirectly through her capacity as a teacher. It is particularly worth turning our attention then to her student Robert Pagès and his thoughts on documentation as a cultural technique.[8]

In his 1955 treatise *Problèmes de Classification Culturelle et Documentaire*, Pagès suggests *isomorphism* as a concept worth considering when defining the cultural role of documentation processes in general, and of classification systems in particular. Examining the value of this suggestion, it is important to recognize the specific perspective on documentation that connects Pagès's disciplinary interest with his overall view on society, marked by an engagement with various Trotskyist and anarchist organizations during World War II and while studying at the documentation program at the Conservatoire National des Arts et Métiers (CNAM) a few years later.[9] It is, however, also important to note that, although informed by it, this engagement does not diminish the stringency of his theoretical construct on documentary processes and the role of classification. As already mentioned, like Briet, Pagès understood documentation processes as cultural techniques. However, where Briet's understanding was limited to a narrow scholarly environment, Pagès expanded the argument in two directions: psychological and broader social movements. Central to Pagès's thinking was an increasing conflict between humanism and a society built around the rationalization and bureaucratization of social processes seen in his own time. Pagès considers the latter a major threat to social progress, and he struggles with the rationalistic character of documentation, as part of a critique of civilization that ultimately builds on the classic philosophical conflict between lived experience and bookish knowledge.[10] In a dramatic sequence he states that

> At a time of mass production (factories), mass politics (parties), and mass warfare (conscription and total war) there also arose in culture the documentary industry of surrogates for experience. Modern societies no longer try to base themselves on competition ("capitalism") but on collective cohesion, which requires a general understanding of the technical and social context.[11]

With such passages and defining statements like "documentation is to culture what machinery is to industry,"[12] Pagès distances himself from his documentation colleagues and instead places himself in the ranks of contemporary critics of modernity such as Martin Heidegger as well as Walter Benjamin in his 1936 essay *The Work of Art in the Age of Mechanical Reproduction*.[13] Still, as Day shows, Pagès's somewhat obstinate approach to classification and documentation theory can be defined as a precursor to later document theory.[14]

So, how does this explicit social critique, if at all, influence Pagès's view on classification in general and classification systems as documents in particular? In *Problèmes de classification culturelle et documentaire*, overall social perspectives and structural-syntactical considerations converge. Classification systems are contextualized within the entire system of scholarly knowledge, and its immediate relation to taxonomical development is problematized by a perceived gap between the rational and the social-psychological—the humane character of life. The critique of modernity that is seen in his earlier publication is here emphasized further, defining not only the role of classification but the character of classification systems as autonomous documents. Once again, the rational paradigm in society and *culture*, understood in a broad anthropological sense, is cast as conflictual. He even goes so far as to describe culture as invasive [*envahissant*] of rigid classificatory structures, in the sense of being subversive. He argues, with reference to Henry Evelyn Bliss, that

> the relation between the sciences (and of techniques) is not isolated, suggesting a salient cultural environment that it [the classification system] has the ability to describe in general. It does not only extend to the sciences and techniques, but to the totality of social activities working in the cultural terrain, and thus it is quite impossible to make a complete enumeration. Bliss claimed that the sciences are "pervasive," each one individually. That is why all cultural viewpoints have the ability to be invasive and egocentric.[15]

This tension between the scientific and the cultural, lived, world is of crucial importance for the understanding of the documentary character of a classification system, as it is in its ability to host that which defies enumeration that its informative potential appears. The structural elements that assure such transgression are found in the notational systems, the syntactical dimension of the semantic-syntactical dialectic emphasized by Begthol.[16] Notation defines the indexicality of the system in lack of a defined content, thus providing the necessary requirement for an autonomous agency of the system. However, documentality hosts not only such immediate and situational agency but historicity and functionality as well, and as Pagès's fellow student at CNAM, Eric de Grolier, later stated, temporal coherence and hereditary traces.[17]

Even if we accept a genealogical or hereditary progression between individual classification systems over time, there are few accounts that describe how this progression occurs other than through the development of certain structural particulars. One famous example of such is the decimal construct of the Dewey decimal classification, formulating a Baconian influence acquired through the classificatory work of William Harris.[18] Pagès takes this discussion forward by suggesting *isomorphism* as an element that helps explain another kind of progression between both universal systems and special classifications in particular institutional contexts. Isomorphism is, in its most general sense, a way for an organization or organizational entity to adapt to its surroundings in order to gain legitimacy. One way of doing this is to adapt to certain governing types of hierarchical structures, not necessarily mimetically but in a way that creates the sought legitimacy for, here, the documentary process. In Pagès's writings, isomorphism is also a way to overcome the problems of applying categorizations related to scientific taxonomy to everyday life and culture. With regard to the classificatory practice at the Bibliothèque National (BN), he suggests that

> the classificatory isomorphism of the BN works in the space between metaphysics and bibliographic classification but is not necessarily limited to these two domains. It can exist also between the kinds of domains that are explicitly classified (schemes) and those that are not (areas of experience).[19]

The ability to define classificatory structures and relations between them as isomorphic is, however, dependent on the ability of a system to define a wide range of subjects, knowledge areas, and areas of cultural experience. This provides an alternative way of formulating the linguistic definition of de Grolier's first- and second-degree documentary processes.[20] What brings them together is a processual focus that replaces the lack of defined content; the informative potential of a classification system is built on the idea of notational or codified isomorphism. That is the only way the documentality of a classification system *can* be defined, and this, to Pagès, manifests itself explicitly in the division between the classification of complex scholarly disciplines and cultural expressions, political environments, or personal experiences. Thus, isomorphism becomes not only a conceptual but perhaps also a practical tool for classification to manage the coercive problems identified in his politically inspired critique of modernity and its "mass" movements. Furthermore, it provides a basis for exploring a way to increased understanding of the problem of the elusive interaction between bibliographic classification and contextual elements—that is, in short, the documentality of classification systems. Thus, before turning to empirical cases, let us consider the concept of organizational or institutional isomorphism in a somewhat broader sense.

ISOMORPHISM AS A BASIS FOR UNDERSTANDING DOCUMENTALITY

Pagès makes use of isomorphism not primarily as a concept of change but as a way to capture the tension between classificatory structures (schemes) and contextual influences (areas of experience). In this way he not only manages to formulate an alternative to the social mechanization he sees documentary processes as parts of but also provide a key to our understanding of classificatory change and development. These ideas, brief as they are, encapsulate an almost precursory quality as they correlate well with the rethinking of Weberian sociological and organizational analysis that took place in the 1980s. In the school of new institutionalism, we again find isomorphism as a conceptual tool to characterize both contextual relations and change impetuses in institutional settings. This takes us to the last element of the given working definition of a document: that it should hold institutional value.

Writing about isomorphism in their widely influential anthology *The New Institutionalism in Organizational Analysis*, Walter Powell and Paul DiMaggio define the concept as "a constraining process that forces one unit in a population to resemble other units that face the same set of environmental conditions."[21] The character of this "constraining process" shows itself in observations that contradict the capitalist assumption that there is a pervasive and increasing variety in the construction and appearance of commercial enterprise and social organization. Instead, DiMaggio and Powell focus on a more complex relation between size, time, and bureaucratization in the progress of society, professions, and the role of administrative tools in institutional settings. What they find is instead homogenization: "In the initial stages of their life-cycle, organizational fields display considerable diversity in approach and form. Once a field becomes well established, however, there is an inexorable push towards homogenization."[22]

We see this development in the history of bibliographic classification as well. The introduction of the Dewey decimal classification in 1876 proved to have a decisively homogenizing effect on the plethora of local classification systems across the US at that time, and the development of the Universal Decimal Classification on the back of Dewey's system only emphasized this. In a discussion relevant to Pagès, Suzanne Briet suggests that classification should be done with "cultural affinity" considered—the organization of documents differ between bookshops, museums, and libraries, and thus should classification accordingly. In arguing for such a practical character of bibliographic classification systems, she denounces what she calls "the organization of knowledge," referring to universal systems such as the Universal Decimal Classification. For Briet, classification systems had institutional value through their direct relation to an immediate library or museum collection. This view was later the subject of intense criticism from Eric de Grolier, who in his 1962 book *A Study of General Categories Applicable to Classification and Coding in Documentation*, instead argued for the need to move away from pragmatic "anarchy" in classification and instead find a universal solution to the needs for subject access based on the, at that time, new computerized possibilities for subject-coded infrastructures.[23] The process of the homogenization of classificatory expressions and forms was already well underway when Briet delivered her argument for local, pragmatic classification systems. Thus, isomorphic processes have long influenced the development of bibliography. But what kind of isomorphic change exerts influence on documentation processes? In their organizational analysis, DiMaggio and Powell identify three main categories of isomorphic processes, based on the kind of influence on, or alignment with, surrounding conditions that tend to dominate: coercive, mimetic, and normative processes.

Coercive isomorphism occurs when an organization and organizational process react to either changes in other directly related organizations or from altered expectations related to cultural and social developments that immediately influence the organization. It may, for instance, be new regulatory or technical requirements imposed by the nation state or other bodies within which the organization is provided legitimacy. The stronger influence a state has on the organization of society, the more homogenized will institutions, organizations, and processes set to uphold that order become. "Thus," DiMaggio and Powell write, "the expansion of the central state, the centralization of capital, and the coordination of philanthropy all support the homogenization of organizational models through direct authority relationships."[24] The above quote from Pagès concerning the internal bibliographic processes at the Bibliothèque National provides a sense of what is meant by coercive isomorphism, and we will see several further examples in the upcoming chapters.

Isomorphism defined as a *mimetic process* is the second category discussed by DiMaggio and Powell. They ask how mimetic processes can be viewed as examples of isomorphic change. The answer has to do with uncertainty. Even in a situation where new external conditions are open for a variety of solutions, new agents still tend to follow already established organizations or institutions and create administrative or business models after these pioneering few. In a bibliographic context, we see this, for example, with technological innovations that set new formal or informal standards for document description and subject organization. Truly innovative models are rare, as even the most groundbreaking ones quickly adapt to older, successful, models. Whether this increases legitimacy or brings other kinds of benefits still begs the question. DiMaggio and Powell conclude that

> organizations tend to model themselves after similar organizations in their field that they perceive to be more legitimate or successful. The ubiquity of certain kinds of structural arrangements can be more likely credited to the universality of mimetic processes than to any concrete evidence that the adopted models enhance efficiency.[25]

The third kind of isomorphism identified is that of *normative processes*. This kind differs from the first two kinds in that these normative processes, in the writings of DiMaggio and Powell, refer to processes of professionalization. Professionalization is about conquering privilege, control, and the interpretation of limits and processes within an institutional setting. Critical elements are the establishment of academic education programs and professional organizations by which standards and mechanisms of exclusion can be defined and defended. Also, at a brief glance, we see how bibliographic classification aligns with such efforts in librarianship, first with the professional definition of librarianship by Gabriel Naudé in 1627, and then later with Melvil Dewey's concurrent founding of the School of Library Economy, the American Library Association, and the Dewey decimal classification. Both aspects, the educational and the organizational, are treated by DiMaggio and Powell as pivotal to organizational development and the homogenization of structural processes within institutions and organizations.

This division of isomorphic forms is analytical, and categories are not mutually exclusive. The processes influencing institutional implementation are complex and intertwining, and particularly the delineation between coercive forces and normative processes seems hard to uphold. I have mentioned here only briefly how these forms of isomorphism can be applied to bibliographic classification and their institutional belonging in a process that best can be described as meaning-creating. When applying this terminology to documents and processes of documentation, one needs to make a transposition from institutionalism to documentation. The coming chapters will show how this can be done, but before we move on, I would like to dwell, if ever so briefly, on the methodological process that will achieve this.

METHODOLOGICAL CONSEQUENCES

Reading isomorphic processes as central for the understanding of classification systems and their ability to exert social agency and institutional influence as autonomous documents requires a methodological approach that takes us back to the question of the mimetic that has run through this entire chapter. Bibliographic classification systems can be seen as mimetic documents in two ways: as objects or as parts of social processes, be they understood as cultural, political, or professional. Both of these perspectives carry their own legitimacy from a document-theoretical point of view, and in the end, they not only inform each other—they require each other. This division between object and process, as the idea of transposition, is open to objection as it is always hazardous to bring a concept from one discursive context to another, and a methodological framework is needed to create legitimacy for such an endeavor. In addressing what can be defined as *isomorphic documentality*, I choose to revisit one of the major influences on the above-mentioned discussions in information science that pronounced a hermeneutic, socially meaningful alternative to established cognition-oriented research practices within the discipline.

In his three-volume work *Time and Narrative* (*Temps et Récit*), French philosopher Paul Ricoeur uses an Aristotelian understanding of mimesis as a foundational concept to describe the relation between narrative texts (mostly fictional), temporality, and historical consciousness.[26] It is beyond the confines of this present study to dwell too deeply over this complex work, but the basic idea that carries Ricoeur's argument, that narrative configurations are tied up in processes that end in a completion of a refiguration of temporal experiences, can still work as a compass. In our case, this means, approximately, that every form of document is engaged in an interactive process with contextual elements that both influence and are influenced by the structural-semantic construct of the document. Documentality is thus at play. The concatenate concept for creating this refigurative movement or process is *mimesis* in any of the senses identified by DiMaggio and Powell. Alas, once again, mimesis is here treated as presentational and processual rather than purely re-presentational, and it is here that we find the Aristotelian influence to be most helpful. Ricoeur writes in the preface of the first volume of *Time and Narrative*:

> The mimetic function of narrative poses a problem exactly parallel to the problem of metaphorical reference. It is, in fact, one particular application of the latter to the sphere of human action. Plot, says Aristotle, is the mimesis of an action.[27]

Ricoeur then goes on to define three distinct interpretations of mimesis:

> A reference back to the familiar pre-understanding we have of the order of action; an entry into the realm of poetic composition; and finally a new configuration by means of this poetic refiguring of the pre-understood order of action.[28]

Here, we find our methodological key. What is described is a fundamentally dialectic process that presupposes one important step in the transposition to documentality: that the structure of a bibliographic classification system is treated not as a random combination of subjects (and relations between them) but as something meaningful that carries social and cultural significance. A classification's order of classes and hierarchical arrangement is similar to the Aristotelian idea of plot, as understood by Ricoeur. From this, it is possible to follow Ricoeur's intentions and adopt a tripartite methodological framework that can bring together documents in accordance with our definition with the open-ended, non-defined content of bibliographic classification systems. In order to meet the problem dealt with in this study—how to capture the social significance, the documentality, of classification systems outside of the information retrieval process—my analysis will follow the basic dialectic structure of prefiguration, configuration, and refiguration.

The first phase, *prefiguration*, paints a nonexhaustive picture of a variety of contextual elements and conditions of relevance for the understanding of a classification system as something more than a working tool. This phase aligns with the modern French documentation tradition's idea of documentation as a cultural technique, but it also addresses the problem of warrant as a basis for adequate classification and subject description. The focus is on social, political, cultural, and institutional influences and relations, all of which are relevant for the construction of individual bibliographic classification systems. The description of these contextual conditions differs from case to case according to what is most pertinent for providing analytical significance. Of specific interest is that which DiMaggio and Powell understand as normative practices in relation to library professionalization, which emerges gradually over the course of time periods of the cases. Professional contexts too develop in diverse guises, but they contribute to defining classification systems as more than tools; bibliographic practice is seen as foundational for professional identity in librarianship.

The second phase of the analysis, *configuration*, focuses on the individual classification system or group of classification systems at the center of each case. The semantic-structural construct—the "plot"—is discussed in a close reading–inspired fashion, and the significance of individual solutions for subject representation is analyzed both in relation to the pronounced contextual conditions and the document-theoretical arguments regarding the visibility of elements providing for a defined documentality.

The third concluding phase, *refiguration*, is governed by a synthesizing ambition, bringing together the various elements of the previous two stages of analysis to a new and deepened understanding of classification systems as documents. This refigurative analysis takes place within each case chapter, but most importantly provides the guiding principle of the concluding chapter of the book, not only giving a renewed picture of bibliographic classification systems and practices but, equally important, pushing for new questions in research on the significance of practices of knowledge organization.

With these three quite open analytical phases, a process is defined that brings together various aspects of our analysis: the document, documentality as a property of documents, classification practices, the problem of representation versus presentation, and the use of isomorphic processes as a way of getting away from a traditional view on both documents in general and classification systems in particular. The model is open enough to be flexible, hosting the need of each case, while still providing for a reasonable interpretation of the social significance of the systems analyzed. It is also open enough to be reinterpreted and even objected to. An important value of hermeneutically inspired analysis lies just here, in the combination of openness and reasonable interpretation. Answers sought cannot be proved in any final way but show one avenue to create an understanding of the complex way in which documents find social and cultural significance that goes beyond their immediate use. So, with this methodological compass, let us embark on our journey across the sea of analysis with the needle set on the harbor of increased understanding.

4

UNIVERSAL KNOWLEDGE, UNIVERSAL LANGUAGE: PAUL OTLET AND THE UNIVERSAL DECIMAL CLASSIFICATION FOR ESPERANTO

Most universal bibliographic classification systems hold within their syntactic-semantic relations seemingly contradictory connections to the local and the universal. As most of classification history revolves around systems being designed for specific libraries, the nineteenth century brings in another element—the quest for universality. Universality in this context means that the definition of subject classes and the hierarchical relations between them should not only fit the practical requirements of one specific collection or type of collection (such as a university library) but also provide a structure that mimetically represents certain non-bibliographically defined views on knowledge. In such a shift, several issues surface, one example being the status of the arts and humanities in relation to "pure" sciences, as an issue of significance and challenge.[1] As a result, it is from this period and on that we can talk about a scholarly field of knowledge organization or, in the words of Paul Otlet, "bibliology." The practical and the universal are often combined quite consciously. A good example of this is the Dewey decimal classification (DDC), prepared between 1872 and 1876, when its first edition appeared in print.[2] Originally appointed to produce a practical subject division for the Amherst College Library, Melvil Dewey developed his subject divisions from the actual holdings of the library. However, as he also wanted the system to meet general requirements that corresponded to his emerging ideas of renovating librarianship in a broader sense, elements of Italian bookshop practices and the works of English philosopher Francis Bacon were included into the system as well.[3] The philosophical connection was used as a basis for legitimacy in a sort of intellectual feedback loop where the subjects drawn from the local Amherst library were organized with reference to Bacon's early seventeenth-century knowledge divisions, that in turn were used to motivate the decimal structure of the system as the most suitable for library use. Such dialectical movements between the practical and theoretical were explored in several systems during this time, albeit none did ever enjoy the success bestowed upon Dewey. The Dewey decimal classification not only proved practical, but it did so in a way that has made it today's most-used bibliographic classification system in the world, used by about 200,000 libraries across 140 countries.[4]

However, parallel to the subsequent interest in Dewey's system in other countries during the first decades of the twentieth century, there was also another project, one that took Dewey's work in a somewhat different direction. Although firmly rooted in a European bibliographic tradition, Belgian lawyers Paul Otlet and Henri LaFontaine used Dewey's structural foundation to develop a classification system not intended for use in specific libraries, but instead in a bibliographic repertory constructed to gather all documented knowledge within an ideological vision of internationalism, seen as a springboard to a new social and intellectual level for humanity. A grand vision, indeed. To organize such a vision and secure its basis in knowledge, a new classification was needed. From a structural perspective, Dewey's system was attractive to the two Belgians, but they needed something more: another kind of classificatory universality, based on semantic abstraction, ontological presumptions, and linguistic synthesis. The result became the *Universal Decimal Classification*, first published in its complete form in 1904.

In this chapter, the Universal Decimal Classification system will take the center stage. I will direct our interest toward the specific cultural environment that developed in central Europe in the 1870s, defining the cultural and ideological preferences of the bourgeoise class until 1914, when World War I brought this very particular period—*La Belle Époque* or *La Fin de Siècle*—to a brutal halt. What we will look at is how one classification system came to represent a documentary embodiment of an idea: a world governed by knowledge, a knowledge society if you will. I will develop the chapter through three phases. As the decades surrounding the turn of the twentieth century have been widely covered by sociological and historical research, I will focus on one specific phenomenon that not only engaged numerous intellectuals, artists, and political representatives but also had a significant element of documentation and bibliography at its core: the idea of internationalism. The internationalist movement had many components functioning as an ideological backdrop to the peace movements, the workers' movements, the Arts and Crafts movement, first-wave feminism, the artificial language movement, and the women's suffrage movement. Politically it entailed the idea, firmly anchored in an odd combination of socialist sentiments and an imperialist understanding of geopolitical realities, that humanity is *one*, and that the only way to progress society in a harmonious direction was to move beyond nationalism and the idea of national borders. Within such a complex context, bibliography came to play an important role.

The definition of bibliography as part of the internationalist construct is discussed in part one. In part two, I focus on the classification system developed by Paul Otlet and Henri LaFontaine as presented in its first practical version in 1905, the *Manuel du repertoire bibliographic universel*, as part of the International Institute of Bibliography in Brussels. There is a vast literature on Paul Otlet and his work, and I will not reiterate the general findings of these efforts here.[5] Instead, I will discuss the documentary agency of classification systems within the vision of a world based on universally accessible knowledge. Thus, part three proceeds toward the significance of the Universal Decimal Classification by showing how it was developed specifically for use within the context of constructed auxiliary languages, another important aspect of internationalism. I do this by discussing an often-overlooked version of the UDC, the *Manuel du répertoire bibliographique universel applicable à la bibliographie de l'esperanto*, uniquely designed to meet the classificatory requirements of Esperanto. This system was published in 1908. The chapter concludes with a reconnection to the document-theoretical discussions in chapters 2 and 3.

INTERNATIONALISM AND THE ROLE OF BIBLIOGRAPHY

The originally intended role of the Universal Decimal Classification system differs from more library-oriented universal bibliographic classification systems in several ways, whereof the most striking perhaps is the visionary context within which it played a pivotal role. Development and expansion of the system was gradual, and the actual publication of it as a singular document in 1905 had only limited significance in that it was by then already part of an elaborate documentary infrastructure and practice conceived by Paul Otlet and Henri La Fontaine as a necessity for the international peace movement. The role of documentation as part of the very heterogeneous internationalist movement during the period between, roughly speaking, 1870 and the outbreak of World War II in 1939 has attracted increased interest in research during the last couple of decades. What brings this cross-disciplinary compound of investigations together is the positioning of documentation as a cultural practice rather than scientific one. This is a scholarly perspective that owes much of its current prominence to Akira Iriye's influential 1997 book, *Cultural Internationalism and World Order*.[6]

In the introduction to her edited volume, *Internationalism and the Arts in Britain and Europe at the Fin de Siècle*, Grace Brockington emphasizes the development of institutional infrastructures as the basis for a culturally defined internationalism through "societies, journals, conferences and exhibitions."[7] She goes on to claim that "cultural practitioners created their own organizations to support and disseminate their work, and to give them a point of contact with like-minded cosmopolitans."[8] These organizations were political, scientific, artistic, and perhaps most of all they carried ideas of a world beyond nationalism with a new society in mind, promoting universalism, solidarity, and peace. The way to establish practical alternatives to the structure of the nation state, more often inclined to muscular, military, and territorial preferences, was through the formation of organizations and alliances between organizations. The output in terms of societies, journalism, conferences, and such needed to be organized and brought together in some sort of superstructure in order to work. What such a superstructure should look like proved contentious and was subject of continuous discussion. The librarian, philosopher, and novelist George Bataille advocated an almost anarchistic, distributed power structure with no real center, while Paul Otlet took an opposite position, arguing for the need of strong, centralized institutions backed by a documentary infrastructure securing the constant need of up-to-date, transparent, and uniform flows of information. Both positions carried significance for the role of documents and documentary processes.[9] Otlet's position tended to correspond more accurately to a practical development of both individual organizations adhering to various scientific disciplines or social causes, as well as to the development of technological innovations enabling new routes of communication and representation, such as electricity, typewriters, phonograms, cameras, and telephones. Such innovations not only proved to be defining artefacts of the creative and entrepreneurial spirit of second wave industrialism; they also came to define artistic and cultural development of the time in ways that, among other things, supported the idea of a new universalism. What they all had in common was the simultaneous character of distributed use as well as centralized infrastructure.[10]

The documentation project of Paul Otlet and, to a somewhat lesser extent, Henri LaFontaine, who was increasingly over time more engaged in politics and the Belgian peace movement, was complex and displayed several developments over a period of three decades. It can be of value to give a brief chronological overview of some of the more significant steps. Otlet started thinking about documentation in the early 1880s as he worked for the esteemed law firm Edmond Picard in Brussels. In 1882, he and Henri LaFontaine of the same firm started to compile a cross-disciplinary social science bibliography for the Belgian Societé des Sciences Sociales et Politiques. As they needed to organize this bibliography, they evaluated a number of existing subject classification systems and eventually reached an appreciation for the Dewey decimal classification. Therefore, Otlet initiated correspondence on classification with Melvil Dewey that in a letter on June 29, 1895, led Dewey to agree to let Otlet develop the fifth edition of Dewey decimal classification according to their specific bibliographic needs.[11] The result was published as the Universal Decimal Classification in 1904. In 1895, Otlet and La Fontaine also acquired funding for the Institute International de Bibliographie, within which they developed the Universal Bibliographic Repertory, which in the mid-1930s consisted of more than fifteen million entries in the form of catalog cards, arranged in accordance with the Universal Decimal Classification system, at that time vastly bigger than its original Dewey counterpart. In 1907, following the publication of their classification system, Otlet and LaFontaine founded the Union of International Associations, with the ambition to create a kind of superstructure within which all internationalist associations and organizations could make use of, and contribute to, common resources such as the universal bibliographic repertory.[12] The last major phase in the common work of Otlet and LaFontaine was in the 1910s, searching for actual architectural solutions to host their work. This effort resulted in the *Palais Mondial* and an even more grand vision that eventually grinded to a halt on the drawing table of the famed architect Le Corbusier—a city of knowledge or a World City that would manifest the intentions of international idealism in the form of boulevards, parks, libraries, and museums. It was a kind of life-size documentation of a dream—architectural documentality before the term was even invented.[13]

The activities of Paul Otlet can thus be said to fall into two periods roughly divided by the late 1910s as World War I led to different perceptions of what social organization and trust and universal knowledge were all about. In the years leading up to the war, documentation and bibliography were explicitly placed as a central part of the internationalist ideas, creating an organizational infrastructure of information exchange. As time passed and illusions and hopes were shattered, pragmatism was transformed into a visionary idea in which documentation had symbolic correspondences with buildings and urban constructs that would house collections and bibliographic data. Both these periods relate in a very direct sense to Otlet's gradually refined understanding of documentation and bibliographic classification.

Bibliography and documentation coordinated the organization of a plethora of cause-specific international organizations that in the early twentieth century existed by the hundreds across Europe. In a report for the International Institute of Bibliography, *L'organisation international et les associations internationales* from 1910, Otlet describes a situation where documentation and information could join fragmented organizations. He argued that his International Institute of Bibliography could serve the role of being an overarching, national and international, institution for bibliographic unification:

> The International Institute of Bibliography is devoted to bibliographic and documentary organization in general, and the coordination of this domain. It is established on a principle of co-operation between national organizations of a [bibliographically] general order (libraries, and national associations), and specialized international organizations (international associations and congresses). The institute develops centralized collections and indexes.[14]

Interesting to note here is the parallel occurrence of a national and international perspective. Particularly in the discussion on the early European documentation movement within information studies, this influence of national bias has rarely been recognized. It is, however, important, as British historian Daniel Laqua has pointed out, to realize that internationalism created a route to national significance and recognition for smaller European countries such as Belgium and Switzerland.[15] In order to achieve the universal element in documentation that may be perceived as attractive and worthwhile for individual organizations, Otlet stressed the reciprocal character of the bibliographical repertory by arguing that the classifications and subject definitions used by the different organizations and associations are the very foundation on which the expansion of the decimal classification system is built. This, emphasized Otlet, leads to the need for international terminological standardization of which the International Institute of Bibliography could be an integral part through its capacity to organize knowledge. In what way the institute could contribute on a practical level is described by Otlet and La Fontaine in an article from 1914, advocating for the development of a union of international associations with documentation at its center. Creating a bridge between some four hundred primarily Belgian international associations, the union was to pursue the following goals:

- Create a federal body bringing together representatives from the individual associations through periodic conferences.
- Establish universal documentary systems, such as:
  - standardization of, for instance, legal procedures, weights, and measures;
  - regulation of the use of documents such as contracts, international rules, and conventions;
  - terminological standards in technical and scientific nomenclature, classification practices, and the use of national languages in international relations; and
  - coordinated publication of journals, reviews, yearbooks, and conference proceedings.

These efforts to create a common ground for the Belgian international associations would be further accentuated by establishing documentation centers, such as an international museum, an international library, encyclopedic archives, and, of course, the universal bibliographic catalog that was at the heart of the International Institute of Bibliography.[16] The mission to connect organizations and associations by means of documentation was due to Otlet's fear of decentralization and "anarchic" power distribution. Documentation not only had the potential to achieve a coordinating infrastructure but also provided a type of common language, manifested through standardized solutions for decision-making and the dissemination of information and knowledge. Reading the works of Otlet, one gets the impression that the rather ferocious intellectual and emotive environment that internationalist endeavors created needed all the coordinating help it could get. However, this was not entirely true. Most associations were already connected by means of documentation both within their chosen subject fields or social causes and between one another in recognition of each association's reciprocal value.

One such example was to be found "close to home," within the inner circle of the International Institute of Bibliography, where Henri La Fontaine's sister, Léonie La Fontaine—rarely recognized in the literature on documentation—was not only a significant force in the development of the institute but an ardent organizer of the feminist movement in Belgium. In this latter role, she was responsible for the establishment of the cross-disciplinary *Office Central de Documentation Féminine* in 1909, collecting documentation on feminism and the women's suffrage movement from associations across the social (science) spectrum. As her role in the bibliographic institute preceded her founding of the feminist documentation center, this was almost immediately incorporated as a subdivision of the International Institute of Bibliography, serving as an example of how social causes could be centrally organized through efforts of documentation.[17]

However, toward building transparency and a common ground on which associations and ideas could meet, there was the need for more than the important practical work of establishing publishing avenues, meeting places, and general standards. A guiding idea was needed. To develop the ideological and epistemological requirements of true universality, all branches of knowledge needed to be collected and positioned in relation to each other in such a way that a higher goal could be achieved—that of a *totality of knowledge*. The totality of knowledge was seen as necessary for elevating humanity to a new stage of solidarity, empathy, and peaceful social relations based on scientific progress. And toward this, a classification system up to this task was needed. As previously mentioned, Otlet had found the inspiration for this in the Dewey decimal classification system, but his ambition went far beyond the practical intentions of the American original. What Otlet required was a classification system that had the documentary capacity to (re)present—and develop—a semantic-structural relation that could only be implemented through treating the classification system as an autonomous document that contained a much larger complexity than what could serve an average library system. Isomorphic properties were required. The Universal Decimal Classification gradually came to fulfill such a purpose (in relation to its original context) and institutionalize such isomorphic (re)presentation of the totality of knowledge as described in the later writings of Paul Otlet, privileged among which were the *Traité de Documentation*, published in 1934, and *Monde*, published in 1935.[18] Classification in the late nineteenth century was still a primarily positivistic endeavor, not least seen in the obvious difficulties Dewey encountered when organizing subject hierarchies in the arts and humanities, which did not easily fit into a the clearer epistemic divisions of scientific knowledge. This was true for Otlet as well, but, as Steffen Ducheyne has shown, Otlet's early understanding of classification as practice, and classification systems as documents, gradually made way as the first decades of the twentieth century progressed for a more reflective, almost metaphysical, perception of his classification system as a structural verisimilitude for the inherent structure of the universe itself, an "unité essentielle."[19] At the very end of his monumental *Traité de Documentation: Le Livre sur le livre*, Otlet comments: "Creating a classification with concise idea-based notation enriches the spiritual with a universal, written language capable of forcefully influence the very shape of thought itself."[20]

The UDC was seen as a powerful language, a document touching on the very essence of thought. Let us look at how this language manifested itself in terms of documentary properties and then see how it was used in the service of another constructed auxiliary language, Esperanto, which indeed could fit Otlet's description of classification in its own right. So, to define the role of classification and the Universal Decimal Classification in its original context, let us turn to the problem of universality through language.

CLASSIFICATION AS A UNIVERSAL LANGUAGE OF DOCUMENTATION

Creating the Universal Decimal Classification out of the Dewey decimal classification was not merely a pragmatic choice for Otlet. Aspects of usage were of course important, not least as Otlet's creation was constructed for bibliography rather than library use, something that allowed for the implementation a wider range of warrants than was the case for most library classification systems. The perhaps greatest innovation in the Dewey decimal classification was the simplification of subject analysis that came with the combination of decimal notation and a "relative index," guiding the user into the classified tables, subject by subject. The index also worked as an authority list, showing what terminology was preferred in the system. However, Paul Otlet took this combination of hierarchies and index entries further by creating an even simpler, yet more elaborate, structural compound in the forms of auxiliary tables allowing *aspects* of the original subject—all for the quest of increased universality. He regarded subject classification as an attempt to create a universal language. In approaching this transformative process, it can be worthwhile to briefly reflect on classification as a language, and language as a basis for an internationalist identity, as this will prove important for the subsequent discussion on documentality and the social role of classification systems as documents.

Classification theorist Elaine Svenonius has written of the "language" of classification as a bibliographic language, divided into sublanguages that (1) describe information as such—that is, content or subject classifications—and (2) that describe its documentary embodiment—that is, the physical attributes of a document. In traditional librarianship, this difference would be the same as that between content-oriented subject classification and cataloging. She describes these linguistic constructs as, on the one hand, work languages dealing with authority control, titles, author names, and subject definitions, and on the other a document language formulating production attributes and information on location of documents in specific libraries or collections.[21] Such formulation of classification as part of a complex of bibliographic languages and sublanguages aligns closely to the idea of the organization of knowledge, and indeed information science as a scholarly discipline too, as working on an epistemological meta-level. In a famous article, Marcia Bates writes that all academic disciplines can be seen as studying different universes of phenomena. The natural sciences study the natural world, the social sciences study the social world produced by humans, and the arts and humanities study the content and context of the creative works of human beings, from philosophy to literature to the arts. Information Science has a distinct universe that it studies also—the world of recorded information produced by human agency. We can imagine all the human activities in studying the above natural, social, and artistic universes themselves producing information entities—books, articles, databases, data files etc.—thus creating a fourth universe, that of recorded information.[22]

This view not only reflects the deep influence of Paul Otlet on today's information science discourse, but more importantly, it creates a sort of feedback loop of the role of classification that has been carved out of his writings. In the formulation of a "fourth universe," the meta-disciplinary character of documentation and the discipline that Otlet called *bibliology*, classification systems are provided documentality as a meta-language based on a grammar of authoritative terminologies and taxonomies across all fields of knowledge. And indeed, we find Paul Otlet proposing a similar view, echoing his period by characterizing a bibliographic classification system as a "vast synoptic outline, divided into classes, divisions and sections, of all the subjects on which it is possible to write."[23] This conception of a vast synoptic outline brings with it associations of confinement, total control, distinction, and discipline. In other words, it presents a picture of absolute centralization.[24] With the completion of the Universal Decimal Classification, Otlet and La Fontaine not only created a vital ingredient for a universal informational and documentary infrastructure of international associations but they also expanded that practical function into something even more visionary: an organizational principle for all types of documents in all disciplines of knowledge. With departure in Dewey's original construction, their methodology for development was built on two central aspects of classification: depth and synthesis. The Universal Decimal Classification displayed a previously unseen number of subjects placed in its hierarchical main tables, and the elements of synthesis were chosen with a nod to the most universal language of all: mathematics. So, let us look at how this endeavor for universality was created in practice.

When the first complete edition of the Universal Decimal Classification was published, it presented relatively few innovations. The Classification's main table structure was taken over from Dewey's system, and the synthetic elements were already at this time present in various library classification systems. What pushed the envelope was instead the level of detail and the consciousness of which the different elements of the system were presented. Unlike Dewey, who in the preface of his system put significant energy into providing a philosophical legitimacy to his very practical and literary warrant divisions, Otlet and La Fontaine related their system to a belief in the permanence of scientific knowledge, not unlike the one by Richardson that I wrote about in chapter 2. The development of new subjects becomes a matter of genealogic offspring from established knowledge rather than paradigmatic shifts presenting established knowledge as obsolete or irrelevant. In this way the structure of the system becomes both stable enough to persist over time and possible to develop as new issues becomes formulated in documents. However, Otlet and La Fontaine also recognized the problem of classificatory bias and that several perspectives on a subject or a fact can influence the perceived content of a document, thus necessitating mechanisms in the system to counteract such distractions from pure knowledge. "The consequence of this observation," Otlet writes in 1896 shortly after the adoption of Dewey's system, "is that a structure of classification numbers is desirable such that to each category of basic ideas which regularly recurs, there should correspond a form of notation with a distinct appearance and a permanent meaning."[25]

To understand how this permanent meaning is achieved, it can be of value to look at how the Universal Decimal System is constructed. It has ten main categories:

0. Science and knowledge, Organization, Computer Science, Information, Documentation, Librarianship, Institutions, Publications.
1. Philosophy, Psychology.
2. Religion, Theology.
3. Social Sciences.
4. *Vacant.*
5. Mathematics, Natural Sciences.
6. Applied Sciences, Medicine, Technology.
7. The Arts, Recreation, Entertainment, Sport.
8. Language, Linguistics, Literature.
9. Geography, Biography, History.

It is a tight schedule. Most striking, of course, is the vacancy in category 4. It has been there from the very beginning, and debated ever since as to what function it serves, as Otlet and La Fontaine rationalized the Language and Literature categories by grouping these two major subject areas together in category 8, thus providing for a common set of subdivisions. The Dewey decimal classification hosts Languages and Linguistics in category 4. The formulation of the main categories here are taken from the now current complete version of the system, the electronic so-called Master Reference File from 2011, consisting of a total of more than seventy thousand classes.[26] Except from the obvious crowdedness in, for instance, category 6, Applied Sciences, Medicine, Technology, it is worth noting that subject areas relating to information, documentation and librarianship are placed in the first category (0), which holds a status of a general documentation division that can be used in various ways across the main tables in the definition of subjects—a practical implementation of Bates's meta-disciplinary "fourth universe." This is the synoptic tower overlooking the succeeding categories of the system.

The vast number of classes that are housed in the main tables need to be complemented with features to capture bias and perspectives, language, space. All these are necessary to establish a correct relation between the content of an individual document and its searchable bibliographic representation. Expanding on the idea of classification as a linguistic construct, Otlet and La Fontaine developed a set of auxiliary divisions applicable in accordance with specific rules across the subject classes. These were equipped with a nonalphabetic notation that made them easy to separate from the actual subject class. Melvil Dewey at an early stage also experimented with such divisions, attempting to compound numerical and alphabetical signatures, leading to solutions like this:

598.2j43d44	Birds in Germany in the 18th century.

The inclusion of letters into the classification was questioned by Otlet, "because the mixture of numbers and letters removes from the classification its decimal and numerical character in which lies both its simplicity and its universality."[27] What he instead suggested was a model where the main tables are transformed into auxiliary indices:

Main table	*Auxiliary table for geographical aspect*
91.4 Geography of Europe	(4) Europe
91.54 Geography of India	(54) India

This made it possible to use geographical, historical, temporal, and formal subdivisions throughout the system without adding extra elements. The only thing added was a set of punctuation marks:

+	Bringing two subjects together.
/	Extension of subdivisions. This connects the first and the last class in a sequence of classes on the same hierarchical level.
:	Relation between two subjects, with the dominant subject to the left of the colon mark.
=	Language.
(0 . . .)	Form.
(1/9)	Geographical division, Place.
(= . . .)	Ethnic division.
". . ."	Time, historical period.
.00	Point of view.
-03	Materials.
-05	Persons.

In this way, Otlet and La Fontaine not only managed to keep their vast system together by using main table numbers as auxiliary means across the system but they also created a codification that provided the fundamentally numerical divisions with grammatical tools making it possible to formulate highly complex subjects within a limited, yet universal, pronunciation. Eventually, Dewey, too, abandoned his alphanumerical attempts and instead introduced a system of auxiliary tables similar (but uncredited) to those of Otlet and La Fontaine, however with a different, entirely numerical, solution for separating main subject tables from auxiliary tables.

One of the most important properties of the Universal Decimal Classification was that it should be possible for the classifier to create complete systems for special collections within, basically, any subject field. It was therefore necessary for the universal structure to speak across disciplines. Over time, this particular feature has proved to contain both advantageous and disadvantageous elements. On the one hand, the system has proved useful for detailed classification in archives and libraries of various sorts; on the other it has led to a somewhat anarchic development of the system as there was, after the demise of Otlet, a lack of coordination between updates in the system. This was a consequence of the original updating and development practices, building on suggestions from scientists and other relevant representatives in the various fields of knowledge. Such suggestions for new subjects or replacements of existing ones were included fluidly, so that with time it became difficult to know which edition was followed in the individual library. However, these problems were mainly caused within the Fédération de Information and Documentation, as it developed after Otlet, thus stretching somewhat beyond the scope of this book.

So, to summarize thus far: developing a classification system for the bibliographical repertory of the International Institute of Bibliography was not only a practical necessity for information retrieval. It was also a central element in the perception of documentation structures and processes, as a central part of an infrastructure was needed to coordinate Belgian internationalist associations and to create an infrastructural network of accessible and useful knowledge. In time, these ideas grew into a global vision, encompassing the idea of a totality of knowledge as a cornerstone in a "Cité Mondial," a World City, which was to control the ferocious nationalist sentiments of the decades leading up to World War I. The Universal Decimal Classification did, however, relate not only to this sense of totality, but to specialists as well. The construction of the system by means of numerical and grammatical notation made it possible to adapt to any specialist field. In fact, this value for specialists was at the very heart of the project, as Paul Otlet made clear already in 1896: "Thus, the encyclopedic requirements of the Universal Bibliographic Repertory can be reconciled with the necessities of special bibliographies."[28] To exemplify how this was done in practice, I will now turn my attention to one of the earliest examples of such a special classification system extracted from the Universal Decimal Classification, the *Manuel du repertoire bibliographic universel applicapble à la bibliographie de l'esperanto* from 1908.[29] In this, Otlet combines the universal ambition of his classification system with another attempt at linguistic universality, Esperanto, the constructed language built and motivated much in line with the ultimately peace-supporting bibliographic project of Otlet and La Fontaine.

THE UNIVERSAL DECIMAL CLASSIFICATION FOR ESPERANTO

Even though Otlet is not known to have practiced Esperanto or any other artificial language in any significant sense, his view on classification as a linguistic construct is in many ways similar to those considerations made by the emerging movement of constructed languages in the late nineteenth century. As such, the idea of constructed languages was not new by this time. However, the thought that both scientific and social development would benefit from unified expressions that counteracted the vernacular Tower of Babel of the European continent gained prominence as part of the progressive movements and associations centered around the idea of international peace.

Throughout its intellectual history, Europe has always struggled with the tension between the vernacular expressions of the peoples and the unified language of politics and science. Such efforts to find a linguistic common ground were always part of the execution of power, whether through knowledge, the church, or in politics—Latin of course being the most obvious example, serving as the main language of social and religious power for more than a millennium. There are other examples too, such as German being used as the administrative language in the Habsburg monarchy, and Sweden's linguistic oppression of its Sámi- and Meänkieli-speaking minorities in the far north into the mid-twentieth century. As the dynastic power spheres of central Europe eventually dissolved and vernacular languages were elevated in status, ethnic and nationalist identities became more pronounced. However, this development also drove the chauvinist sentiments that came to dominate public discourse and political actions in the early twentieth century. Constructed languages were all part of an intellectual movement that wanted to thwart this progression toward seemingly unavoidable conflict. These planned languages appeared in several shapes. The concept of pasigraphy can help us understand this.

A pasigraphy, writes Pierre Janton in his history of Esperanto, "is a purely visual writing system." These are not languages that are to be spoken, but pure notations and grammars with representational functions. I discussed this type of linguistic form in the first chapter, which Jack Goody attributed to classification systems within his anthropological studies. Janton shared Goody's view by addressing classification systems as being at the very origin of planned languages:

> The universal language projects that appeared in increasing numbers from about 1650 on used as their starting point the Cartesian postulate that 'invention of the language depends on true philosophy.' Posited on the classification of ideas, they constituted coherent systems ordered around sets of fundamental concepts.[30]

Examples of classificatory structures include the decimal classification system constructed by Melvil Dewey that in this context led the way to another project, *Translingua*, a planned language that developed its numerical structure into one that could accommodate full linguistic expression. In a comment on the translingual script, Erich Funke writes that

> the most practical and formative principle of a neutral and logical "international" system of symbols seems to be the decimal system which has been utilized in several a priori languages and which Melvil Dewey has most successfully applied in his bibliographical classification. The limitations of Dewey's ingenious and widely used system lie in the fact that it contains no verbs and that many fields of human experience cannot easily be organized in units and subdivisions of ten concepts.[31]

This last point is a well-known issue in the critique of both the Dewey and the Universal Decimal Classification systems. However, Funke continues, probably without realizing that he was establishing the type of link between bibliography and social agency that Otlet so longed for:

> Due to the absence of verb symbols and syntactic patterns, it [the Dewey system] does not permit the formulation of sentences. It might, however, be used as the basis of an a priori language if properly modified and if supplemented by number symbols for verbs and by a simple grammatical system.[32]

This resembles the kind of modifications that were introduced into the Universal Decimal Classification as auxiliary tables, forming a kind of simple grammatical structure in its representation of subjects. Thus, Otlet's definition of his classification system as a kind of language was part of a larger movement, and although most planned languages never got out beyond a very limited circle of initiated few, some did indeed find larger numbers of users and followers.

Two of the most successful were *Volapük*, created by Johan Martin Schleyer in 1880, and *Esperanto*, compiled seven years later by Lazar Ludwik Zamenhof. Between the two, Esperanto went on to become the one with the largest degree of dissemination into the general consciousness of ordinary people, while Volapük, although elegant in its construction, never quite managed to achieve general recognition and eventually dissolved in disagreements over how it should be developed.[33] What is more interesting is how they connected to the general sentiment of the times, the late 1880s and the following decades. Schleyer, a Catholic priest, was motivated by new communication technologies—telephones, railways, postal systems—that all created a bedrock for a unified language that would facilitate the exchange of information internationally. Zamenhof's motive for engaging in the development of Esperanto was similar to that of Schleyer's, but it included a social ethos that the latter seemed to lack—Volapük was almost exclusively a language for the emerging European middle class. Zamenhof brought with him the concrete experience of growing up as an Ashkenazi Jew in Bialystok, in what is today northeastern Poland, close to the borders of Lithuania and Belarus. Here, daily life was dominated by a tense linguistic environment dominated by Yiddish, Polish, German, and Russian, each representing various social layers of racial, social and religious conflicts. Janton concludes that "[Zamenhof] was not an ivory tower linguist. . . . Human divisions and conflicts had caused him great suffering, and so he saw the creation of an international language as simply a first step toward a more general goal of peace."[34]

Not unlike Esperanto, the Universal Decimal Classification was discussed by its creator not as a language with an ideal but an ideal with a language. Therefore, it is not surprising to see Otlet follow up on Zamenhof's 1905 publication of the *Fundamento de Esperanto*, consisting of a sixteen-rule grammar and the original Esperanto dictionary originally published in 1894 under the pseudonym "Dr. Esperanto," with a classification system designed exclusively to cover the rapidly growing body of Esperanto literature, in time for the creation of the World Federation of Esperanto Associations in 1908. For Otlet, Esperanto was a solution to the endeavor to democratize the language of congresses and assemblies of international associations, as the common choice of English, French, or German as official languages inevitably brought cultural biases into their work.[35] Furthermore, the publication of the *Manuel du répertoire biblipgraphic universel applicables à la bibliographie de l'esperanto* proved a good case for how the Universal Decimal Classification could be used as a special classification for a limited range of subjects while still maintaining its universal character. In the preface of this system, Otlet describes it as a win-win situation; Esperantists get a bibliographical tool suited for their needs, and these adjustments are introduced into the system rendering it "un caractère complètement international."[36] The classification itself focused on two major fields of knowledge: language and linguistics (4), and literature and belle-lettres (8).

Of course, these seem intuitive enough, but they host a number of interesting and sensitive considerations. Let us look at how they are divided in the system.

Main class 4 Language and Linguistics consists of a hierarchical division constructed uniquely for this classification:

4 Philologie. Linguistique.
4.0 Questions linguistiques diverses
 4.08 Espèces diverses de langues
 4.089 Langues artificielles
  4.089.0 Généralités et projets généraux
  4.089.1 Volapuk
  4.089.2 Esperanto
  4.089.3 Langue Bleu (système mixte) de Léon Bollak
  4.089.4 Autres systèmes mixtes
  4.089.5 Projets généraux et prjets mal définis
  4.089.6 Systèmes a priori
  4.089.7 Idiom natural (Systèmes a posteriori)
  4.089.8 Autres systems a posteriori.
41 Philologie genérale
42–49 Philologie Spéciale des langues usuelles

Following this main division that situates planned and auxiliary languages in the general science of linguistics, the system deepens those parts that are specifically relevant for Esperanto, 4.089.2, by making explicit both semantic and syntactical elements in a unique division, renaming the main class for artificial languages:

4.089 Philologie spéciale des langues artificielles
4.0892 Philologie de 'Esperanto

Here, directions are included on how to create more sophisticated and specialized notations:

4.0892	[(0), (.), "", xx,:] *Généralitiés.*
4.0892-	*Questions particuliéres.*[37]

These aspects [Questions particuliéres] are then accounted for in a division that ranges from the orthographical to educational requirements:

4.0892-1	Orthographie.
4.0892-2	Étymologie.—Derivations.
4.0892-3	Lexicologie—Dictionnaires.
4.0892-4	Synonymes—Homonymes.
4.0892-5	Morphologie—Grammaire—Syntaxe.
4.0892-6	Prosodie—Métrique—Versification.
4.0892-7	Dialectes. Patois—La langue aux diverses époques.
4.0892-8	Études et enseignement de la langue.

As for further divisions, these aspects of Esperanto in turn vary significantly. 4.0892-4 has no subdivisions at all, while 4.0892-5 consists of no less than 112 subdivisions on three levels.

In this classification, Otlet took a step back from his decision to leave the main category (4) vacant in the Universal Decimal Classification, situating Language and Linguistics in category (8) together with Literature. The overall idea is that these knowledge fields can be divided in similar ways and that subjects concerning linguistics, languages, and literature overlap. This is, however, a deviation from the original Dewey division that in this special classification system proves difficult to uphold. Instead, in division 4.0892 Otlet returns to the system's Dewey origins, applying the divisions made in the Dewey decimal classification class 420, English Philology. The division, seen here in the eighth edition from 1913, distributes as follows:[38]

420	English Philology.
421	Orthography.
422	Etymology. Derivation.
423	Dictionaries. Idioms.
424	Synonyms. Homonyms.
435	Grammar,
426	Prosody
427	Dialects. Early forms of language. Slang.
428	School books. Texts for learning the language.
429	Anglo-Saxon.

Incorporating the Language and Linguistics category in Arts and Literature in the Universal Decimal Classification was one of the most controversial changes from the Dewey system made by Otlet. It is particularly noteworthy that he returns to the Dewey division almost *verbatim*, as the other aspect of Esperanto that is expanded upon in the classification system is precisely that of literature. That literature gets a refined treatment in the Esperanto classification is a good example of a subject sensitivity that characterizes the Universal Decimal Classification as a whole, but it proves even more accentuated when used in a special classification. Literature was a fundamental ingredient in the early development of Esperanto. It was important for Zamenhof in his efforts to create a language that not only related to scientific terminology, which was the prime object of, for instance, Volapük, but instead reverberated into all aspects of life—not least literary. While building the Esperanto movement several literary works were translated quite early on, and this helped develop the language by confronting it with "real" problems. Translations abounded: *Eugene Onegin, Peer Gynt, Gösta Berling, Kalevala, Faust, Othello, Oedipus Rex,* to only name a few, were all translated into Esperanto during the years surrounding the turn of the century, along with original works in Esperanto published either as solitary monographs or anthologies. Esperanto theater made its first original mark in 1910 with five-act drama *Gustav Vasa: historia drama in kvin aktoj* by renowned esperantist and teacher Reinhold Schmidt from Breslau (today Wroclaw, in southeast Poland).[39]

Introducing the Literature category into his Esperanto classification, Otlet stressed the intersubject correspondence principle of the Universal Decimal Classification, thus providing literature in Esperanto with notational number 8.0892, Littérature de L'Esperanto. The main division here distributes as follows, based on the original Universal Decimal Classification division from 1905:

8.0 Écrits sur la littérature.
 8.089 Littératures des langues artificielles.
  8.0892 Littéraure Esperantiste.
   8.0892 (0) Subdivisions communes de forme et de généralistes.

8.0892 (A-Z)	Œuvres particulières classes par noms d'auteurs.
8.0892.01	Esthétique littéraire de l'Esperanto.
8.0892-	Œuvres particulières, classes par genres littéraires.

In this last class, literary genres are further divided as follows:

8.0892-1	Poésie.
8.0892-2	Théâtre, littérature dramatique.
8.0892-3	Roman. Nouvelle.
8.0892-4	Essais.
8.0892-5	Éloquence.
8.0892-6	Lettres.
8.0892-7	Satires.
8.0892-8	Miscellanées, Mélanges littéraires, Fantasies littéraries.

As most of the Esperanto literature at this time consisted of translations, this relatively fundamental classification, formulated according to the same structural properties as the division in (4), was complemented with a division of original languages, taken from the 1905 edition of the full system:

82 à 89	Littérature des langues national diverses.	
	82	Littérature anglaise.
	83	Littérature allemande.
	84	Littérature française.
	85	Littérature italienne.
	86	Littérature espagnole.
	87	Littérature grecque
	89	Autres littératures diverses.

Otlet richly commented on the literature class, primarily on how to build numbers to fit the needs of Esperantists. To the above division 89 [Autres littératures diverses], he adds that "les divisions sont les mêmes que celles de 49 *Philologie des langues diverses.*"[40] And reasoning on how to treat translations of classical works, he gave directions with concrete examples. For instance, he wrote that a translation of *Hamlet* by Zamenhof could be treated in either a fully expressed way or with abbreviations:

Full notation: 8.0892 (Zamenhof -41—Shakespeare -7—Halmleto -032): 82 (Shakespeare -7—Hamlet -031)

Abbreviated notation: 8.0892 (Z -41—S -7—H -032): S -7—H -031)

In examples such as this, Otlet aligned himself not only with the economizing principles of the Universal Decimal Classification but also with the general tendency among planned languages to economize language as such. It is therefore hardly surprising to see that Otlet maintained an open door toward these languages over his entire career, building his documentary and classificatory theories in relation to them long after the Esperanto classification was produced. In his 1934 treatise *Traité de Documentation*, he maintained the strong bond between planned languages and the bibliographic language of documentation. Documentation needs to meet the requirements of several kinds of languages:

> In language as in documentation, we distinguish between that which is spontaneous, familiar and ordinary: vernacular language; that which is cultivated, figurative, aesthetic: the literary language; that which is rational and precise: scientific language. These three languages are, as they are constructed, talked, but the latter two, the literary and the scientific, are increasingly written.[41]

The tripartite division of languages as either vernacular, erudite, or scientific is problematic for documentation, which in one way or another must cover them all. It proved to be a similar kind of challenge for planned languages as well, and while some, such as Volapük or Ido, focused on establishing a new scientific language, Esperanto provided a grammar for a more holistic approach, addressing the differences between various levels and types of languages as something in need of bridging. This is likely the reason for Otlet's focus on Esperanto at the expense of other planned languages that, at first glance, would seem more appropriate for a bibliographical project such as his, concentrating on promoting social relevance for mainly scholarly output. Another reason is, of course, which I have touched upon previously, the common ground between Zamenhof and Otlet in attempting to merge knowledge with social action and universal peace. The existence of a language with adequate bibliographical counterparts, such as the proposed classification system, is a prerequisite for taking these projects forward. Action is needed in the short term, but, more importantly, a language such as Esperanto and bibliographical tools such as the Universal Decimal Classification are made for the support of a long-term development that may take generations. Otlet considered the prospect of a generational overturn in his *Traité de documentation* as a question of mass education: "An international language is a complementary sign of a universal civilization. Men are members of one unity within which they understand one another. The international language should be chosen by a qualified group and be taught as obligatory in schools."[42]

He further states that there is a never-ending tide of new languages developing, but that Esperanto is the one with the most sustainable properties in building the bridge between common people and these new educational initiatives aiming at comprehensibly "créer une langue philosophique et scientifique universelle."[43] Interesting to note is that Otlet never extended his obvious fascination over Esperanto into the language itself. His exemplary use of the Universal Decimal Classification as a basis for organizing Esperanto in the *Manuel du répertoire bibliographic universel applicables à la bibliographie de l'esperanto* stayed safely within the realm of the French language. There is no known translation of it into Esperanto. There seems also to have been very limited, if any, interaction between Otlet and Zamendorf. At the World Exposition in Paris 1900, Zamenhof was one of the stars, giving a widely recognized public presentation on Esperanto, while Otlet was placed only a few meters away showing off his world bibliography. Down the hall, Melvil Dewey stood in the American Pavilion. It is likely that they all at least met in person on this occasion.[44] The fates of Otlet and Zamenhof were to become similar. After the challenges to the internationalist movement brought on by World War I, the Nazis eventually declared Esperanto part of the "International Jewish Conspiracy" and targeted Zamenhof's family for extinction. In 1940, as the Nazis created havoc in Brussels, Otlet's life's work was looted and carried away by the occupiers. He never recovered and died as a broken man in 1944.

CONCLUDING REMARKS

As the multitude of internationalist associations grew into a movement of social change during *La Belle Époque* in the last three decades of the nineteenth century, the need for a centralized documentation service gained increasing importance. Today, the bibliographic project of Paul Otlet and Henri La Fontaine stands as one of the most persistently researched phenomena of this era. Not just for its ability to foresee a future where information sharing would become a key feature in international contacts of all sorts, but more for its provision of an archetypical infrastructure. At the center of attention in this case has been the Universal Decimal Classification, which came to manifest a way to organize knowledge aligned with the ideology of internationalism and, in the case of Otlet and La Fontaine, the peace movement. Building on a vision to create bibliographic representations of all scientific knowledge, classificatory structures were normatively adapted to fit the current ideals of knowledge distribution within internationalist associations and social movements. Governing among those ideals were centralization and hierarchic modes of organizational structure. In this way, the Universal Decimal Classification represented a manifest documentality, well in line with the definition of an autonomous document as an inscribed social act. Its documentality is seen in a representational dialectic between structure and content, proven in practice not just through the general divisions of the full system, but even more so, perhaps, in special classifications created from the full system created to meet the requirements of individual disciplines or social movements. The example discussed in this chapter, the special classification for Esperanto and Esperantists, is telling of how this alignment was created by means of documentary integrity of the classification.

The ambition of the Esperanto movement to create a language that could unify the scientific community across disciplines, as well as literary and vernacular use was matched by the structural properties of the Universal Decimal Classification. Not perhaps primarily through the decimal structure as such, but rather through parallel syntactical elements that allowed for notational transfers between different fields of knowledge. This flexibility conjured up a connection between the machine-bureaucratic social ideals of the time—"the steampunk version of hypertext," as the founding editor of *Wired Magazine*, Kevin Kelly, once called it—a rationalistic and positivistic representation of a knowledge ideal of social progress and predictability. This connection between the mechanistic and bureaucratic is exactly what was submitted to critique by Robert Pagès a few decades later as he found that the intellectual efforts of Otlet and later classification and document scholars would feed not only a military arms-race, but also a dehumanizing technocratic discourse. However, analyzing the documentary value of the Universal Decimal Classification, we also find a side that corresponds to a vision dressed in a positivistic, hierarchical robe, perhaps hiding an idealistic spirit that perhaps even Pagès would succumb to. This is also what makes Paul Otlet's creation unique. Rarely do we see pronunciations such as those that Otlet formulated in his search for a legitimacy to his universalist endeavor for world peace based on a new world order. Applying the categorization made by DiMaggio and Powell, the Universal Decimal Classification represents an isomorphic refiguration of classificatory conventions most closely aligned with *mimetic processes* manifested in parallel to the construction of pasigraphic planned languages, claiming rationally expressed universality. In the light of this, Otlet's classification for Esperanto literature becomes even more interesting as Esperanto displays use well beyond the mathematical and grammatically abstract. Instead, Esperanto is a language that is very much alive, an aspiring change agent and the designated classification shows such sensitivity in action, in that it not only manages to create a relevant classificatory representation of the literature on and about Esperanto, but furthermore a classification with a unique documentary agency through an isomorphic (re)presentation of a defined specialist area of knowledge while maintain the meaning-carrying properties of the universal classification system.

In the next chapter, I will address the opposite movement of the same period, the building of new national identities on the back of industrial, entrepreneurial, and technological progress. Through the case example of the Swedish SAB system, I will discuss nationalism and the use of libraries and library classification systems as parts of a sociocultural infrastructure with which to formulate nationalistic sentiments in the construction of a novel, democratic system. In this politically contentious and dramatical process we will find Éric de Grolier's idea of classification systems as anticipating future trends—in this case, Sweden as a culturally coherent modern nation.

5

NATIONALISM AND DEMOCRACY: PUBLIC LIBRARIES AND BIBLIOGRAPHIC CLASSIFICATION IN EARLY TWENTIETH-CENTURY SWEDEN

The Universal Decimal Classification system that was at the center of attention in the previous chapter was developed as a theoretical construction, taking established bibliographic practice as a point of departure for a system that would align with a certain defined agency. As part of an explicitly internationalist culture, Paul Otlet and Henri La Fontaine used their bibliographical institute, and the bibliographic tools developed therein, to promote and facilitate work to counteract abiding nationalist sentiments at the turn of twentieth-century Europe. In this chapter my analysis will remain in this period, although extended somewhat both back and forward, but I will focus on classifications that fed national identity. I will turn my attention toward the elusive relation between the establishment of a new social order and the development of a nationally defined library practice manifested through a unique bibliographic classification system that brings yet another meaning to the concept of institutional value of documents. The so-called SAB system (SAB—the Swedish Library Association) was published in 1921 as one of several initiatives to bring together a public library infrastructure during the establishment of new institutional relations in the emerging Swedish democracy.[1] Limits were drawn immediately. What I am dealing with here is a national system, designed to meet the needs of Swedish public libraries at the ideological crossroads between romantic-nationalist sentiments and industrial rationalism, so significative of the first decades of twentieth-century west Europe.

The modern public library is essentially a twentieth-century institution, although its antecedents can be traced back to the mid-eighteenth-century Enlightenment ideas that took hold of liberal and progressive social movements across Europe as well as being part of the constitutional fabric of the US. In more or less every country, its ascendance has been due to a developed library system, connected to democratic breakthroughs.[2] Of course, public libraries exist—and in many cases developed simultaneously—also in societies that were, and are still, not fully democratic, but only in democratic systems have they thrived as institutions for individual education and *Bildung*. However, it is important to stress that also the character of the democratic connection differs significantly between countries. If we follow the ideals governing public libraries over the last hundred and fifty years or so, we can see that that they have changed in relation to the variety of political specters that have come to build the political systems in different countries. Wallace Koehler states that "the relatively recent support of public libraries and library associations for a multiculturalist approach is of very recent etiology. . . . Public libraries and library associations have at times resisted liberal trends, just as they are today resisting more conservative trends."[3] In whatever environment they appear, they do have their origins in the Enlightenment trust in knowledge as a force for the betterment of the everyday life of ordinary people to move society toward higher states of civilization—basically, the idea of social evolution.

In this chapter, I will discuss classification for public libraries in Sweden through a historical prefiguration, focusing on two related processes: (1) the tension between state control and self-educational popular movements at the turn of the nineteenth century and the first decades of the twentieth century, and (2) the question of a claimed Swedish bibliographic tradition and its conflicted relation to American influences on classificatory practice and, more generally, bibliographic control.

BUILDING DEMOCRACY, BUILDING LIBRARIES

Swedish democracy is not defined in a constitution written by a handful of "founding fathers," nor is it the result of revolution. Instead, the implementation of democratic practices was introduced under the influence of educational ideals from the Enlightenment, first formulated within the state church in the early nineteenth century and eventually through the emergence of alternative social structures within three major popular movements—the Labor Movement, the Sobriety Movement, and the Free Church Movement—at the turn of the twentieth century. These movements were all parts of the international network of progressive social cause organizations that were discussed in the previous chapter. Swedish legislation opened gradually for a more educated and participating citizenry during the whole of the nineteenth century, with the most crucial reforms being the Public-School Act in 1842, mandating six-year primary school education for *all* children, and a series of constitutional reforms on the rights to vote, taking place between 1909 and 1921, which gave women full rights to vote and uphold public office. In this development, supported by maturing ideas about the value of post-school self-education, libraries carved out a sometimes-conflicted position between norms and values that both were emancipatory and guaranteed the maintenance of established power structures.

PUBLIC LIBRARIES DURING THE NINETEENTH CENTURY

The first libraries in Sweden that in any modern sense can be described as public libraries were founded as parish libraries in rural communities by local state church priests, inspired by the ideas of the Enlightenment that had entered the country not least through the writings of Immanuel Kant. After the first official public library was founded in 1799 by Magnus Hjortsberg in Kjula, a municipality some ten kilometers east of the city of Eskilstuna, others soon followed across the country in increasing numbers during the first two centuries of the nineteenth century.[4] At this point in time, Sweden was a poor, rural country suffering from a war-stricken eighteenth century, geographically consisting of today's Sweden including, until 1809 Finland, and, between 1814 and 1905 Norway through a legislative union. The country was still decades away from the rapid industrialization and urbanization that would characterize the later part of the century. Society was divided into two very distinct spheres, one public, represented by the state, and one private or "civil," containing family and parish life. In 1832, a legislation that ratified this division was introduced, thus creating a model that allowed for a strong municipal self-government that in a developed form is still in effect today. This division made the question of public support to libraries problematic, as they were placed in the private, or civil, sector of society, thus making them regulated and recipients of funding on a local level, rather than a national one. The first time an issue concerning state funding of public libraries was discussed in parliament was in 1828. Already from this first initiative, the role of public libraries was to complement an insufficient school system. By establishing libraries, the church took on a responsibility to educate the rural population, not least in a moral sense. There was, both politically and religiously, a belief that material and social progress of the country would become possible through a morally educated population. To control this development, the suggested form for state support was by means of directed purchase of books made by the local clergy. Due to the strict social division between the public and civil sector, parliamentary motions suggesting concerted efforts to establish a national library infrastructure during the nineteenth century were all dismissed.[5] One issue that simultaneously helped and complicated the role of public libraries was the emergence of a uniform popular school system, instituted by the Public-School Act of 1842, which guaranteed a secular elementary school for all Swedish children. In many municipalities, the parish library effectively became also the school library, while in others it provided books as a means for continued education *after* elementary school, as a sort of popular education initiative.

Parish libraries were during the second half of the nineteenth century an established local institution, functioning either within or in close relation to elementary schools. They were run by the clergy, often in collaboration with local village teachers, and they generally consisted of small collections, sometimes simply a handful of books of officially sanctioned moral stature. Governmental disinterest for state support meant that library development became increasingly intertwined with that of the somewhat more regulated school sector. One example, which I will return to as it is of bibliographical interest as well, is that the acquisition of books became increasingly uniform, as the Public-School Authority from 1870 produced a uniform catalog from which parish and school libraries had to buy their books. From this time and on, public libraries thus came to represent official authority and taste, which they provided to the ignorant rural public as a means for their presumed moral elevation. However, during the final decades of the nineteenth century, parish libraries became increasingly obsolete and deteriorated rapidly. The industrial revolution brought pervasive changes in Swedish society from 1870 and onward, resulting in people moving to the cities with their promises of prosperity, along with major emigration, primarily to the US. Both of these migratory processes drained the rural areas of people, and new social class structures emerged in the cities, causing huge social problems. The emerging industrial society spurred political movements so as to meet the requirements of the current conditions, creating a bedrock also for social cause movements that were able to attract significant masses, as the public began to direct their educational and cultural needs away from the traditional, rural-based, parish institutions and toward the democratic ideals of the future.

POPULAR MOVEMENTS, *BILDUNG*, AND LIBRARIES

The two decades surrounding the turn of the twentieth century were, in Sweden, characterized by rapid change, social unrest, severe poverty, and sharp political divisions. Prerequisites for representational democratic governance were unfolding gradually, and traditional social structures were correspondingly dissolving as various groups in society prepared themselves for roles in the emerging democratic societal structure. Cultural policy historian Anders Frenander writes that "'the social question', that is poverty, abysmal living conditions, alcohol abuse, and other concerns primarily afflicting the poorer layers of the population, could be remedied in different ways. Increased industrial activity, and 'moral re-armament' were addressed by various parts of the bourgeoisie as a recipe."[6] This points to one side of the "social question" at the center of political debate. Influence over society from traditional aristocracy decreased as a new entrepreneurial class emerged, eventually transforming into the materialistic middle class that would come to define the latter half of the twentieth century. Although the ruling classes shifted, the threat from the increasingly organized working class remained. It needed to be cultivated, which leads Frenander to conclude that "the State power and the leading social elite regarded the existence of libraries as something positive. They were seen as significant popular education institutions, hearths of, and dissemination hubs for, the culture of the leading social classes."[7] This is important to recognize. As Swedish democracy was not formulated by a single constitution or decree but developed gradually through redistribution of power to the rural and working classes, along with systematic institutional reformation (not least in the educational sector), cultural priorities in terms of aesthetics and canonical priorities are often somewhat overlooked. These were almost without exceptions governed by the social establishment, both on local and national levels. The taste and choices of the bourgeoisie were offered through the new, modern libraries. Such cultural formation (*Bildung*) attempted to shape the thought, knowledge, and behavior of the working and rural classes in Sweden.

Bildung—bildning in Swedish—is not a concept that lends itself easily to translation. Radical feminist and progressive pedagogue Ellen Key, one of the few internationally recognized Swedes of the era, famously described *Bildung* as "that which is left when all we have learned is forgotten."[8] In an American context, *Bildung* is perhaps best understood as a form of the liberal arts, in the sense recently developed by Martha Nussbaum in her defense of the humanities as an educational basis for all other knowledge fields. Bildung refers to the development and education of an individual into an emphatic and compassionate participant of society.[9] In the period of interest to us here, the self-organizing efforts of the social classes strove for increased social power and democratic influence, and these were to a large degree channeled through two of the major popular education movements: the sobriety movement and the workers' movement, both of which hosted significant library activity to support their pedagogical and ideological practices. Swedish historian Bernt Gustavsson identifies three distinct ideals of *Bildung* within these two movements, with different approaches to, basically, the same bourgeoise cultural heritage: citizen education, self-education, and neo-humanistic personality formation.[10] These ideals should be seen as versions of learning connected to the perceived need to be on the one hand collectively educated enough for social and political participation and, on the other, individual in the sense that *Bildung* and self-education is necessary for personal growth and formation. Educational and cultural efforts of the workers' movement and the sobriety movement functioned as alternatives to the official school system, which by 1900 was divided in two: the first being public school level education for the lower classes of society and the second being preparatory to higher education for the upper classes. The alternative pedagogical practices of the popular movements would become important for the legitimacy of the Swedish modern public library.

Of the three versions of *Bildung* defined by Gustavsson, the citizen education ideal is the one perhaps most explicitly associated with the goals of the trade unions and the workers' movement. Educational efforts, culminating in 1912 with the establishment of *Arbetarnas bildningsförbund* (The Workers' Educational Association), were directed toward the immediate needs of knowledge for a social overtake and democratic participation.[11] Literature on social issues and economic conditions was prioritized, while fiction was used as a means to share experiences of various social conditions. The Workers' Educational Association, as most popular movements, used study circles as its main pedagogical form, albeit first initiated in Sweden in 1906 by Oscar Olsson, a prominent leader of the Swedish branch of the International Good Templar Movement.

In the self-education and the neo-humanistic ideals as implemented by the Swedish sobriety movement's ideal of self-formation, fiction, arts, and aesthetics played a much more prominent role than in the workers' movement. Artistic expressions were seen as the very bedrock on which the ethical and moral components of both private and public life are built. The educational ideals for citizenship found their roots in the notion of self-elevation, similar to that which was expressed by Immanuel Kant in his famous introductory sentence of *What Is Enlightenment?* from 1784: "Enlightenment is man's emergence from his self-incurred immaturity."[12] The self-educational and neo-humanistic ideals of later *Bildung* found their roots in a more romantic notion of the morally strong individual, which, for example, Wilhelm von Humboldt formulated in his vision of the university as a place for personal and moral growth. *Bildung* transcended class in the sense that any person could achieve a culturally coherent moral and ethical standard in his or her life. Within the popular education movement, such standards were used as tools for personal, political, and social emancipation. Art, history, and that which we today understand as the humanities, were seen not only as disciplinary sites for knowledge but as tools for putting men and women on equal social standing. Considering these educational ideals together, there was something subversive in the way they used the classical cultural heritage, hitherto used by the nobility, to emancipate the working class and, not least, women. By establishing an educational structure as an alternative to a primary school system that was perceived as repressive and reproducing established norms and values, self-education was used to counteract severe social injustice. The movement went in two directions: inward toward the home, and outward into society through new institutions, public libraries being one, creating a public sphere combining classical severity with home-like warmth. These two directions were represented by two women who each in their way influenced new views on family ethics and libraries, Ellen Key (1849–1926) and Valfrid Palmgren (1877–1967). Both used similar self-educational ideals to rewrite the meaning of how poverty, lack of proper schooling for children, and social influence of adults, should be met—Key by looking at the child within the family context and Palmgren also by looking at the children's societal situation. For Key, *the living room* was the actual place of peaceful, educational self-improvement, while for Palmgren it was a metaphor for what the library could be in a society where many children lacked the real thing.

It important to recognize that both Key and Palmgren represented an upper-class, conservative, even philanthropic strain in Swedish social thinking and practice, not unlike that of Paul Otlet and Henri La Fontaine. In the wider political discussion, conservatives opposed and fought every step of the democratic implementation and gave way only to pressure from groups that were long denied actual influence but were too large to neglect. Gradually, the struggles of these rural and working-class groups gained political representation, primarily through the increased influence of the social-democratic party and the liberal party. Ellen Key earned international recognition through her book *The Century of the Child*, first published in Swedish in 1900, and soon translated into more than ten languages, making her an intellectual of note across Europe. Her radical vision was one where the child was seen and treated as an individual and allowed to bloom and develop through play and curiosity, while being given moral and ethical foundations in a loving home under the care of benevolent paternalistic parents. In this aspect, Key's writing bears resemblance to that of Jean-Jacques Rousseau. In other writings, she further emphasizes the value of the home as the cradle of learning and education that in its comfort and aesthetic ideals contrasts widely with the social reality of most children at the time. Not least in the rapidly growing cities with their abysmal conditions for the working class, the ideals of *The Century of the Child* were hard to even imagine. From a pedagogical point of view, however, the book was groundbreaking. It emphasized ideas of learning and knowing that were radically different from the public school system, offering an alternative to the repressive pedagogical methods. It was based on, simply, encouragement and trust—equally applicable to children and adults, regardless of economic or social status.

Valfrid Palmgren held a similar ideological position as Key, but she took it in another, more practical and perhaps less anachronistic, direction. Palmgren was not a philosopher or an intellectual, nor an educational theorist, although she was the daughter of a school headmaster in Stockholm. She was a politician and a librarian who used her conservative political influence to work for the establishment of a national public library infrastructure that would serve both children and adults as a complement to current school conditions. She promoted the children's library as an alternative space, a "home" for children to read in and discover themselves. For adults, the library should function as a continuation of school, driven by the same curiosity as the child's. In 1907, Palmgren undertook a journey to the US financed by the Swedish Ministry of Education to study American public libraries as institutions and practices. She summarized her impressions in a travelogue, *Bibliotek och folkuppfostran* (Libraries and popular upbringing), which, when it was published in 1909, immediately became a standard text for the emerging public library movement in Sweden. Her book builds a strong argument for the implementation of an American-based public library model in Sweden, with libraries located in every municipality. She is particularly attached to the idea of letting libraries become a sort of second living room where children can go and, basically, receive opportunity for comfort and self-education much in the same way that Ellen Key wanted to see in the homes. Palmgren, however, argued that during the current hard times, most children did not have the material standards that Key's ideas demanded. Instead, libraries would become the prime self-education institutions in society as they would connect the local hardships of everyday life with the ideas and works that have defined Western, and more specifically Swedish, cultural history.

Public libraries had in 1905 been allowed limited state funding. Primarily parish libraries, but also a small number of popular educational organizations maintaining libraries for their members, were eligible for financial support in the form of book purchases. Such a model had its reason. The sobriety movement and labor organizations had become increasingly formalized in their efforts to facilitate individual learning and foster their members into becoming ready not only to partake in democratic decision-making but to develop a lifestyle imbued by the ideas of Enlightenment and *Bildung*. This had led to adjustments of certain tastes and priorities of what people should read, and the chosen form of subsidiaries further emphasized the need for a uniform standard of what was considered as good and useful literature. Palmgren was engaged in the promotion of "good" reading and regarded libraries as the perhaps the most important tool to provide the working classes with quality literature. Her work did not go unnoticed and in 1911 she was appointed to make a public investigation of the current state of the Swedish library system and provide suggestions for its improvement.[13] The investigation resulted in increased state engagement in, and control over, the Swedish library sector. The Library Act of 1912, which can be seen as a manifestation of Palmgren's ideology, is today considered to be the starting point of the modern public library system in Sweden. Economic compensation for book purchases was increased in relation to the levels from 1905, and librarians were directed into buying from a new national Union Catalog listing current literature in various disciplines along with fiction and poetry. I will soon return to this catalog in detail. The Union Catalog was administered by a newly installed authority, the Library Consultant, with the responsibility of supporting local library development and providing uniform directories and advice on bibliographical and managerial issues in order to create a coherent infrastructure and practice of public libraries all over the country.

SWEDISH PUBLIC LIBRARY CLASSIFICATION SYSTEMS BEFORE 1920

One important aspect of the library movement led by Valfrid Palmgren was a devotion to securing the prerequisites for a strong nationwide infrastructure of connected library units while another, and perhaps the most important, involved the content of library books. To gain control over the holdings of the libraries, both the state, through the Library Consultant, and the popular movement organizations published officially sanctioned booklists for libraries to choose from for funding eligibility. Several bibliographies and catalogs, guiding both parish and popular movement librarians to pertinent scientific titles and morally high-ranking fiction, were in circulation when the Library Consultant Union Catalog appeared in 1915. I will here only bring to attention some of the most influential ones.

P. A. SILJESTRÖM'S CLASSIFICATION OF BOOKS FOR PARISH LIBRARIES

One of the earliest efforts to create a national bibliographic standard among parish libraries was a classified catalog published by Per A. Siljeström in 1859. In an article in the popular pedagogical journal *Läsning för folket* (Reading for the people), he provided advice on how to build and maintain a parish library, advice that also included a list of recommended books.[14] Siljeström was a teacher and a social-liberal member of Parliament. He was strongly engaged with issues concerning school development and the freedom of religion. He argued forcefully for the separation between school and church, a question that had gained prominence after the Public-School Act in 1842. From an ideological position built on the ideals of the Enlightenment, he advocated for secular libraries in accordance with a formulation in the Public-School Act. His idea was that parish libraries should be established as a complement to schools for older children—public school was only six years—and adults wishing to pursue a will to further education. It was thus reasonable, he argued, that parish libraries should follow the secular path of the schools rather than that of the church in such a division. In 1867, in a development of the Public-School Act, the municipality was able to take control over, and inspect, public libraries as well. However, when his library advice was published, parish libraries were still a concern for the local clergy and as such often neglected, even if in pure numbers, new parish libraries were founded in ever more municipalities.[15] The titles suggested by Siljeström were important as in the late 1850s there was still no coordination between municipalities, churches, and schools outside each individual parish. This lack of consensus created a need for advice and guidance among priests, teachers, and librarians alike. The subject division presented in Siljeström's article is thus one of the first divisions intended for the *secular* parish libraries that we have. It consists of the following categories:[16]

- Miscellanea (including literature on popular education and libraries).
- Religion.
- Political Science and Economy.
- History and Biography.
- Geography and Travelogues.
- Natural Sciences and Agriculture.
- Health Studies and Medicine.
- Fiction.

The list consists of 270 titles, whereof fifty are fiction. This, in itself, is worth mentioning as the library provision for fiction was, during most of the nineteenth century, subject to continuous debate and questioning, mostly on moral grounds, not least by the clergy tending the libraries. The division itself is rudimentary, but it served its purpose well as most parish libraries in the 1860s maintained very few books. Few had the means to reach the numbers of books in the catalog itself. The quantitative expansion of collections that would come within libraries founded by the sobriety movement and the labor movement was still a decade away.

Structurally, however, there are a few things in Siljeström's classification worth mentioning. Fiction is placed last, indicating that it was not a priority for the libraries, even if, as mentioned, the included titles in that category were quite substantial in numbers. Even if religion were placed first among the actual subjects, the preceding miscellanea class included popular education and library-oriented titles. This, together with the rest of the disciplines gave precedence to such subject areas such as economy, political science, health studies, and medicine, which shows an Enlightenment-inspired belief that even the smallest libraries could, and should, be aligned with current scientific development. Siljeström's subject division proved in this sense to be a wedge opening a way forward in a political and religious environment that had yet to follow suit. Only a few decades later, the situation would be very different, and the ideas that Siljeström advocated for would spread into the popular education movement and their significantly larger library catalogs and bibliographies.

THE CLASSIFIED CATALOGS OF STUDENT ASSOCIATIONS HEIMDAL AND VERDANDI

The labor movement and the sobriety movements both gathered their pedagogical efforts around a limited set of document forms and practices: public lecturing, study circles, the publication of minor popular treatises [småskrifter] on current social and scientific topics, and, as support to all of these, libraries. These practices converged in an intention to provide an alternative educational route for adults from all walks of life. Famous scholars, professionals, and intellectuals crisscrossed the countryside, giving lectures that were then printed and distributed for use in individual self-study or collectively in study circles, and as a consequence, libraries developed. At the turn of the twentieth century, these collected pedagogical practices and tools functioned as a close to complete alternative infrastructure, preparing the rural and working population for democratic participation in a way that may define them as precursors to what is today called *critical pedagogy* as developed by, among others, Paulo Freire and Henry Giroux.[17] When, eventually, state subsidiaries were introduced for libraries and popular movements, the advantages of this structure were seen not only by the popular educational organizations themselves, but within the ruling classes as well, as the philanthropic character of conservative efforts was aimed at avoiding the spread of revolutionary incitements by political discussion and development. Two of the most prominent organizations that developed support for these dual aspects were the student associations at Uppsala University, Heimdal and Verdandi, which were devoted to popularizing scholarly efforts through debate, lectures, publications, and the establishment of libraries. Heimdal was founded in 1891 as a conservative student union, while Verdandi, founded in 1882, attracted students of liberal or social-democratic sympathies. Among their many parallel activities was to establish union catalogs for use in public libraries, both their own and parish libraries.

Verdandi published four editions of its public library catalog between 1899 and 1908, as part of a self-proclaimed public library movement, where the organization encouraged the founding of local libraries across the country. Compared to its contemporaries, the Verdandi catalog is substantial, with its fourth edition consisting of 2,973 titles organized under an elaborate classification system.[18] The catalog also consists of an essay with practical advice on how to establish and organize a public library and, from 1905, information on how to fill in the forms when applying for state subsidiaries.

The Heimdal catalog is in many ways similar to Verdandi's even though it stems from a different, more paternalistic ideological standpoint. It was published in two editions, the first in 1899 and the second in 1905. From 1906, Heimdal received state funding for their nationwide library development program. Just as with the Verdandi catalog, a, for its time elaborate, classification system was developed. Parish libraries had begun to decrease in numbers and deteriorate in quality during the 1870s, and by the time these catalogs were published, the popular library sector consisted mainly of secular municipality libraries and, primarily, labor movement libraries. New libraries were founded and organized across the country, giving new priorities to ideological interpretations of popular adult education efforts within the social framework of modern industrialism. In the preface of the second edition of Heimdal's catalog, we are instructed as to the value of subject accuracy: "In plan and structure, the second edition differs from the first only slightly; as that, this is developed under the guidance and advice of concerned professionals in various subject groups."[19] It goes on to comment that the consequences of increased literature production within various subjects leads not only to a widening of already existing subjects but "the establishment of a new subject category, National Economics and Social Literature, which due to the increased interest for the relevant societal problems should properly be able to defend its place [in the system]."[20]

The classification systems developed by Heimdal and Verdandi exerted significant influence on the knowledge organization practice of Swedish public libraries during the first two decades of the twentieth century. However, and I will soon return to this, they also cemented a division between libraries that used one or the other system, effectively undermining the unifying ideals that lay beneath the political initiatives on library development through the state subsidiaries. The two classification systems are interesting to us as they present a distinct break with the traditional parish library ideals seen in Siljeström's division, not only in the order of their main classes but in their degree of division detail as well. I here present the main categories of both systems in parallel:

Verdandi		Heimdal	
I	Fiction.	A.	Fiction.
II	Children's literature. Youth literature	B.	Linguistics.
III	Linguistics.	C.	Literary history. Art history.
IV	Literary history. Art history	D.	History. Biography.
V	History. Biography.	E.	Geography. Travelogues. Ethnology.
VI	(a) Geography. Travelogues.	F.	Religion. Church history.
VI	(b) Maps.	G.	Philosophy. Ethics. Psychology.
VII	Natural Sciences.	H.	Education. Pedagogy.
VIII	Medicine. Hygienics.	I.	Natural Sciences.
IX	Popular Philosophy. Religious Studies.	J.	Agriculture. Economy—practical manuals.
X	Pedagogy. School issues.	K.	Jurisprudence. Political Science.
XI	(a) Social issues. Economics.	L.	Economics. Social issues.
XI	(b) The sobriety issue.	M.	Books for children and adolescents.
XII	Jurisprudence. Political Science.		
XIII	Agriculture.		
XIV	Miscellanea.		
Norwegian and Danish literature in original languages.			

The Verdandi and Heimdal classifications bear significant similarities. They are both made to handle the popular educational needs of society during the first decade of the twentieth century. By and large, we find the same main divisions in approximately the same order, but there are a few things worthy of comment. Both organizations are founded by student organizations at Uppsala University, by this time one of the largest universities in northern Europe. Neo-humanist thought is prioritized in both systems, seen in the pronounced representation of fiction, history, literary and art history, and linguistics. In the Verdandi catalog, fiction for adults, children and adolescents, classes I and II, account for 1,198 titles, which is 40.27 percent of the complete catalog. If we count the five first classes, approximately corresponding to what we today count as "humanities" subjects, the numbers are 1,688, that is 56.74 percent of the entire catalog. This is a drastic shift of attention from the religious focus of the parish libraries. At the end, the Verdandi catalog includes a class for "Norwegian and Danish literature in original languages." This is interesting not only because it is added without a notational figure but also as it reflects a sentiment of respect for the Nordic languages as autonomous yet connected—few Swedes at this time could probably read Danish, and even fewer municipality libraries held Danish books. At this time, however, there was among certain groups, primarily within the universities and among conservatives, a strong romantic sense of a common Nordic identity and a joint destiny stretching both back and forward in time. Paradoxically, it may seem, in the midst of this romantic enthusiasm, the legislative union between Norway and Sweden was dissolved in 1905, a process that did not pass without ideological conflict and significant reevaluation of the national and Nordic sense of identity in Sweden.[21] That this occurred the same year as the first state subsidiaries for libraries, and library-developing associations such as Verdandi, should not be seen as a coincidence, as the political left supported the national sovereignty of Norway. Treading lightly on the path of speculation, one might suggest that this kind of marker is lacking in the Heimdal classification due to the organization's conservative affiliations.

In the Heimdal catalog, the dissolution of the Norwegian-Swedish union is not visible in such a direct sense. Structurally it differs from the Verdandi equally by having somewhat fewer main classes, but instead some finer subdivisions within most of them. In this sense we may consider the Heimdal classification somewhat more developed than the Verdandi system. Particularly class J, *Agriculture, Economy—practical manuals*, has a deeper division than its corresponding class in the Verdandi system:

J Agriculture. Economy—practical manuals.

1. General agriculture.
2. Animal husbandry and dairy farming.
3. Hunting and fishing.
4. Forestry and gardening.
5. Practical manuals.

These are subjects that were relevant in municipalities outside of the cities, where library expansion was significant. At the time of their catalog publications, both Heimdal and Verdandi established libraries across the country, not just in the cities, thus in many municipalities replacing the parish library as the most relevant. This class on agriculture is one of the first examples of user sensitivity that would come to characterize the emerging public libraries. Simply put, this was what many library users in rural Sweden needed and wanted to read about at the time. In many ways, it still is today. From a classification theory point of view, we here see a good example of cultural warrant being defined within the tables of the system.

Both classification systems make mention of specific social issues, directing interest to what is at the center of interest for respective organizations. Interestingly, they don't mention the same issues, and so it is possible to discern a class aspect in the difference. The Verdandi system mentions the sobriety question among its main categories, in class XI(b) in connection to XI(a) *Social issues and Economics*. The Heimdal system also, as seen above, provides a similar main category, L *Economics and Social Issues*, with one specified subdivision: the home ownership movement and housing issue. Both questions relate to the effect of widespread alcohol abuse, poor living standards, and the connection between them, issues that were high up on the political agenda in Sweden during the first decades of the twentieth century. However, the two systems present us with slightly different ideological overtones. The labor movement and the sobriety movement went much hand in hand in their efforts to create educational opportunities for the rural and working classes by prioritizing the sobriety issue above all else. Socially and economically, the Heimdal classification emerged from a different position, being a documentary manifestation of a more conservative interest for social issues in the cities, where the housing issue by many was seen as a kind of root problem for all educational and social efforts. We see this in the library discussions well. In *Bibliotek och folkuppostran*, Valfrid Palmgren devoted two full chapters to the American library buildings, and she emphasized the need also for Swedish politicians and librarians to care for the room as such in order to not only create a space filled with books and activities that keep people from lesser valuable pursuits, but to create a sense of home, calm and dignified, where citizens of all classes could rest and take part in the offered "beautiful and lovely world, closed to them by the repulsive conditions of everyday life."[22] She did this from a privileged position, as a conservative, guarding a highly specific neo-humanistic set of values within which the public library was a vehicle in the struggle for social improvement. Bad schools, bad living conditions, bad habits—they were all thought to be cured by active and present libraries in the local community. Palmgren's view on library development was basically a belief in the applicability of a copy-pasted version of the American *Public Library Spirit*, and her approach was duly paternalistic. However, her interests were primarily governed by social and moral concerns, and thus bibliographical matters were less pronounced. So, when we look at the bibliographical development in the wake of the gradual implementation of state subsidiaries for public libraries in 1905 and 1912, we need to look elsewhere. The divided, scattered even, situation represented by the Verdandi and Heimdal classifications was not viable, and with the establishment of the Library Consultant Office in 1912, things would start to change.

THE DEWEY DEBATE AND A "SWEDISH CLASSIFICATION TRADITION"

As the SAB system was published in 1921, it became immediately significant, but in terms of innovative bibliographical thinking and the defined institutional value of a national classification system, the installation of the Library Consultant Office in 1912 was perhaps more important.[23]

Besides being a support and control authority, the Library Consultant took on a normative collection management role with the publication of a new national Union Catalog (*Grundkatalogen*), which was published as singular catalogs in 1913, 1914, and 1915, whereafter it was included as a current supplement in *Biblioteksbladet* (Swedish library journal), published by the Swedish Library Association. The role of the Union Catalog was to present book titles available for purchase, making local public libraries eligible for state support in accordance with the Library Act of 1912. It was also used by the Library Consultant to take control over the scattered bibliographic practices among public libraries, both in terms of documentary description and subject division for local catalog use. Earlier catalogs such as those by Verdandi and Heimdal were thereby made obsolete from, more or less, one day to another. Practice was, however, defined in relation to what had been developed in these earlier iterations. In the earlier catalogs, there had been signs of a conscious bibliographic theoretical treatment and structuring. In the Verdandi catalog, for instance, a brief essay by Axel Hirsch was published providing advice for the management of a public library, and indeed, one section was dedicated to the "Grouping of books":

> The grouping of books usually causes considerable trouble, and concern thus requires that this work is done so that it will not have to be redone in some time, in part or in whole. Therefore, arrange, also in the smallest libraries, the stock of books in certain groups according to subject content, so that fiction books will be in one section, books on science in another, etc. The grouping used in the Verdandi catalog can be considered fully sufficient also for bigger public libraries, but as the stock of books increases, one achieves better clarity by, in the catalog, defining several subdivisions. . . . Of course, this does not mean anything for the books' original subject attribution.[24]

However, this little crash course in basic library classification is one of a kind before 1912. With the Union Catalog, things changed, and a new discussion emerged. The choice of a national classification system, which was the real effect of the Union Catalog, was not one that would be taken lightly. There were several options, the most obvious being the implementation of the Dewey system, by this time internationally accepted, structurally authoritative, and used by both Danish and Norwegian public libraries. In both these countries, use of the Dewey system was a direct result of study journeys to the US much like the one undertaken by Palmgren in 1907.[25] Primarily Danish library representatives such as Andreas Schack Steenberg argued forcefully, also in Swedish, for the use of the Dewey system.[26] The principal argument was that this would facilitate Scandinavian bibliographic exchange now that Sweden, as its neighbors had already done, formulated a national coordination of the public library sector. There was, however, one problem with this principal argument. Denmark and Norway had adapted the Dewey system to their national needs in very different ways. In Norway the Dewey system was used in its original American version translated to Norwegian with only minor, necessary, adjustments made concerning various local needs. Denmark chose a different path. Adjustments in the original system were so wide-ranging that they resulted in a uniquely Danish system, distinctly national in character. The National Library in Copenhagen even decided not to call it the Dewey decimal classification, but instead DDK—the Danish decimal classification. The Library Consultant Office and most of those in the Swedish library sector were not particularly impressed by either solution. There was only one vocal advocate for a Swedish adaptation of the

Dewey decimal classification in the professional discussion. The influential Gothenburg school librarian Alvida Sandberg published in 1915 a book on school library management, *Bibliotek och biblioteksskötsel: En hjälpreda för bibliotekarier i skolbibliotek och mindre boksamlingar* (Libraries and library management: A guide for librarians in school libraries and other minor book collections), in which she argued forcefully for the use of the Dewey decimal classification in Swedish public and school libraries.[27] Her arguments were both practical and ideological: as school libraries in Sweden echoed both ideals and practices of American librarianship, as introduced by Palmgren, she found it only reasonable to also use the Dewey decimal classification in school library catalogs. Sandberg also considered the simplicity of the decimal principle for subject division as superior to any of the solutions she had seen in any previous Swedish efforts published in various book catalogs, including the Library Consultant's Union Catalog. The Dewey decimal classification was by this time already in use at three major libraries in Sweden: the Stockholm Children's and Youth Library (founded by Valfrid Palmgren), the Jämtland Library in Östersund, and the Malmö City Library. These examples were also briefly acknowledged by the library consultant Fredrik Hjelmqvist, first in an article in *Biblioteksbladet* in 1916 and later in the preface of the SAB system, albeit as examples of bad, or at least insufficient, bibliographic practice.[28] Even though there are no published records stating their reasons, one may speculate why these libraries had chosen Dewey in the Swedish library environment. A qualified guess is that the Stockholm library was strongly influenced by the ideals and work of Valfrid Palmgren in a very immediate sense. In Malmö, the decision to implement the Dewey decimal classification was a result of extensive travels in Norway, Sweden, and Germany by its first manager, Hans Emil Larsson, as part of preparations for the founding of a new city library in 1905.

The argument against adopting the Dewey system as a national classification can be divided in two parts: (1) a general skepticism to everything "American," and (2) the idea of an existing specific Swedish tradition in cataloging and classification. Although general critique was recurring, both consider the American influence with some benevolence, accepting the obvious value it had on current library practice, mostly in public libraries and school libraries. In bibliographical terms, however, this was deemed insufficient if it were not adjusted to the local needs of small municipality libraries. From a larger perspective on these arguments, Swedish librarianship could be seen as an extension of a Central European, primarily German, tradition both in practical and cultural terms. A representative formulation is seen in a review of Alvida Sandberg's book written by Royal Library librarian Gustav Adde in *Nordisk tidskrift för bok- och biblioteksväsen*:

> Even if Swedish public libraries have a lot to learn from the American free public libraries there is reason to question the value of imitating everything that is in use there. By this is meant, particularly, how American libraries used the Dewey Decimal Classification system. There is of course nothing to say against the basic idea of this system, but the fundamental rationale for division of the various areas of human knowledge is far too influenced by Anglo-American views, by Anglo-American conditions in general, for it to be adopted by our Swedish public libraries.[29]

Too American. Any analysis of the cultural bias of the Dewey decimal classification will confirm that Adde's critique bears some relevance from any non-American perspective. Looking at the different solutions in Norway and Denmark, the argument for Dewey as a basis for Nordic bibliographic collaboration is without doubt weak. It is worth mentioning here that Melvil Dewey argued for the rational universality of his "procrustean ten" but he did not emphasize any intention for his system to be used in other countries than the US.[30] However, the "too American" argument runs deeper than simple pragmatic concerns. In the mid-1910s, World War I ravaged the European continent, and the nationalistic sentiments that developed in what Benedict Andersen defines as a post-dynastic Europe reached deep into the roots of national identities, and so also in Sweden.[31] Thus, the argument was not only against the foreign, here in the shape of American bibliographic practice, but for the national. The direct reference to what is claimed to be a Swedish tradition in library classification practice should be understood as a significant cultural indicator.

Except for the sporadic advocacy of the Dewey adaptation, discussions on how to create a national bibliographic standard as part of the emerging institutional structure of libraries never really considered any alternatives but to construct a classification system that was uniquely designed to work in the Swedish environment. In itself, this was no surprise. On the contrary, it seemed a reasonable position to take. The problem was that the presumed Swedish tradition was far from self-evident. In order to keep what was seen as a continuous practice, the authority of public library pioneers such as

Valfrid Palmgren and Alvida Sandberg was taken over by a more administrative and conservative group of librarians, representing the Royal Library and the Library Consultant Office. Thus, when the request for a national classification system was raised by Frithiof Berlin, head of the Malmö Workers' library, at the annual meeting of the Swedish Library Association in 1917, the task was assigned to the Library Consultant Office, through which a working group should be formed. The request itself was met by unanimous consent, and there were no documented discussions concerning possible alternatives. It is as if the discussions of 1915 and 1916 had already been closed and the Dewey decimal classification was ruled out as an option. However, we do have evidence that indicates that the Dewey option would be kept alive, not as a solution but as a standard against which each solution in the national system was to be measured. But not only that—structural elements from the Dewey decimal classification would in fact make their way into the new system. I will consider this evidence in just a while. First, we need to ask wherein lay the substance of the suggested national tradition.

The preface of the SAB system reveals some of the structural properties of such a tradition, arguing that an alphabetical system is superior to a decimal in terms of hospitality, and that it is easier to fit local conditions, administrative structures, and the like in a nationally designed system. These arguments formed a response to the brief Dewey discussion of 1915 and 1916. A more detailed insight into the matter, also of ideological interest, is given in a reminiscence piece published in 1950 by Fredrik Hjelmqvist, the first head of the Library Consultant Office, and *de facto* responsible for the construction of the SAB system:

As for the classification, I had in the spring of 1913 turned to the Head of the Royal Library, E. W. Dahlgren, and consulted with him concerning the most appropriate system. He was benevolent and interested and suggested that one should use the system of the "Accession catalog". This advice was followed. Thus, it is this system that is reflected in the Union Catalog. No principal objections were raised by [the SAB classification] committee, however, some changes were desirable in certain details. First and foremost, it concerned the standardization of the geographical division, following that in Dewey's system and the Danish Decimal Classification. Another area, where the committee decided on far-reaching completions and changes was the detail division of the main categories. For this one turned to specialists in various areas, all accounted for the preface of the first edition of the classification system. In addition to this, we took account of the current divisions in the Royal Library and Lund University Library. From this, it should be apparent that our guiding principle in constructing the classification system stems from a desire to not construct a set of rules that deviated from Swedish library classification.[32]

This quotation is important for several reasons. Firstly, it confirms that the discussions concerning the best option for a national system took place well within the confines of the national and university libraries. Secondly, it reveals that despite the open skepticism of the Dewey decimal classification, the Union Catalog already at its publication in 1915 had overtaken practices of divisions from Dewey and implemented them as improvements of the geographical division, in line with the way these were treated in the Danish version of the system. This is important because it is not mentioned in any of the contemporary sources available to us. And, thirdly, yet again the reference to a "Swedish library classification." Looking at how such a Swedish tradition was formulated, it is obvious that it mainly rested on the uncontroversial idea that an alphabetic division of main categories is easier to work with, mainly in small libraries, than a decimal one. Theoretical considerations rarely go beyond this. However, claiming notational properties as the basis of a national tradition is a weak form of argument, as the alphabetical divisions are consciously introduced in the 1915 Union Catalog. Its main division is presented as follows:[33]

A. Book industry and librarianship	J. Biography
B. Religion	K. Geography (with Travelogues, Ethnography and Anthropology).
C. Philosophy. Aesthetics.	L. Jurisprudence. Political Science (with Statistics, National Economics, and Social Issues).
D. Upbringing. Education.	M. Technology (with Mining and Metallurgy).
E. Linguistics (with Writing and Rhetoric).	N. Economics.
F. Literary history (with Literary Critique).	O. Military and Naval Sciences. Gymnastics and Sports. Games.
G. Fiction.	P. Mathematics. Natural Sciences.
H. Liberal Arts (with Music and Theatre).	Q. Medicine.
I. History (with Cultural History).	

I will comment on this division in just a while. *The Accession Catalog* was first published by the Royal Library in 1886, and thereafter expanded and revised annually. By the time of the SAB system in 1920, its subject division consisted of thirty-one main categories—with numerical notation![34] Alphabetical notation could be found in some parish library catalogs, but these were so limited that they could not be used as a basis for any defined traditional practice. They must be regarded as the result of local pragmatism in municipality libraries or within popular education movement libraries. Thus, claiming a Swedish tradition in library classification is a cultural signifier, indicating a need for identification necessary for the new public library infrastructure to come together on a national level, a way to use classification as a means to formulate a defined Swedish identity. The problem was not the functionality of the Dewey decimal classification, but the self-perception of Swedish librarians.

The disparate practices of public library classification in the pre-1912 period, illustrated by the Heimdal and Verdandi classification systems, were replaced by the SAB system in 1921, based on the Library Consultant's Union Catalog, which in turn was based on the subject division of the Accession Catalog of the Royal Library. Considering that decisions were made already in 1913, and that Dewey's influences could be seen already in 1915, the SAB system did not provide much new, but it had one single issue that makes it culturally, ideologically, and not least, document-theoretically interesting: it is the first classification system in Sweden that was published as a solitary document. The Union Catalog was, as were the Heimdal and Verdandi catalogs, relevant only in relation to the books that were listed as eligible for purchase by public libraries. The SAB system presents us with an autonomous documentary structure on par with the Dewey decimal classification—a singular contribution to the international plethora of bibliographic classification systems.

THE SAB SYSTEM: EUROPEAN IDEALISM CLASSIFIED

A first version of the SAB system was published in *Biblioteksbladet* in 1920, partly with the aim of indicating the coming full system that in the following year would be published as an autonomous publication, and partly to provide an indication of how primarily small municipality libraries should implement the new classification. This prototype version was complemented with a brief comment directed at librarians working in small library environments, stressing the need for a classified catalog in such libraries as well. The comment reassures that division beyond the main categories "are to be used only if one may consider the stock of the library make such a special division desirable."[35] What is seen here is the final step in making the Heimdal and Verdandi classifications obsolete. The main categories of the SAB system, as presented in 1920, and finally in the full version of the system are the following:[36]

As seen, it is a developed version of the classification found in the Union Catalog, this time without the attachment to a list of books. As this system comes forth as an autonomous document, how can we read its agency, and what is the specific documentality of its structural-semantic relations? I will proceed by briefly commenting on the overall structure of the main categories, and then move on to comment on some illustrative subdivisions in order to establish the cultural, political, and institutional value of this system.

Swedish classification and educational scholar Maj Klasson characterizes the division of the SAB system as deeply ideological and a clear indication

A. Bibliography and librarianship	L. Biography and Genealogy
B. Miscellaneous	M. Anthropology and Folklore
C. Religion	N. Geography
D. Philosophy	O. Social Sciences and Law (incl. National Economy and Statistics)
E. Upbringing and Education	P. Technology
F. Philology	Q. Economy (incl. Industry, Trade, and Communications)
G. Literary History	R. Gymnastics, Sports, Games and Play.
H. Fiction	S. Military Sciences.
I. Art (incl. music and theater)	T. Mathematics
J. Archeology	U. Natural Sciences
K. History	V. Medicine.

that the academic side of the Swedish library sector, with the Royal Library as its highest institutional representation, had "won" the classification battle over the more progressive public library movement.[37] The sequence of the system's main categories can roughly be divided into three super-categories, revealing an underlying epistemological kinship to a *Bildung* ideal based on idealism, humanism, and romanticism—a sharp contrast to Dewey's industrious rationalism. This philosophical and educational position becomes even further accentuated when grouping the main categories (excluding the two introductory categories A and B that are of more generic miscellanea character):

- Man, as spiritual and intellectual being (C, D, E, F, G, H, I)
- Society, as structure and practice (J, K, L, M, N, O, P, Q, R, S)
- Nature (T, U, V)

The order indicates a descending movement from the divine in Cb *the Bible,* passing through humanity and society and down to the sick animal (the last class in the system is Vq *Veterinary Medicine*). This division contrasts with the kinds of classifications seen in the libraries that in all other aspects were bedrock for the public libraries in Sweden at this time. Labor movement libraries focused on the social sciences and economics, while temperance movement libraries relied on pedagogical literature and fiction as primary means for *Bildung*—that is, for educational orientation and individual moral growth. The structured idealism of the SAB system is interesting in several ways. The system is explicitly designed to support work in public libraries inspired by American ideals as parts of a progressive social vision based on popular education to reach the full potential of the recently (and still at this point developing) institutionalized democracy. The documentality of the system does, however, reach out in two seemingly opposite directions in terms of what institutional and cultural value it appears to promote. Implementing a new social system, here reform-based deliberative democracy, in a country takes time, and in Sweden progress was fragile. Women, for instance, were not allowed to vote until 1921. One might argue that institutions, such as schools and courts, needed to find a balance between established tradition and renewal, and so they needed to (re)organize and determine ways to (re)produce. Such a balance was upheld in a very direct way within the tables of the SAB system. The sequence of its semantic relations as seen in the main categories and the underlying syntactic structure of the system leans toward the conservative in at least two ways:

1. The order of subjects represents a continuation of an antiquated order maintained by the National Library in its accession catalog. This order relates to a general cultural identification with the German cultural sphere, leading back to the idealism of the early 1800s. World War I had effectively put a stop to the cultural and scholarly environment of the *Belle Époque*, and even though this period played out differently in different countries and parts of Europe, it maintained an idea of an ideal society in which scholarly institutions represented continuity and stability and wished to do so in the future as well.
2. The classification committee's reference to a Swedish tradition is in fact one that voices the priorities of the university libraries. This is a political and ideological marker against an adoption of American ideals and documentary techniques, perceived as being done perhaps too uncritically within the more progressive parts of the public library movement. Set in a wider social frame, this is the time when a fundamental shift occurs that introduces American entrepreneurial and educational ideals on a broader scale not just in Sweden, but in most Western European countries. Libraries and educational institutions sometimes used subtle means to counteract this development—the SAB-system can be seen as one such means.

However, the picture is complex. For most, the system displays in its hierarchies and subject syntheses the Eurocentric colonial values and priorities of its period, not unlike those seen in other classification systems constructed in the preceding decades such as the Library of Congress classification or the Universal Decimal Classification. There are, however, certain elements in the SAB system that also point forward, toward values and structures that belong to the emerging democratic system of Sweden at this specific point in time. I will here comment more in detail on certain aspects of two main categories: E. Upbringing and Education and O. Social Sciences and Law. In the first of these, I will concentrate on the placement of popular education, and in the latter, I will identify two temporal demarcations that placed the system in the midst of social and ideological situations: the placement of various political movements and the classificatory pronouncement of neo-Malthusian ideas. First, however, let us turn to the issue of education and pedagogy. The first level subdivision of E. Upbringing and Education presents like this:

E. Upbringing and Education.

Ea. Pedagogy and methodology

- Eb. History of pedagogy and the educational system: general and specific periods.
- Ec. History of pedagogy and the educational system: Sweden.
- Ed.-Er. History of pedagogy and the educational system: Other countries (geographically divided).
- Es. Works on specific pedagogues.
- Et. Reformatory upbringing (Tvångsundervisning).
- Eu. Teaching of the abnormal (Abnormundervisning).
- Ev. General Popular Education.
- Ex. The Art of Living (Coupling etc.)

This class is dominated by three sections on the history of pedagogy and educational systems. The most interesting is perhaps the second of these, covering this broad topic in relation to the Swedish conditions (Ec). As I mentioned earlier, the Library Consultant Office and the state subsidiaries of 1905 and 1912 gradually increased both state funding and ideological control over popular movement libraries that formed alternatives to the nationalization of public libraries. This development was not uncontroversial, and Oscar Olsson, one of the leading ideologists of the Good Templar Order's educational efforts, treated this as a kind of treason, which forced an abandonment of the organization's alternative status in order to become eligible for state subsidiaries. In the SAB system, we see the alternative popular educational movements placed as parts of the official educational structure in Sweden. Class Ec has four further subdivisions, following a path from small children to adulthood:

Eca. Primary Schools (with Ecaa. Kindergartens)

Ecb. Popular Education.

Ecc. Advanced Primary Schools (Lärdomsskola)

Ecd. Universities.
Ecf. Polytechnics (Fackskolor)

Of particular interest to us here is Ecb. Popular Education, which gathers together specific types of schools and educational institutes outside of the official school ladder. Among these, Ecbc. Folk High Schools (Folkhögskolor), and Ecbe. Workhouses (Arbetsstugor). Folk High Schools were, and are still today, the primary educational institutions of the popular educational movements as they established themselves across the Scandinavian countries in the 1870s and 1880s. The Good Templar Order, The Workers' Study Association (ABF), and several free churches established folk high schools as alternatives to the official school system, primarily for their member adolescents and adults. The placement of these in the midst of the hierarchies of the official school system is, if not consciously, a provocation and a challenge to the alternative identity fostered within these movements. The workhouse was another alternative pedagogical institution founded across Sweden in the late nineteenth century promoting the education of, and caring for, children whose two parents needed to work over the often-vast distances in Northern Sweden. They responded, often in the form of philanthropical initiatives, to a need created by rapid industrialization, which took many women into the labor market with no one to look after their children. In many places, however, the workhouses institutionalized child abuse, not least in the far north, where Sámi and Tornedalian children were subjected to forceful language assimilation by being prohibited to speak Indigenous Sámi languages or Meänkieli, the language of Tornedalians.[38] In no way were the working houses parts of the official educational system, but they became emblematic of the language assimilation policies in the north.

A possible influence from the Dewey system is found in Eu. Teaching of the Abnormal, which in the SAB system is subdivided Eua. Blind; Eub. Dumb (*dövstumma*), and Euc. Mentally defective. A similar division, albeit somewhat more detailed, is found in Dewey class 371.9, with the problematic addition of, for example, 371 .97 Special Types such as Freedmen, Negroes, Indians, and Orientals.[39] Such time-bound biases and racisms are recurring throughout both systems, however with different emphases. The SAB system tends to work with silence and negligence rather than outright racist classification. For example, neither Sámi nor Tornedalians are mentioned as classifiable in the relative index (another Dewey-inspired first in Sweden). The only place where they are present is under religion in Cg. Church Organization and Pastoral Care, as objects for missionary work, so called *Lappmission*—Lapps being a long-used derogative term denoting any non-Swedish-speaking Northern Indigenous people.

The class on education is of sociological interest. The development of the school system, along with the change in the political system provided the national library infrastructure with a prominent role as cultural progression left the romantic-nationalist sentiments of the first decade of the twentieth century for an industrial identity characterized by rapid change. This new Sweden did not emerge through revolution, but incremental reinstitutionalization, where new meaning was given to several traditional institutional settings. One category in the SAB system that reflects this development is O. Social Sciences and Law. Its second-level division is distributed accordingly:

O. Social Sciences and Law (incl. National Economy and Statistics)

- Oa. Social conditions in general.
- Ob. International Jurisprudence (incl. Peace Movement).
- Oc. Constitutional Law.
- Od. Public Administration (incl. Municipality Administration).
- Oe. Jurisprudence.
- Of. Finance (incl. Finance Law).
- Og. National Economy.
- Oh. Social Issues.
- Oi. Statistics (incl. Population Policy)

The Social Science category in the SAB system is one of the most elaborate and contemporary in the system. It organizes a large variety of subjects of which most are expected, but some are worth commenting on. Looking at the sequence of the main division, we find that International Law is given a prominent position, even before domestically oriented subjects that are placed within Oc. Constitutional Law and Od. Public Administration, both of which relate explicitly to the political and administrative foundation of the Swedish society. What is perhaps even more striking is the inclusion of the Peace Movement in class Ob. The classification system was developed during World War I and immediately after the Versailles Peace, and this made its mark in two distinct subdivisions: Obc. Peace Movements and Arbitration, and Obd. The League of Nations. This can be understood as a proactive classification. The League of Nations was founded as late as 1920, with the intent of promoting international peace and avoiding a future world war. As a neutral state, Sweden was invited to join the League of Nations during spring 1920, and it submitted its application in March of that year. Perhaps this is a classification created to anticipate future trends, as de Grolier claimed?

If the Peace Movement classification in the SAB system is both contemporary and points to the future, the main class Oh. Social Issues instead places us firmly in the political reality of late-1910s Sweden. I have earlier in this chapter pointed to the various choices of specific social issues that were prioritized in the Heimdal and Verdandi catalogs, while arguing that they reiterated their respective ideological belongings. The SAB system provides us with a completely different approach, clearly aiming at covering the entirety of what sometimes is summarized under the term "the social issue." It is therefore of value to see the complete subdivision of this class:

Oha. The Labor Question.	***Ohak. Employment service and unemployment.***
Ohaa. General labor legislation.	**Ohb. The land legislation issue and Georgeism.**
Ohab. The history of the labor question.	**Ohc. The housing and home-croft question.**
Ohac. Salary and wages.	**Ohd. Emigration.**
Ohad. Working hours.	**Ohe. The Cooperation Movement.**
Ohae. Occupational safety.	**Ohf. The poverty relief question.**
Ohaf. Work by under-aged.	**Ohg. Philanthropy.**
Ohag. Women's labor.	**Ohh. Childcare.**
Ohah. Work in the home.	**Ohi. The sobriety question.**
Ohai. Employers' organizations and Workers' organizations.	**Ohj. Women's rights question.**
Ohaj. Labor dispute, compromise, and arbitration.	**Ohk. The social security question.**

This classification is an example of documentality as mimetic representation, in the sense that it holds up a mirror in which to see Swedish society during the time of the development of the SAB system. It is inclusive, but there is also an obvious priority to the complexities presented by questions stemming from the labor movement agenda. Half of the entire class is dedicated to issues directly related to the labor movement. The labor question is placed as first subdivision, which is a mark of priority, but perhaps first and foremost should be read as a hierarchical placement in the sense that in the late 1910s dramatic shifts had taken place in labor, marked by rapid industrialization and urbanization, and this should be seen as a root cause for several of the other issues dealt with in this subject division. Prior to the industrial take-off, Sweden had been one of the poorest countries in Northern Europe, far behind in social development in most parts of the country when compared to other nations. That made it particularly ill-equipped to deal with the sudden urban migration that increased from the 1860s and onward. When Valfrid Palmgren and other library and popular education pioneers refined their efforts, they mostly did so in social terms, meaning that public libraries had to find their place among the pressing issues of sobriety, housing, poverty relief, and childcare. As Swedish society gradually over the decades built a social security system that would provide a safety net for most of these issues, libraries had their part to play. The substance of this subject division from a social and ideological, and even a national, perspective is that it provides us with a map of the most pressing issues of the day. In this way, the bibliographic classification system responded not only to a literary warrant but to cultural and institutional warrants as well.

The mimetic character of the main category O. Social Sciences and Law is visible also in other parts. In Oa. Social conditions in general, we see a political division that separates socialism, communism, and anarchism from "general" politics (Oab), placing these in a separate class, Oac. This is proof of how a classification system can work as a distinguishing mechanism reproducing a silent norm while producing a separate, defined alternative representation. The democratic reforms of the late 1910s called upon the establishment of a symbolic and ideological space within which legitimate political discussions could take place. By the time of the completion of the SAB system, this political norm was understood as consisting of conservative, liberal, and social-democratic parties, while more revolutionary-oriented socialists, communists, and anarchist movements were separated out to represent alternatives that should not be part of the Oab. General Politics class. Another norm reproducing classification, of a somewhat darker note, is the last class of the Social Science and Law category, Ois. General Population Policy. Each of the main classes of the system is followed by instructions on what to include and what not to, and for this class we are instructed that this is the place for literature "for and against" neo-Malthusianism. This may seem like a well-balanced instruction, but looking at the social practice connected with population policies in Sweden during the first decades of the twentieth century, this class bears connotations that go well beyond such balanced expressions. Neo-Malthusianism, basically claiming that social and economic problems in society could be solved by limiting the birth rates among the population, primarily among the lower, more socially demanding, classes, enjoyed great success in several Western European countries during the decades surrounding the turn of the twentieth century. In Sweden, a specific brand of this idea took root, connecting it to vast programs of birth control, eugenics, and ethnic oppression, albeit not without critique.[40] Neo-Malthusian ideas were among those that would legitimize both major programs of birth control, sterilization of working class women, and eugenics programs, primarily in the far north where Sámi and Tornedalian people were subjected to phrenological assessment in the quest for a distinction between these and a pure Swedish-Nordic race.[41]

CONCLUDING REMARKS

The development I have sketched in this chapter is one where bibliographic classification relates to specific types of library institutions with defined positions in the process of achieving social progress. The various iterations of classificatory structures discussed gradually developed autonomy from dependencies on literary warrant to a socioculturally warranted documentary autonomy. In the 1890s, by the time of the first Verdandi catalog, this transition had reached a point where *the legitimacy* of classificatory practice as a basis for classification system design was proclaimed as a response to the need of the institution of the local public library, rather than the literary warrant of the books listed in the catalog. When the SAB system was published in 1921, the transition was completed, and legitimacy through the Union Catalog published by the Library Consultant Office was replaced by reference to (1) the best way of how to organize knowledge in general, manifested in the arguments concerning the Dewey classification system, and (2) mimetic social and institutional (re)presentation and (re)production.

As the classification systems discussed in this chapter form a relatively coherent narrative, represented by their immediate and value-based connections to the various stages of public library development, it is possible to apply an isomorphic positioning in relation to Powell and DiMaggio's typology. While in the previous chapter we discussed the classificatory work of Paul Otlet as an example of coercive isomorphism, we can here identify a much more complex development. The intimate relation between classification and library development not only represents the institutional value of the proposed working definition of classification systems as documents but furthermore provides an example of normative isomorphism, seen in the movement from literary warranted classificatory structures to more autonomous ones, motivated by and mimetically reproducing sociocultural warranted conditions. This normatively isomorphic movement is also manifested in what can be described as almost the opposite of coercive isomorphism: the refusal to submit to the processes of others. The reluctance to adhere to the Dewey classification adoptions in Denmark and Norway is undoubtably an act of institutional integrity, but also a truly significant cultural demarcation in that it lends both institutional (library) practice and classificatory structural-semantic constructs to the cause of national identity and cultural belonging. The SAB system and its prehistory proves an interesting example of how the documentality of classification systems can develop over time to align with not only a fully integrated institutional value but how a classification system can develop as a representational and reproducing document in itself, here understood in terms one attempting to represent a national identity and positioning public libraries as central hubs for education and cultural identification.

Having spent this and the previous chapter addressing classifications developed, more or less, in the same conflicted cultural environments in Europe during the decades of the turn of the twentieth century, I will now broaden the perspective both in geographical and temporal terms. In the next chapter, I will discuss the long history of Jewish bibliographic classification. Jewish bibliographic classification moves freely across countries and continents, but it is tightly connected to strong cultural and religious institutions and practices. It has been transformed through pressures from surrounding social conditions, whether we find ourselves in fifteenth-century Spain, seventeenth-century Netherlands, nineteenth-century US, or twentieth-century Germany and Israel. Regardless of which and where, Jewish culture is built through documents and documentary practices, and thus, through bibliographic classification.

6

BIBLIOGRAPHIC CLASSIFICATION IN JEWISH CULTURE AND THE PROBLEM OF THE HOLOCAUST

While the cultural settings in the two previous chapters were firmly rooted in a European, bourgeoise context, I will in this chapter turn to a context far more nuanced and complex. Judaism is at the same time one of the great religions of the world and at almost every location and point in time one representing a popular minority, with the notable exception of contemporary Israel. This position at the fringes of mainstream society, be it Christian or Muslim, has over the millennia defined Jewish thought and practices. It is beyond the scope of this book to cover the philosophical, ritualistic, historical, and geographical entirety of Judaism. Instead, I will focus on the limited but central aspect of Jewish identity connected to its self-image as the "People of the Book." The aim of the chapter is not to write a condensed history of Jewish bibliographic practices, a topic covered by several scholars before.[1] Instead, I wish to direct interest toward changes that have taken place over time, as Jewish librarianship, bibliography, and book culture adapted to cultural, philosophical, and ideological changes in relation to similar non-Jewish developments. In practical terms, the relation between Jewish and non-Jewish classification systems will be the primary object of analysis, a relation complex enough to be used as a commentary on the documentality and documentary isomorphism of these systems. Of particular interest are the questions of the role of documentality in Jewish classifications and the tension between mimetic representation and isomorphic change in their various iterations. I will also discuss the emergence of new Jewish classification systems in the twentieth century, in Europe during its first decades, and then in the US during the 1950s and 1960s, in order to identify various ways that the cultural trauma of the Holocaust has been addressed as a subject, among others, within the classificatory hierarchies and divisions.[2]

In general library histories, Jewish libraries and the organization of Judaica are for the most part ignored or, at best, treated as fringe issues. There is an equal rift toward the general European and American library development from studies on Jewish library history as well. This is despite the fact that during several historic periods exchange and influences have gone both ways in terms of general library practice and, particularly perhaps, the organization of collections by means of subject classification, on shelves and in catalogs. That Jewish libraries have not been as isolated as generally assumed in historical accounts opens the possibility of relating their practices to general, non-Jewish trends in bibliographic classification. Thus, it becomes possible to subject them to more theoretically inspired analyses than one taking departure only in the representation of specifically Jewish collections, instead establishing the narrative of the movement from contextual prefiguration over structural configuration to integrated refiguration in addressing the documentality of the systems. The history of Jewish library classification is one relating to not only the personal preferences of individual rabbis, secular collectors, or the educational needs of yeshivas or religious practices. Instead, it places Jewish librarianship in the midst of a development that stretches across borders: professional, confessional, philosophical, cultural, and geographical.

THE PROBLEM OF IDENTITY AND THE SOCIABILITY OF LIBRARIES

The relation between Jewish and non-Jewish parts of society has always been, and in many countries and cities still is, complex. There is no one position taken by the Jewry toward the non-Jewish secular, Christian, and/or Muslim majority in any given period of time, and the same goes for the popular majority acceptance of the Jewish minority. As with most minorities, there is a profound "us" versus "them" approach underlying

Jewish social identity. The level and character of this opposition varies on a spectrum from near total assimilation to open conflict. The level of assimilation and distinction is, as I will show as we enter the discussion of post-Holocaust classification, a matter of concern also for librarianship and the organization of knowledge, historically directing its efforts toward erudite individuals and groups within the rabbinate in the educational context of yeshivot. Before I enter the concrete discussion of Jewish classificatory practices, I need to develop a prefigurative understanding of Judaism in terms of social and cultural identity in a way relevant to the documentary properties of the classification systems discussed in the subsequent exemplifications. I will do so through a brief expansion on Anselm Strauss's concept *Social World*,[3] and *Enthnorace* as a basis for collective identity as defined and discussed by Gerald Izenberg.[4]

Racial essentializing has always carried complexity between the role of genetic distinction and moral perception. Jewish minorities have been racially defined in Christian societies since at least the Spanish conquest in the late fifteenth century. While contemporary American society builds its ethno-racial identity markers around issues based on color, Jewish definitions are not based primarily on external or physical attributes, but on moral and religious inferiority. Izenberg writes:

> In the cases of French aristocracy [the pre-revolutionary Frankish/Gallic descendant conflicts in France] and European Jews, where there were no immediate obvious physical markers, differences were "naturalized" by rooting them in "blood", a precursor of modern race theory, but naturalization was accompanied by the drive to discover visible distinguishing marks that reached maniacal extremes in the twentieth century in Nazi "racial science."[5]

This "drive" also contains efforts that connect whatever traits have been perceived as proof of physical distinction with cultural and moral demarcation. In Jewish history, communal self-definition has either developed as a response to such external processes or internally around the objects of rituals, religious practice, or as parts of everyday life, for instance in the form of rules for eating. Seen as primarily social rituals, these demarcations of identity have been used both for collective identity and defense against perceived external threat. They have also included identification of the majority in much the same way applied by the majority on Jews, providing moral attribution to both Christians and secular social expressions.

We shall see this appear in the subsequent classificatory exemplification in subject divisions such as "Righteous Gentiles" in the process of formulating the trauma of the Holocaust into a meaningful historical narrative.

That processes establishing and essentializing collective identities may resemble each other from the perspective of those in power as well as those of the oppressed fits well with legitimizing strategies of competing social worlds as described by Strauss. Relating such strategies explicitly to Jewish classification practice, both historical and contemporary, most of them are found in the legitimacy of solutions in the address of Jewish versus non-Jewish classificatory standards. Strauss only explicitly refers to Judaism once, letting Hasidic Jewry exemplify "Theorizing" as a legitimation strategy: "The interpretative elaboration of some [Jewish social worlds] is tremendous—commentaries being made on commentaries, with specialists who work mainly at embroidering on this commentary itself."[6] Can bibliographic classification systems be seen as commentary documents such as the ones Strauss is referring to as the basis for legitimacy by theorizing? If so, how does that relate to concepts of documentality and isomorphic change? The second legitimating strategy worth mentioning here is "standard setting, embodying, evaluating." The core of Strauss's argument is that some standards relate to a concept of authenticity that should be defined for instance in "even seemingly straight forward documents like catalogs" as "authentically reflective or representative or appropriate to the character of a given [subworld] or [social world]."[7] In my analysis of classification systems I will show how such claims on authenticity play out explicitly in the relation to non-Jewish classificatory standards and procedures, most explicitly perhaps in the twentieth-century ambivalence from the Jewish classificatory community toward the Dewey decimal classification.[8] This complexity has, however, a long history leading at least back to the introduction of the Aristotelian divisions of knowledge to the Sephardic Jewry in Spain and Portugal during the fifteenth century before the Catholic expulsion in 1492. Over time, book culture developed a central standing in socially defined Jewish culture providing avenues to influence and acceptance in powerful majority groups as well, something used by Jewish representatives both as a means of sociocultural distinction and assimilation.

Vanessa Freedman, a Judaica scholar and librarian at the British Library, claims that the semantic, meaning-making aspect of Jewish classification practice is best seen if it is placed in relation to developments that concern the broader society or historical periods.[9] This is not necessarily an obvious stance to take. Jewish librarianship relates strongly to the unique position of the written document in Jewish religious practice and social culture.[10] This also applies to the development of its classification systems—the People of the Book is indeed The People of Classified Books. The specific character of document collections as found in Talmudic comments, Halakah, and Mishnah, originates from their specific organization, internally and in relation to each other. These relations were for a long time the preferred organization of Judaica collections whether they were assembled in yeshivas or by (more or less) secular collectors. Inter-Jewish practices play a decisive role in the development of libraries, but as the cause of history has led the various centers of the Jewish diaspora to change and develop, influence from surrounding social structures have made their way into classificatory practice. Eventually this influence came to reformulate, for instance, Aristotelian philosophy and ethics in the development of Judaica literature and its organization in libraries. One example of this is provided in Joshua Teplitsky's account of the life of prominent eighteenth-century Jewish book collector David Oppenheim, working to support central European Jewry by collecting and archiving both its intellectually important and ephemeral documents on life, faith, and daily practices in the zeitgeist of pre-Enlightenment central Europe:

> His [Oppenheim's] distinctive collection took on a larger valence, both symbolic and functional, as well. The world of books in early modern Europe encompassed more than individual affection for cherished volumes. Bibliophilia belonged to a wider apparatus of learning, documenting, and archiving that played a significant part in early modern social life. Possession of a consolidated 'archive' of the documents of Jewish life served a function much like state archives had since their inception in the Middle Ages: they accumulated ever more knowledge about diplomacy and the peoples who resided in the territories under the state's authority.[11]

This function within the Jewish community gave Oppenheim a significant position as a provider of social stability and identity. Teplitsky writes, "Acquired with family wealth and symbolic of courtly influence, the library was used by both Oppenheim and a constituency of rabbinic and communal leaders to shape the legal, ritual, and daily lives of an even wider array of ordinary Jews in early modern Europe."[12] The significance of placing Jewish library practices in relation to general library development by addressing functions both of formal kinds ("state archives") and the guidance and shaping of daily lives in the Jewish community should not be underestimated. This latter role for Oppenheim's library to, at least indirectly, influence "ordinary Jews" is not altogether dissimilar from the morally informed function of early modern libraries such as, for instance, the subscription libraries of Georgian Britain, contemporary with Oppenheim's work, promoting new (secular) moral codes and "sociability" in developing social stability both locally and nationally.[13]

As we approach classification systems and practices of Jewish libraries, it is important to keep in view their relation to a wider social and professional community, as this is something that has been largely ignored by research. In so doing, it will come as no surprise that the perhaps most intriguing and complex developments in Judaica classification correspond to points in time where significant changes in non-Jewish knowledge production, library practices, and political and ideological transitions also took place. The first problem is, of course, one of range—which systems also deem as significant—when and where.

ARISTOTELIAN INFLUENCE, *SIFTEI YESHENIM*, AND THE TRANSITION TO MODERN BIBLIOGRAPHY

In a chapter of his *Books on Fire: The Tumultuous Story of the World's Great Libraries* devoted to the century-long predominantly Christian proclivity for burning Jewish books and libraries, Lucien Polastron indicates a traditional principle of order for the holdings of Judaica libraries: "The reader with means collected only the books of Maimonides, Galen, Averroës, Claudius Ptolemy, Avicenna, Aristotle, and Hippocrates and arranged them around the Bible or the Talmud."[14] For a long time this was true. As in secular European bibliography and librarianship, a more profound thinking about subject classification developed in Jewish environments during the second half of the sixteenth and early seventeenth century.

Sometimes described as the Age of Bibliography corresponding to the Age of Description in the natural sciences, with its urgency to develop tools for scholarly definition, the subject classification of documents as collections grew in the early modern period.[15] Knowledge production promoted new ideals of science and bibliographical analysis based on empirical discovery. Classification systems of Judaica showed specific characteristics early on in this development. On the one hand, they were what today is called special classification systems in the sense that they did not claim the kind of universality that later came to characterize, for instance, the Dewey decimal classification, first published in 1876. On the other hand, they *did* claim a distinctive universality as almost any subject is possible to define from a Jewish perspective. It was a universality that could be formulated as being simultaneously defined *by* and *of* Jewish culture in the world. This seemingly contradictory feature also provided a basis for a complex and ever-changing relation between Judaica systems and library classifications informed by first Christian, and then later, secular norms and values.

In his brief, oddly unfinished albeit detailed, paper on the early history of Jewish bibliographic classification, David Levy points to the difficulties of establishing an origin of Jewish libraries and archives.[16] It was not until the Tannaitic period (circa 10–220 C.E.) that indications of classificatory structures reflecting the relation between the theologically defined laws and daily life practices emerged more regularly when the oral tradition, the so-called Oral Talmud, was written down and codified in the Mishnah, Tosefta, and Talmud. Judah ha-Nasi, the presumed editor of the Mishnah, divided this into six main "orders," constructed for retrieval of advice on argumentation and ethical guidelines[17]:

- Zeraim (prayers, agricultural regulation)
- Moed (laws relating to Shabbat and festive calendar)
- Nashim (rules for family relations, marriage, and divorce)
- Nezikim (civil and criminal law)
- Kodashim (sacrificial and temple practices, dietary regulations)
- Tohorot (laws on "purity," concerning for instance the dead, food, and the body)

These six main orders were further divided into a total of sixty-three "tractates," although the exact number is disputed. The division of the Mishna and the Talmud maintained a major influence on the classification of knowledge in the Jewish community throughout the medieval period. During this period, Christian libraries developed a strong dependency of the Aristotelian division of knowledge as well, interpreted in library environments as the *Trivium et Quadrivium*, which I commented on in chapters 1 and 2. It remains a matter of controversy how this influence also made its way into Jewish thought and its organization of knowledge or whether the influence went the other way. Indeed, it has been questioned whether Aristotelian philosophy of knowledge *at all* formed the basis for Judaica classification in any explicit sense. Levy mentions that while Christian (monastery) libraries developed the *Trivium et Quadrivium*, Jewish scholars organized subjects in accordance with another tripartite division found in the *Hobot ha-Lebavot*, a philosophical work written by Bahya ben Joseph ibn Pakuda, published in Hebrew circa 1080 C.E.[18]:

- the Tanakh (commentaries, lexicons, grammars, Masoretic works)
- rabbinic law and responsa
- philosophy and theology

Still, it is fair to claim that the Aristotelian division of knowledge has proved significant in the shaping of Jewish thought throughout the medieval period, not least in classifications made by prominent thinkers such as Avicenna and Maimonides. Wolfson introduces his investigation on Jewish classification of knowledge by stating: "The classifications in Jewish philosophical literature follow on the whole from the Arabic models and are consequently Aristotelian in principle."[19] That they are Aristotelian "in principle" does not, however, mean that they adopt the *Trivium et Quadrivium* division, but rather that Jewish philosophical writing developed in accordance with the three basic Aristotelian forms of knowledge—theoretical sciences, practical sciences, and productive sciences—following the ambition of Jewish philosophers to classify and explain knowledge and the world from the perspective of the Torah. One such alternative division, albeit arguably more archaic, was the so-called Seven Pillars of Wisdom, referring to Proverbs 9:1, "Wisdom has built her house; she has hewn her seven pillars." These pillars appeared in various forms during the Middle Ages, usually divided into two main categories:

- mathematics
    - arithmetic, geometry, music, astronomy
- philosophy
    - physics, theology, politics

This division was further complemented with metaphysics and developed in both Arabic and Jewish organization of knowledge into a tripartite of metaphysics, mathematics, and physics as "superior, middle and inferior."[20] Such divisions have a strong resemblance to Christian scholastic philosophy and medieval bibliographic practice. It is not until the theocratic worldview was challenged that a change would occur, and that change was, in bibliographical terms, seismic. The transition from premodern to modern Jewish bibliographical thinking appeared in a very concrete sense in 1680 with the publication of the first printed Hebrew bibliography compiled by a Jewish bibliographer: *Siftei yeshenim*, designed and compiled in Amsterdam by book printer Shabbethai Bass.[21]

Siftei yeshenim was published during a period when book culture, Jewish and non-Jewish alike, adapted to print technology and with that the development of new conventions for authorial authority and paratextual components such as frontispieces, page numberings, colophons, and indices. Even as *Siftei yeshenim* appeared more than a century after Konrad Gesner's *Bibliotheca Universalis* from 1545, its impact on Jewish culture became significant. Teplitsky writes that, "in enumerating all extant Jewish books, it [*Siftei yeshenim*] mapped the horizon of Jewish literary culture and expressed an emergent ideal of what a library could be."[22] The full comprehensive bibliography materialized a transgression that propelled the book-based Jewish culture from the necessarily local character of manuscript collections to the universality of print culture and the subsequent growth of libraries, both in terms of institutional numbers and volumes of content. It was a shift crucial for the modern idea of cultural "totality," which now for the first time became imbued in Jewish identity as part of its modernization. What *Siftei yeshenim* represented was, thus, "a shift from the medieval perspective to the modern of the knowledge of all texts, or from the medieval fragmented library awareness to early modern comprehensive library awareness. What enables the shift, and advances it, is the general bibliography."[23] When addressing the subject organization of *Siftei yeshenim*, it is worth remembering that it was addressed to a distinct user group in Jewish scholarship, set to function within what would eventually emerge as modern Jewish culture. It is, however, important to notice here that "Jewish culture" as a formulation of a collective identity apart from strictly confessional identification markers does not appear among the European Jewry until the late eighteenth century with the development of the so-called *Wissenschaft des Judentums* movement in today's Germany.[24]

Bass formulates the highly original subject classification in *Siftei yeshenim* as a gate with two doors, which are both divided into ten "indices" (classes). The first of these doors is the Written Torah ("The Right Door"), consisting of the Torah, the prophets, the Writings, and some commentaries with indices founded on the Ten Commandments. The second door is the Oral Torah ("The Left Door"), consisting of the six orders of the Mishnah and their tractates, with the discursive units of the Babylonian and the Palestinian Talmud. Both categories are further divided into ten classes based on a mixture of form and content (subjects). To give insight here into to the vastness of the project, here is a simplified version of the ten indices of the Left Door of *Siftei yeshenim*, following Bar-Levav[25]:

- the six Orders of the Mishnah, the Babylonian and Paliestinian Talmud
- various comments on the Talmud, explaining the Mishnayot, Tosafot, and Avot
- books of algebra, astronomy, astrology, palmistry, physiognomy, music, and demonology
- books on the fundamentals of faith, casuistry, and dispute
- books of customs and laws
- books of responsa on laws and decisions, riddles, and their solutions
- books of human medicine, the nature of man and beast, animals and fowl, the quality of precious stones
- books of acronyms, numerology, and acrostics
- books of legal explanations and novellae in specific orders, such as that of the Talmud, the Turim, or following the order of Maimonides
- books of rules of Talmud, the building and vessels of the Temple, the Tabernacle, of musical instruments, books published in Yiddish and other languages

For books that did not fit any of these divisions, an index was created, open to potentially expanded classifications based on, over time, literary warrant. The inclusion of this early kind of relative index is a clear sign of the influence on the *Siftei yeshenim* from the Swiss School of Bibliography that developed from the work of Konrad Gesner, as well as other efforts in contemporary non-Jewish bibliography. But not only that: despite its obvious originality, this is one of the first classification systems to establish what may, in Birger Hjørland's terms, be called an "informative potential" in a bibliography through the complex relations between the various Jewish records organized in its divisions.[26]

Bass's work is indeed considered the first "modern" bibliography on Judaica designated toward addressing the rabbinic and scholarly Jewish community, but it was not the first bibliography of its kind organizing Judaica. The relation between Jewish and non-Jewish Judaica and Hebraica bibliography was during the late seventeenth century both sensitive and complex, and one that would benefit from further scholarly investigation. Blair traces conflicts and discussions back to, at least, the establishment of Latin-Hebrew biblical concordances in the fifteenth century, where the Christian division of the Bible in chapters and verses first made its way into the Hebrew versions of the Torah.[27] Jerchower and Lerner trace influence on Bass from Johann Heinrich Hottinger, a Christian Hebraica bibliographer, working within the early seventeenth-century Swiss School of Bibliography, cultivating the heritage of Konrad Gesner.[28] Although Bass explicitly refers to the eleven-category classification of Judaica in Hottinger's *Promtuarium, sive Bibliotheca Orientalis* from 1658, its influence is only indirectly acknowledged by Bar-Levav in his study of *Siftei yeshenim*. Hottinger on the other hand was, besides his non-Jewish contemporaries, influenced by several early Jewish bibliographical efforts, such as those of Menasseh ben Israel and Johannes Buxtorf's *Bibliotheca Rabbinica nova*, published in Basel in 1613.[29]

BETWEEN THE UNIVERSAL AND THE CULTURALLY SPECIFIC: THE TWENTIETH CENTURY

Moving forward in time to the very different set of complexities of the twentieth century, the idea of totality has changed. Development has taken us from the premodern conceptions of bibliographic classification systems that build on an existing body of documents, whether in specific collections or such as seen in the *Siftei yeshenim*, the complete occurrence of works in Judaica, to the idea of capturing the ever-growing amount of literature in a comprehensive system that on the one hand semantically encapsulate a collective identity and, on the other, syntactically provide avenues for expansion. In his "Libraries" entry in the 1906 *The Jewish Encyclopedia*, Richard Gottheil writes that "in modern general libraries the books on Jewish subjects are not always shelved apart from the main collection, special sections for Jewish subjects being provided for merely in the various sections."[30] The ability to overlook the publication of Judaica is lost due to the dramatic increase of publications during the nineteenth century and the inclusion of Jewish literature and subjects in larger secular, non-Jewish collections and classifications is, within circles of Jewish librarianship, perceived as a problem that now needs to be addressed. However, in the first decade of the century, some of the largest libraries maintained separate Judaica classifications, several of which are enumerated by Gottheil; The Bodleian Library, British Museum Library, The Vienna Kaiserliche Hofbibliothek, and the New York Public Library. All these manifested singular systems set apart from the overall subject divisions. The most prominent subject division of all was at this time perhaps the Freidus System used at the New York Public Library. This system was first used in 1906 but not published in its entirety until 1929 by Joshua Bloch in a memorial book for Abraham Freidus.[31] The order of its main categories presents as follows:

P.	Manuscripts. Book Rarities. Works of Reference.	PM.	Ethics
P*.	Reserve books (to 1600).	PN.	Doctrinal Theology
PA.	Bibliography. Literary History.	PO.	Post-Talmudic Schisms and Dissensions
PB.	General Works.	PP.	Philosophy.
PC.	Hebrew language. Aramaic.	PQ.	Kabbalah. Chasidism.
PD.	Hebrew Bible.	PR.	Folklore.
PE.	Archæology.	PS.	Belles-Lettres.
PF.	Pre-Talmudic Literature and Sects.	PT.	Dialects and their Litteratures. Languages.
PG.	Christianity.	PV.	Secular Sciences.
PH.	Talmudic Literature.	PW.	Geography. General History. Biography.
PI.	Halacha.	PX.	Jewish History.
PK.	The Ritual.	PY.	The Jewish Race ethnologically and sociologically.
PL.	Homiletical Literature.	PZ.	Jews and Gentiles.

The Freidus system represented a new way of thinking about bibliographic classification in that it was partly built on literary warrant but still mostly met the needs of both Jewish and non-Jewish readers as part of the cosmopolitan New York environment of its day. The most striking element is perhaps not the main categories themselves, but the depth of the system. The twenty-six main categories consist of, between them, more than five hundred subdivisions. In terms of semantic articulations, it is worth noting that this system is the first to explicitly refer to contemporary issues concerning Jews as an ethnological and sociological "race"—a way of distinguishing the Jewish community from the majority society on the terms of the latter.

Although various systems approached the universal ambition of the Freidus system in a highly diverse manner, they all had two things in common: they aspired to some degree of classificatory originality, and they provided examples of warrant expansion, from traditionally being based on literary warrant to being based on cultural identity. Such assumptions not only define modern classification practice. They also provide guidance for how to study classification systems as documents with agency—that is, as part of historically situated environments. Not least do they become of relevance in a discussion that emerges later in the twentieth century, where Jewish classification practice becomes forced to adapt to a world where scientific modernist attachment is no longer a viable option.

POST-HOLOCAUST CLASSIFICATION

The classification of Judaica in the post-Holocaust period takes a somewhat different path, more in line with Jack Andersen and Laura Skouvig's formulation of classification practice as a "social and political activity."[32] The cultural shift that characterizes Jewish identity in the decade following the near annihilation of the European Jewry during World War II is complex and contains numerous perspectives that are not possible to account in this book. In the late 1940s and during the 1950s, the cultural epicenter of Judaism moved from (East) Europe to the US, and with that a desire to universalize events of the war that most Americans, and American Jews, were not personally afflicted by. Most important of these, of course, was the Holocaust. Sociologist Jeffrey Alexander describes two ways of addressing the Holocaust in the attempts of writing it into a longer history of Jewish experiences: a progressive narrative (primarily seen in the United States) and a tragic narrative developed within the European Jewry.[33]

Within the progressive narrative in the United States, much of the trauma process that developed out of the Holocaust took shape as a kind of externalization, as shown by Jeffrey C. Alexander in his discussion of moral standards. The Holocaust is, in this shape, formulated as a catastrophe among others that happened to the European Jewry. This externalization eventually made the processing of the original experience possible through, for instance, aesthetic expressions and popular culture. Novels such as William Styron's *Sophie's Choice,* Gerald Green's mini television series *Holocaust,* and Steven Spielberg's movie *Schindler's List* are examples of works that have contributed to the universalization of the Jewish experience of the Second World War. The Jewish response to such efforts has been diverse, as has that of the American public:

> This quality of compulsory returning to the trauma drama gave the story of the Holocaust a mythical status that transformed it into the archetypical sacred-evil of our time. Insofar as it achieved this status as a dominant myth, the tragedy of the Holocaust challenged the ethical self-identification, the self-esteem, of modernity—indeed, the very self-confidence that such a thing as progress could continue to exist.[34]

Another way in which American society processed the trauma was to insert the Holocaust into what was perceived as similar events in the American society, such as systemic racism and the Black civil rights movement, a sort of cultural internalization that Alvin Rosenfeld finds expands the Holocaust into a general pattern of man's inhumanity to man: "This tendency to relativize and universalize the Holocaust has been a prominent part of the American reception of Holocaust representations from the start."[35] Already from the late 1940s, there has also been, partly in parallel to, and partly in stark opposition against, the attempts to make sense of the cultural trauma within a universalistic framework, a movement within American Jewry to reformulate the Jewish cultural identity as one constantly moving forward with eyes set on the state of Israel as a fulfilment of a Zionist vision. Still, American Jewry in the middle of the twentieth century has not been a coherent group. Instead, as Yehuda Bauer states in the introduction to his book *Out of the Ashes: the Impact of American*

Jews on the Post-Holocaust European Jewry, all forms of interpretations of the Jewish faith and cultural identity exist in parallel, with certain class differences attached to wherefrom people originated: German descendants were mostly reform-oriented middle class, while Jews from or descending from Eastern parts of Europe cultivated a more orthodox position.[36]

The tragic narrative described by Alexander denounces the universalization of the Holocaust experience, not as the American Zionists do but as a uniquely Jewish experience that has no previous or contemporary point of comparison, but that instead represents a kind of end of history. There is no way around the near absolute annihilation of the European Jewry, and as a cultural trauma it is embedded deep in the European experience of social and cultural oppression exclusively directed toward the Jewish minority. One of the voices of this narrative is Polish-British sociologist Zygmunt Bauman who has addressed the Holocaust not as an event but as a result of the bureaucratization of society, a rational consequence of systemic administrative routines and practices implemented by the Nazi rule, making ordinary people do unordinary things.[37] The demystification of the Holocaust provides not only in analytical terms, but political as well, a very different reading of the conditions facing both European and international Jewry than that of the progressive narrative. The systemic aspect of the Holocaust shines through in the research efforts we have concerning the destruction of libraries during the Nazi era, not least in Poland.[38]

These two narratives, or understandings, giving shape to the cultural trauma that developed among the Jewry during the decades immediately after World War II have also impacted the way the Holocaust should, and could, be included in Judaica classification systems. In her analysis of seven twentieth-century Judaica classification systems, Bella Hass Weinberg distinguishes three strategic approaches according to which systems are constructed—approaches that we can see accentuate after the war[39]:

- the use of existing classes concerning Jews and Judaism in general classification systems, such as the Dewey decimal classification or the Library of Congress classification;
- the use of general systems, but adopted to the needs of Judaic libraries; and
- the construction of systems that reflect the explicit needs of Judaica collections with only limited regard for general systems.

These strategies are useful as theoretical tools, which I will discuss in the remainder of this chapter.

Using existing general, non-Jewish systems inevitably presents problems of bias and trust. One such example is the conflicted class on Judaism in the Dewey decimal classification, which is the singularly most recurrently referred to among Jewish classification systems. Starting off as class 296, Judaism in the Dewey decimal classification has been somewhat developed but is still a subject of comparative religion within a system explicitly based on Christianity both in syntactical priorities and semantic subject definitions, such as "Old Testament" instead of established Jewish vocabulary for the same group of texts. Aspects of Judaism that are not necessarily related to religious practice or historical events end up deep in the system with long notations. The same kind of problems apply to the Library of Congress classification, where the class BM (Judaism) calls for further development in most Judaica libraries. Weinberg has addressed American systems in a discussion on classification and use in synagogue and Jewish school libraries. However, the practice of adopting locally or nationally established general systems seems to be valid in other environments as well. David Shavit notes that the Library Centre established in Warsaw, Poland, in the mid-1930s serving Yiddish libraries up until the German closure of all libraries in the city in 1939, "adopted the decimal system," which in this case most likely refers to the abridged version of the Universal Decimal Classification that at this time had found its way into libraries in several central European countries.[40] However, not all Jewish systems relate to the major international decimal systems. In Sweden, one Judaica collection is organized by a classification system based on the SAB system that I discussed in the previous chapter. This system was constructed exclusively for the extensive Judaica collection of Carl Vilhelm Jacobowsky (1896–1986).

The Jacobowsky collection, developed from the early 1920s and on, became one of Europe's largest private collections of Jewish history, not least consisting of Swedish and Scandinavian Jewish ephemera. The collection was sold to Uppsala University Library in 1966 and is still today the backbone of the library's collection of Judaica and Jewish materials.[41] The main categories of the systems are ordered as follows[42]:

A.	Bibliography, Jewish	M.	Anthropology and Statistics
B.	Miscellanea	N.	Travel, General
C.	Judaism, General	O.	Jurisprudence, Jewish Legislation
D.	Philosophy, General	P.	Geography, Palestine, Israel
E.	Education, Pedagogy	Q.	Economy, Diaspora and Israel
F.	Philology	R.	Sports, Recreation
G.	Literary History	S.	Military Sciences, Israel
H.	Fiction	T.	Mathematics
I.	Art	U.	Natural Sciences
J.	Archeology	V.	Medicine
K.	History	Z.	Zionism
L.	Biography, Genealogy		

Jacobowsky, while working as librarian at the regional library in Östersund and later the diocesan and provincial library in the city of Skara, used the Swedish national SAB classification system as a basis for his collection, with adaptations to fit the requirements of Jewish subjects, aspects, and terminologies. The alphabetic main class sequence is kept intact, with additional notation in numbers specifying Jewish perspectives and literatures. The only exceptions are classes P Geography, Palestine, Israel, replacing Technology in the SAB-system, and Z Zionism. Class Z is nonexistent in the SAB system.[43]

The Jacobowsky system displays convergences between the needs of the collection *and* cultural warrant, combining the cultural identity of the European Jewry with the German-influenced *Bildung* tradition of Swedish librarianship. Usage of a generally adopted classification system, adjusted for Jewish libraries, is not uncommon, but relations between warrants vary, as can be seen when we turn to two separate interpretations of, and adaptations to, the Dewey decimal classification: *Classification for Judaica: As Used in the Judaica Department of the Jewish National and University Library,*[44] designed by German-Israeli intellectual Gershom Scholem in early 1920s

Jerusalem, and the *Weine Classification Scheme and relative Index for Judaica Libraries*,[45] designed by Judaica librarian Mae Weine and first published by the Association of Jewish Libraries in the US in the 1960s.

TREATING DEWEY: THE SCHOLEM AND WEINE CLASSIFICATION SYSTEMS

Using the Dewey decimal classification as a blueprint for organizing Judaica is not an easy task. Every classification system bears traces of individual and cultural bias, and Dewey's system is no exception. The literature on Melvil Dewey and his system is vast, so here it suffices to mention that Dewey was, as he designed and published his scheme in 1876, firmly rooted in the very specific New England White Anglo-Saxon Protestant (WASP) elite cultural environment of Northeastern US. Not only is his system structurally influenced by Christianity but it prioritizes Christian ethics as well. On a personal level, Dewey took these ethics seriously enough to over time develop an increasingly open anti-Semitism, most likely inherited early on from his religious and cultural local environment.[46] So, despite the obvious advantages of using the Dewey decimal classification, arguably it being the most developed and well-known classification system, there remains an element of irony in it being subject to transformative interest from the Jewish library community in the search for a pertinent system fitting the needs of Judaica libraries.

Although arguably innovative and elaborate, Gershom Scholem's adaptation of Dewey decimal classification for use in Jewish collections bears a similar kind of bias, not by means of content, but in the influence of the personal ideological preferences of its designer. Gershom Scholem was a leading European early twentieth-century intellectual, a Zionist, and a close friend of Walter Benjamin. Born in Berlin, he moved to Palestine in 1924 and took up a position at the National Library in Jerusalem, leading him to his 1927 groundbreaking work on Judaica classification.[47] He left librarianship after only a few years to instead build a long and distinguished academic career as perhaps the leading authority on Jewish mysticism. In his classification system, this was visible in the way he went into detail in the various classes, scattered over the Dewey decimal classification, that were subjected to change and adaptation. In her analysis of these adaptations, Vanessa Freedman discusses the depth of divisions on sects, religious movements, and mysticism in class 296.6, noting that the mainly chronological division of the class is inclusive by intention, however at the expense of both perceived usability and topical consensus.[48] Here, we find for instance the placing of the Zohar (296.652) preceded by other works on the Kabbalah, implying that Shimon bar Yoḥai could not have been its author, a sensitive positioning that goes against the established understanding within orthodox Judaism at the time. Weinberg points to other problems related to cultural warrant in the system, such as the equation of Jewish nationalism with Zionism in 933.6.[49] Defining cultural warrant in a system like Scholem's is delicate as there is obviously a strong influence of the preferences of the designer himself. Freedman points to this also in the treatment of Ashkenazi over Sephardic Jewry in the system, along with an emphasis on Hebrew and Yiddish, while Ladino is not mentioned at all.[50] The cultural aspect here comes into play when the arguably individually biased system eventually was made official with its implementation in a general Israeli library setting, in Scholem's case, the Jewish National and University Library in Jerusalem. Today, this library no longer uses the Scholem system but has instead developed the Library of Congress classification for the organization of its collection.

A few decades later, the Weine classification scheme was developed in the US in the early 1960s. It was designed to fit the needs and requirements of primarily small Judaica libraries in schools or synagogues. In her preface to the seventh edition of the system, as printed in the ninth edition of 2013, Mae Weine justifies the use of Dewey decimal classification. Faced with the option of either the Library of Congress classification or Dewey, the latter was chosen because of its familiarity "even to school children," although adaptations were needed to avoid the "drawbacks which librarians in the Jewish field have long struggled with."[51] Adaptations have primarily been made in the divisions for religion, Jewish education, and history. The history class is particularly interesting because Weine was of the first generation of classification systems that needed to address the Holocaust in its original design. The overall history category presents a relatively straightforward account of the major events in Jewish history with, for example, z902 medieval period covering the period from the destruction of the Second Temple in 70 C.E. to the French 1789 *Déclaration des droits de l'homme et du citoyen* promoting the liberal ideal of an egalitarian society without distinction between races or religions.[52] This chronological division is partly repeated, but from a different perspective in z940 History of Jews in Europe, a class dominated by the Holocaust (z940.4). In this class, Weine has created an order that mirrors the structural entirety of the system, thus establishing a sense of the permeating weight of the Holocaust in the history of Judaism, starting the class with encyclopedias (z940.403) covering numerous aspects, including artistic expressions with Holocaust themes, such as film (z940.474), art and music (z940.477), and drama, poetry and fiction (z940.478). In the geographically divided part of the history category, the system focuses on mainly three countries that are assigned further subdivision. z943 Germany is almost entirely focused on the twentieth century, including the history of Jews in Austria (z943.6), Czechoslovakia (z943.7), and Hungary (z943.9). The division of the history of Jews in Russia is similarly focused on the twentieth century, under z947 History of Jews in Russia and Poland, including Lithuania, Latvia, Estonia, and Polish Galicia. The class includes divisions such as z947.121 Soviet Jewry Movement, including the *Refuseniks*, Jews who were declined permission to emigrate to Israel during the Soviet period. The class ends with those who managed to do so in z947.9 Soviet Émigré Experience and Dissenters. Class z950 Israel elaborates on numerous aspects of historical and contemporary relations that have influenced, and continue to influence, the state of Israel up until today. Like the divisions under Holocaust, the classification of Israel mirrors the basic structure of the complete system with classes ordered in the following way:

z951 Zionism (1869 1948, theoretical, philosophical, and so on)
z952 Religion in Israel
z953 Social organization in Israel (including social institutions, social problems, cooperatives, and so on)
z954 Economic conditions
z955 Science in Israel (includes archeology, natural science, and the Weizmann Institute)
z956 Applied science in Israel (includes medicine, hospitals, agriculture, ecology, and Technion)

z957 Arts in Israel (includes art, music, theater, film, museums, architecture, and dance)
z958 Cities and regions in Israel (includes geography, travel, and history)
z959 Jews in the Middle East

The section on Israel does not primarily concern these topics related to Judaism, save the fact that its first class is Zionism, but more concretely designated Israeli relations, conditions, and versions of them. For instance, z952 Religion in Israel consists of classes that could be described as the sociology of religion in Israel, such as z952.1 [Religion's] Relations with state. The same can be said about the organization of z955 and z956, concerning science and scientific institutions in Israel. These two classes collect topics on the social organization of the sciences in relation to educational and public research institutions, including an explicit mentioning of the internationally renowned Weizmann Institute of Science, located in Rehovot (z955). z953 Social Organization in Israel puts significant focus on Israel-Arab relations from pre-1700 until today, with special mention of z953.236 Terrorism, z953.24 Immigration and Emigration, and z953.25 Palestinians, Including the PLO.

Using established universal classification systems as seen in these examples enables collections of Judaica to connect to the knowledge structures of surrounding society. As documents, the classification systems may become facilitators of assimilation, seen primarily perhaps in the Weine system as it is designed for use in American libraries. However, it also entails problems, most apparent in the need to construct more detailed classes relevant for Judaica libraries than allowed within the original non-Jewish systems, whether the Swedish SAB system in the Jacobowsky collection or the Dewey decimal classification system in Gershom Scholem's system. These systems prove the point of Amy Scoppert,[53] distinguishing two main shortcomings in universal systems that create a need for more specialized divisions and structures: (1) the problem of facilitating browsing, and (2) bias and plain inaccuracy, such as when Jews are placed as a narrow term within Christianity in the Library of Congress subject headings for Judaica, as pointed out also by Weinberg.[54] In the aftermath of the Holocaust, and in parallel to Weine's efforts, other classifiers found such shortcomings unsurmountable, and therefore chose a different path to the organization of knowledge in bibliographic classification systems, in order to present the Jewish experience, historic and contemporary, on its own cultural terms.

FROM THE TANAKH TO ISRAEL: THE ELAZAR AND THE STOCKHOLM JEWISH LIBRARY CLASSIFICATION SYSTEMS

In the introduction to their *Classification System for Libraries of Judaica*, David and Daniel Elazar argue for such cultural integrity, stating that "any attempt to organize knowledge must be rooted in fundamental principles of the field it seeks to organize."[55] In the Elazar classification, developed over several years during the 1950s and 1960s, eventually with its first edition published in 1968, this endeavor to present Jewish "fundamental principles" should be seen in relation to the postwar, post-Holocaust environment of the American Jewry. As mentioned above, this was an environment with strong, albeit not unifying, Zionist tendencies taking shape in the late 1940s and the 1950s.[56] The basic structure of the Elazar system is syntactically inspired by the Dewey decimal classification in that it uses decimal divisions with a point after the third notational digit. However, that is where similarities end. Main categories present as follows:

001–099 Bible and Biblical Studies
100–199 Classical Judaica: Halakah and Midrash
200–299 Jewish Observance and Practice
300–399 Jewish Education
400–499 Hebrew, Jewish Languages and Sciences
500–599 Jewish Literature
600–699 The Jewish Community: Society and the Arts
700–799 Jewish History, Geography, Biography
800–899 Israel and Zionism
900–999 General Works

This system has a high degree of specificity, but due to a lack of generalized form divisions and therefore transparent possibilities for synthesis (even as it contains numerous "see also" directions between the various parts of the system), it presupposes significant knowledge of Judaism from its users. Notable in comparison with the Weine system, which is the one of those discussed here with most similar syntactical elements, is Elazar's significantly different semantic construction, seen in both its overall structure and its individual classes. Let me highlight two examples: Zionism and the division of the Holocaust. Elazar places Israel and Zionism as one of its ten main categories (800–899), where even if Zionism is closely related to Israel in the Weine system as well, as seen above, elevating it to main class status is a clear sign of the classifier's ideological intent. When comparing the treatment of the Holocaust, there are differences as well. Elazar treats the Holocaust specifically in class 736 The Nazi Holocaust (1933–1945) following 735 The Contemporary Era (20th century-), as a concern within the general history of Judaism, and not as specific for Europe. Significant for the Elazar treatment of the Holocaust is that it does not deal with it in factual or aesthetic terms (film, drama, and so on) as seen in Weine. Instead, it primarily emphasizes the lived experience of victims, seen in divisions such as 736.4 Refugees and Rescue, 736.41 Righteous Gentiles, and 736.5 Personal Narratives, 736.92 Survivors, and 736.93 Second Generation. This is a very palpable way to formulate the cultural trauma of the Holocaust, not only in Germany and other directly afflicted countries but also within the international (American) Jewish community. The experience of suffering is a force binding together the Jewish people throughout much of its history, and the formulation of classes in the Elazar system taps into that stream of cultural and religious identity.

This element of exclusive identity permeates the totality of the Elazar system. Adaptation to Jewish culture and tradition is, however, found not only in the details of the system but in the overall structure as well. In their introduction to the system, brothers David and Daniel Elazar present the reader with an alternative way of reading the relation between the main classes, through a "non-linear" order, with primary and secondary connections binding them together, forming a strong ideological narrative, at once revealing the general idea of knowledge construction within Judaism: "The ten major classes and the ninety-nine divisions within them are designed to elucidate the overall structure of the classification system. However, they may also be used as a complete classification system in miniature."[57] This means providing not just a comprehensive structure but indeed a set path of knowledge between the origin (Torah) and goal (Israel and Zionism) of Judaism. It is interesting to note that in a reflection over the design and development of the system published in the journal *Judaica*

Librarianship, David Elazar published a graphic representation of this nonlinear structure resembling the Sefirot but considered it intuitive enough to not comment on.[58]

The need for a singular classificatory expression, to compensate for the requirements of universality that systems like the Dewey decimal classification or Library of Congress classification fail to address, is in most library contexts and Jewish systems treated as a pragmatic necessity. This pragmatism can also be formulated as an ideological toolbox with which to design structures that reproduce the spiritual or intellectual environment within which a certain system is to be used. Other examples reflect other needs, perhaps less dominated by a political agenda than those of the Elazar brothers, instead creating structures that emanate from survival and a perceived need to maintain literatures lost to the annihilation of the central European Jewry in World War II.

Turning our attention back to Europe, and a part of its periphery largely unafflicted by World War II, at least in terms of library destruction, we find another classification system of interest that in many ways displays the same desire for exclusiveness as the Elazar system. However, the expression turns out very differently. Tensions such as those described above, between ideology and pragmatism, are found in the classification system of the library compiled and developed for the Jewish congregation in Stockholm, Sweden. The collection is unique in that it is one of the very few Jewish libraries in Europe that was untouched by the war, much due to the neutrality principle of Swedish foreign policy at the time, keeping the country to some extent out of the immediate battle zone of central Europe. The library was assembled gradually through gifts and purchase of private collections, and an exact date for its founding has proved difficult to establish. Sax dates its founding to 1883,[59] Norrby prefers 1895,[60] and we have a, from what we know, first guide to the library printed in 1899 with opening hours, lending rules, and recommended readings.[61] In 1928, Carl Vilhelm Jacobowsky, whose own classification system was discussed above, was assigned to build a nominal catalog from the holdings of the Stockholm Jewish library.[62] During the following years, the system developed gradually, albeit changes have been largely undocumented. In the early 1950s, the rabbi and professor Kurt Wilhelm together with the librarian Raphael Edelmann designed an updated system for the library, at this time consisting of approximately ten thousand books and pamphlets. This iteration of the system resembled the Freidus system in its structural-semantic relations. Since the late 1990s, the following order of its twenty-nine main categories (category 14 is still today vacant) have been used to organize the holdings of the library:[63]

1. Manuscripts and Rare Books	16. Development of Judaism
2. Bibliographies	17. Women's Studies
3. Miscellaneous	18. Cultural History
4. Philology	19. History
5. The Bible: Tanach	20. Biography
6. Archaeology	21. Literary History
7. Pre-Talmud Literature	22. Fiction
8. Judaism's Relation to Other Religions	23. Art
9. Talmud	24. Jurisprudence
10. Halacha, the Law.	25. Political Science and Sociology
11. Agada	26. Natural Sciences and Medicine
12. Cult, Worship Order	27. Geography
13. Jewish Theology	28. Anti-Semitism
14. -	29. Zionism and Israel
15. Philosophy	30. Nazism.

A product of the same post-Holocaust period as the Elazar and Weine systems, but in a distinctly different cultural environment, some elements in the Stockholm system are similar to those in the two American systems, while others differ. The movement from Torah to modern Israel correspond in some ways to that of the Elazar system. If we exclude classes 1–4 and 30, there is a movement from 5 The Tanakh to 29:9 (contemporary) Jerusalem. Unlike the Elazar system, this movement is not commented on by any available sources. Rather, it is treated as an inherent direction of the historical, social, and cultural experiences of the European Jewry. The question of what are defined as historical Jewish experiences in the Elazar and the Stockholm system is complex regardless of perspective. This complexity is perhaps most apparent in the classification of the Holocaust. Where we can point to the internalized universalization of the American rewriting of the meaning of the Holocaust in the Elazar system, the Stockholm system is tuned in a different key: the Holocaust is not treated as Jewish, but as something external, afflicting, manifested through class 30 Nazism, gathering all mentions of the Holocaust in the system, almost in the form of an appendix. This is further emphasized in the subdivision, which presents as follows:

30:1 Eye-Witness Accounts
30:2 The History of World War II
30:3 Nazism: Biographies
30:4 Concentration Camps and Ghettoes, Various Sorts
30:5 SS, Wehrmacht and Gestapo
30:6 The Holocaust, Medical Experiments, the Euthanasia Program
30:7 Resistance Movements
30:8 Nazism, Different Countries
30:10 Nazism, Miscellanea: Art as War Trophies, Film, The Righteous, Escape from Justice etc.

Class 30 in the Stockholm system works almost as a miniature classification system in its own right, and the various aspects of the Holocaust as a historical episode, period, and experience, whether structural or individual, is in no way treated as anything Jewish but entirely as belonging to the Nazi political movement—it is about perpetrators, not victims. It is a subject division unique in character, and it does not disturb the cultural coherence of the other categories in the system. The Stockholm system comes forth as a classification of resentment, as well as one of cultural integrity.

CONCLUDING REMARKS

Classification practices and the design of classification systems intended for use in Jewish libraries and bibliographies of Judaica have, throughout history, developed strategies and structures in relation to:

1. a need for distinction against social majorities that largely and persistently throughout history discriminate the foundations of Jewish beliefs and social organization from various ethno-racial positions, and

2. ideals of classification and subject analysis in Christian-biased, non-Jewish bibliography. These relations are complex, and two main approaches are discernible in the examples of this chapter. The first acknowledges the possibility of adapting existing non-Jewish classification system for Jewish use; examples here are the DDC and the Swedish SAB system, as redesigned by Mae Weine and Vilhelm Jacobowsky, respectively. The second way of relating to non-Jewish systems design is by rejection, even in cases where certain syntactical elements are transposed, such as the decimal structure in the Elazar system.

These strategies correspond to various degrees of social assimilation. In the American systems, such correspondence can be seen in, for example, the position of the subject of Israel in a classification system. In the Weine system, arguably directed toward institutional assimilation with the American library sector, classes covering Israel, as shown above, are integrated in a general historical class, ending with Jews in the US. In the Elazar system, the semantic level of the system carries meaning through a unique movement toward Israel as an endpoint, not just for the system but for Jewish history as such. These two ways of framing Israel within the tables of the systems enable us to highlight a sublime hermeneutic refiguration in the relation between the classification systems and Jewish cultural integrity. This is also seen in the transformation of European social strata and classes as they take new shapes in the US after World War II. For instance, Jewish groups descending from Germany often established themselves as a reform-minded middle class, while those from more orthodox environments in eastern Europe tended to stay in lower-income ranges as workers or in handicraft professions. In this latter group, the Zionist vision of Israel as a destination of Judaism traditionally has evoked a stronger sentiment.[64]

Regardless of which approach is adopted, there is a common denominator in the attempts not only to represent the production of Judaica or the holdings of certain libraries or collections but in finding a way to let the subject divisions work as parts of the formulation of Jewish history and present cultural identity. To function as document retrieval tools, bibliographic classification systems need to make sense both to librarians and general users. This sensemaking is achieved through document representation in the formulation and structuring of subject entries, but not only. They also have a *presentational* aspect that goes beyond the instrumentality of their function, which positions them as documents with specific agency, formulating cultural and sometimes political identity autonomously. This can be seen in the early example of radical restructuring of Jewish identity and knowledge in the *Siftei yeshenim* as the hegemony of Aristotelian classification is broken in the seventeenth century. It can also be seen in the radically different formulations of the Holocaust in the Weine system, the Elazar system, and the Stockholm system, even as a fundamental agreement on the classificatory movement from Tanakh to Israel is discernable in the two latter systems.

As could perhaps be expected in any prolonged time frame, some things are lost, but some are kept, building a stronger fundament for classification. It is therefore possible to point to a convergence between a defined cultural warrant and a developed hermeneutic refiguration in the tension between classification structures and contextual semantics. Furthermore, a development from a mimetic representation to an isomorphic change component proves most visible in the treatment of the Holocaust. These converging movements are all complex, and together they form a point of departure for me to take us on into some concluding remarks, connecting the analyses made in the previous two chapters. In the final chapter, I will attempt to bring the observations made into a meaningful understanding of the documentality of bibliographic classification systems more generally.

7

THE MIMETIC AND THE ISOMORPHIC

I have now reached the point where it is time to conclude and ponder what can be said about the cases discussed in the three previous chapters as examples of a wider problem of classification. The basic proposition that has informed the progression of this book states that there exists a connection between (1) the classification system as a document, (2) its institutional context, and (3) the progress of distinct social processes within which classification systems achieve documentary agency that reaches beyond pure subject representation and that, in turn, can earn social significance to these systems *as documents*. When I have written about the documentality of classification systems, this is what I have meant.

That this connection exists is not in itself new knowledge. Information science research has known this for a long time. However, in most of this research, classification systems have been viewed only as information retrieval tools, designed to connect information users with their desired information. Rarely have the classification systems themselves been considered as social documents of autonomous integrity and value. This connection between the systems and their instrumental and intended function informs analysis in a certain way. By understanding how various iterations of structural-semantic relations interact with surrounding contextual factors, we become better equipped to evaluate and improve them. In this book, I have attempted to look beyond this functionalist perspective with the help of a theoretical foundation inspired by document theory, institutional theory, sociology, and anthropology—besides, of course, classification theory as developed within information science. The ambition has been, simply, to capture something new that not only informs us about information systems but, more importantly, tells us about *documents* and the social agency that can be ascribed to them. The issue at hand is not whether there exists a relation between classification systems and their defined contexts or warrants—be they institutional or political or cultural—but how these relations exert influence on the representational ability of the systems. Therefore, I started this book with the question:

How do bibliographic classification systems, seen as autonomous documents, (re)present social and cultural norms, values, and processes beyond their immediate use as information retrieval tools?

Returning to this question now, six chapters later, it appears that there are some dimensions that come forth that are worthy of commenting on before I come to an end. In this brief concluding chapter, I will focus on two of the most important dimensions of the analysis: (1) the relation to surrounding societal conditions as seen in the tension between mimetic representation and isomorphic change, and (2) the question of how to conceptualize the documentality of bibliographic classification systems. Ultimately, of course, my reading of these two issues or dimensions influences an understanding of bibliographic description, subject analysis, and classificatory structures that sees classificatory structures not only as instruments for actions but as autonomous documents that can be of value for the future development of new forms of tools, as we go full circle and reframe a new kind of usage in new document environments.

BEYOND MIMETIC REPRESENTATION

There is a need to move beyond the image of information systems in general, and classification systems in particular, as mimetically representational. In a post-humanist scientific environment such as the one dominating information science discourse today, we cannot settle with a static representational, functionalist, perspective. Instead, there is a need to find processual descriptions that provide a more complex understanding of how historically situated classification systems not only contribute to the mimetic reproduction of contextual environments but carry with them presentational abilities that may help us to better understand the contextual factors as well. The question is, of course, whether such static relation has ever existed, and if so, much classification research, including some of my own early works, has missed the point by not allowing processual aspects to be included in the analysis. The analysis I have conducted in this book, inspired by the hermeneutic methodology of Paul Ricoeur as used in his analysis of the complex relation between time and narrative, takes its departure from the original Aristotelian definition of mimesis as plot. A plot is, by definition, a process or progression, so when institutional theory picks up the mimetic terminology as one of its isomorphic iterations as exactly that, a processual concept, it should come as a no surprise. But what is the consequence of the shift from representation to presentation in the understanding of mimesis when we consider the analyzed classification systems from Belgian internationalist movements, Swedish ambitions for national coherence, and Jewish cultural self-definition?

The first observation to be made is on the very vastness of cultural influence on bibliographic classification systems when they are read as autonomous documents. The complexity of this influence goes beyond that of Clair Begthol's cultural warrant in that she, as most information science researchers, presupposes a one-way influence on the structural-semantic construct of the system as an information retrieval tool. In the cases where the representational aspects stem from the system itself, influence is mostly considered as articulated through the views, needs, or ideology of the system's designer. And strong authorial influence does exist, also in the systems in this book. This is perhaps most obvious in the work of Gershom Scholem and Vilhelm Jacobowsky, both men with clear visions of how certain issues and collections should be structured. However, we have also seen that most relations are more complex than this. As we disconnect the systems from their intentions and functions and let them speak to us as documents, a movement takes place away from the traditional mimetically defined presuppositions to a process-oriented development of isomorphic character. Let me show this by revisiting some of our examples.

When Paul Otlet addressed the Esperanto community with a specially designed classification system for Esperanto literature based on the Universal Decimal Classification, he achieved two goals. First, he found a way to establish the ideological and institutional value of the original system that he developed explicitly to meet the universalist claims of the socially progressive environment within which both he as an individual and his bibliographical project were situated. Secondly, he proved the social value of the system by connecting it to another system of universalist abstraction, a planned language designed to replace, or at least complement, vernacular languages and bind together different kinds of linguistic practice, such as everyday use with scientific terminology. By choosing Esperanto as one of the first (perhaps *the* first) special versions of the Universal Decimal Classification, the system itself provided, through its documentality, an isomorphic iteration that moved in two directions:

1. It underscored social agency through structural-semantic coherence, pertinent terminology, and mathematical-linguistic abstraction in a way that underscored the universalist character of the planned language movement as well as other social causes that the Institut International de Bibliographie was aligned with.
2. The isomorphic process directed itself toward bibliographic practice as such. Otlet's conscious development of the Dewey Decimal Classification should not be confused with the authorial intents we have seen, for instance, by Gershom Scholem or the Elazar brothers. Otlet thought beyond himself and considered what elements of existing bibliographic practice could be built upon for the achievement of a universalist vision that placed the Universal Decimal Classification as only one iteration in a chain connecting informational structures of social cause organizations with the grand vision of the World City, the Cité Mondial, where structural-semantic coherence and universalist abstraction were to be taken to their most grand and complex extremes.

In Otlet's work, a bibliographic classification system was meant to work autonomously as a documental structure progressively aligned with the development of internationalist and universalist ideas and organizations. In this way, an isomorphic documentality was inscribed in the very structure of the system.

We find isomorphic properties also in the other cases. What brings them together is an interpretative alignment to the external sociocultural environment that not only responds to needs of users or collections but also stems from the chosen classificatory structures as definitional of isomorphic change processes on an institutional level. Two versions of this are seen in the case studies: the first is a classificatory arrangement in subject description that aligns with a defined social progression reproducing certain ideological values—that is what happens with the development of the Universal Decimal Classification into special systems such as the Esperanto example. The second version presents us with classification systems as parts of an explicit counterreaction to established norms and practices, be they cultural or institutional. These reactions appear when there is a perceived need to make a distinction that sets out cultural or political identities as something other than what is either expected from a professional practice or a need to create a classification system that reproduces a specific cultural expression. To achieve such distinction, unique syntactic-semantic relations are created through the order of main categories. These in turn create opportunities for subject hierarchies that establish identification points pronouncing cultural and institutional environments within which the systems are to function. We have seen how classification systems contribute to such cultural self-definition in the case of the Swedish SAB system and in some of the Jewish systems discussed, most notably in the *Siftei yeshenim* and the Elazar system. These systems also provide examples of documentary isomorphism in the sense presented by Robert Pagès as discussed in chapter 3, simultaneously presenting a mimetic representation of a defined rationality, and reproducing a spirit of opposition, not perhaps in the anarchistic way of Pagès, but through the refusal to submit under the pressure of external rationality. In the Swedish example, this plays out as a refusal to accept an arguably reasonable advocacy of a local adaptation of the Dewey decimal classification as suggested by, for example, Norwegian and Danish library representatives. The SAB system is attributed a symbolic agency in the subsequent reference to a real, or not, Swedish bibliographic tradition that contradicts the Americanism of the Dewey decimal classification. In this way, the SAB system becomes part of an institutional isomorphic process aligning public libraries with unifying nationalist policies that, at the same time, were the bedrock for the emerging democratic, modern country of Sweden at a time when it developed from being one of Europe's poorest countries to becoming one of the continent's richest. The construction of the SAB system is also a clear marking of a national integrity toward the other Nordic countries, not least after the dissolution of the Norwegian-Swedish state union in 1905. The library sector used its main bibliographic classification system as a tool to retain a sense of national pride by creating a document that carried significance beyond its immediate use on the shelves and in the catalogs of Swedish public libraries.

The Jewish classification systems struggle with the same kind of hesitance toward adaption to international or professional practice norms among non-Jewish environments, albeit with a cultural heritage that goes far beyond nationalism. Instead, as seen in the development of Jewish bibliography at the time of *Siftei yeshenim* in the 1680s, classification is used as a boundary object that on the one hand excludes non-Jewish comprehension and, on the other, provides exclusive access to the organization of knowledge as being reproduced by the records and charters of early Judaism. This exclusiveness is apparent in the *Siftei yeshenim*, which today appears to us as a classification system that displays a high degree of cultural and documentary agency and integrity. Actual use of the system has been limited, but its influence on subsequent Jewish classification systems has been significant, if not in actual class replication then in cultural intent. When the Elazar brothers worked out their classification system in the 1950s US, they took a stance toward non-Jewish classification that was, in terms of cultural integrity, like that of Schabbatai Bass. Of course, bibliographic environments differ, and with Elazar's appearance on the bibliographic scene, it was—as in the Swedish example—natural to define opposition against international professional practice in the form of the Dewey decimal classification. Just as Bass did, the Elazar brothers constructed the subject hierarchies of their system with explicit reference to Jewish intellectual history. The way it was made was to maintain an isomorphic, benchmarking approach by keeping the parts of the Dewey decimal classification that fit their needs and deviated from that structural norm in a way that emphasized the systems reproduction of Zionist ideas of social progress. In both the *Siftei yeshenim* and Elazar examples, bibliographic classification systems are used as tools to emphasize and pronounce cultural preferences and structures in order to elevate a collective sense of integrity among relevant parts of the Jewry—both those relating to professional practice and perceived user needs.

Turning back to the categories of isomorphism suggested by Powell and DiMaggio, it is possible to discern how bibliographic classification systems display complex relationships with their intellectual, cultural, and political environments through strategies that are intrinsically bound to their structural-semantic properties as documents. While Otlet's work with the Universal Decimal Classification reveals mimetic processes to govern both ideals and practical construction of the systems, the Swedish and Jewish examples exemplify different types of coercive isomorphism. However, as the prime attribute of coercive isomorphism is that adaptation takes place by aligning the isomorphic entity (institution, practice, document) with an authoritative best-practice or otherwise privileged example, there are among the examples in this book those that go in an almost opposite direction, aligning with larger cultural or political processes. The *Siftei yeshenim* and the SAB system both prove that the external coercive interpretation of a suitable subject classification, such as the Hottinger classification in the late seventeenth century or the Dewey decimal classification in the early twentieth, can act as a springboard for making classificatory statements that *deny* the coercive character of these systems. This refusal and the subsequent development of culturally and politically unique classification systems can be characterized rather as a kind of inverted coercive isomorphism. The new systems immediately become culturally authoritative through their documentary properties. If such a conclusion can be accepted, it leads to a potentially new and more pronounced understanding of the documentality of bibliographic classification systems, as not only the acts of refusal but also their alignments with social progress, are not necessarily visible in actual library or bibliographic practice, but rather as the systems are interpreted through analytical tools that understand them beyond their instrumental information-retrieval functions. To further such an observation and secure its legitimacy, I need to proceed with a brief concluding comment on that which has been the main cause of this book—the documentality of classification systems.

THE ISOMORPHIC DOCUMENTALITY OF CLASSIFICATION

In many ways, the disconnection between document and use is easier to understand with some historical distance. Bibliographic classification systems are not exempt from this. In the first chapter I showed this by reference to the work of the anthropologist Jack Goody, who in his work on classification systems and lists evoked a cultural understanding of social conditions through analyzing the content and structure of classes and categories in a variety of classification systems. In his analyses, the systems appear as documents, stemming from their structural-semantic relations that carry sociocultural significance. In this present book, I have not dealt with the same historical span as Goody, and I have also limited my analysis to classification systems used in bibliographic and library practice. Such systems are constructed—as is all classification—for use. Applying a document-theoretical perspective on bibliographic classification systems requires that the tool perspective is replaced by one that considers the systems as something of value in themselves, as autonomous documents. In doing that, I have used a hermeneutic approach, not unlike the analytical procedures in literary studies or other traditional humanistic interpretation. However, the document-theoretical perspective also requires an understanding of what a document is as such. In establishing such an understanding, I have proposed a working definition of a document that could inform the treatment of classification systems as disconnected from their immediate bibliographic use. This definition stipulates that *a document is an inscribed reification of social acts with an informative potential of institutional value.* The elements of this definition are worthy of further consideration in light of the insights learned from the above analyses.

There is an apparent tension between a document being an inscribed reification of something and this something being a social act. This is fundamentally the tension between the mimetic and the isomorphic. Most documents are rule-based. Classification systems are good examples of this. Most documents are identified as documents because of the regularity that this inscription/reification implies. This structural coherence is what document research calls indexicality, the defining properties of a certain kind of document, that which makes it possible to be identified as, for instance, a passport, a map, a wedding certificate, or a classification system. Indexicality, expressed in the relation between structure and semantic content, is then contextualized in two ways, through informative potential and through institutional value. Both these components of the definition are inherently processual and progressive. The informative potential of a document changes over time and in relation to users, as does the external and internal perceptions of a document's institutional value. This is evident in the classification systems discussed in this book.

There are interesting differences between how the relation between indexicality and the informative potential of a document are treated and emphasized in classification systems. Two examples that emphasize the structural/inscribed reification aspect of a document are the Universal Decimal Classification and the SAB system. In his expansion of the Dewey decimal classification, Otlet attempted to create an advanced indexicality by means of an abstraction that could correspond to the universal claims of the political and idealist environment of which he was part. He needed to distance the system from public library use and extend it into a more complex bibliographic environment, primarily focused on scientific literature. However, it is not a system that is based exclusively on scientific warrant. Its informative potential can be seen in its treatment of Esperanto, as we have examined, in ways that move beyond scientific subject divisions, as the mathematical abstraction principles of the original system are used to distinguish the specialized system in a way that can be used to formulate the progression of the planned language literature based on the system's properties as a document. In the Swedish example, a similar albeit opposite relation is seen. The rejection of the Dewey decimal classification for a national system simultaneously favors a structural reification and a progressive isomorphic informative potential. The explicit aim was to introduce a classification system that (1) structurally reproduces a hereditary progression of earlier Swedish systems (although few older systems actually consist of comparable structural properties), and (2) is able to meet the informative potential of social progress, which at the time was pushing the country in the direction of industrialism and strong nationalism. The combination of these elements merged through the system's immediate institutional value as it was placed as a centerpiece in the ongoing re-institutionalization of society—a process that allowed for the prominence of public libraries as representatives of new democratic and educational ideals. In this process, the SAB system exerted significant influence through its arguably isomorphic documentality.

The Jewish systems display a variety of relations between inscribed reification and institutional value. Crucial in this variation is the informative potential of the systems as documents. There are basically two groups here. The *Siftei yeshenim* and the Elazar system both use structural elements to create cultural distinction, in the former case by displaying a hereditary organization of knowledge going back to the Talmud and Mishna, and in the latter through contemporary references aligning with defined Zionist ideas. In these examples, the informative potential is embedded in large cultural movements that in many ways are superior to practical aspects, such as those defining institutional value. The other group gives priority to institutional value over informative potential. The Weine system does this by explicit reference to the general knowledge of the Dewey decimal classification and it chose not to deviate from the original system in more ways than necessary in order for collections to host Jewish books and periodicals. This created a system that encourages intuitive use rather than a priori cultural distinction. The Stockholm system displays a somewhat similar semantic approach, but rather than adapting to the general Swedish classification practice, as does the Jacobowsky system, it aligns to the immediate institutional context as part of the Jewish congregation center in Stockholm. These approaches create forms of informative potential that are perhaps, in terms of cultural distinction, more limited in scope than for instance the Elazar system, but at the same time they are easier to use in individual libraries as they contribute to institutional identity in a more pronounced way. We see this in the way that Mae Weine explicitly constructed her classification for Jewish school libraries, which was more important than manifesting a unique Jewish cultural identity or social world within the hierarchies of the system.

Documents are ultimately cornerstones of social institutions and carriers of meaning for myriads of social worlds intertwined in the fabric of society. Most have a limited range and a relatively clear-cut relation to either use or contextual environment, built on complex relations between structural and semantic conventions. As I have shown in this book, by choosing one type of document and analyzing that particular type's properties, its ability to create informative potential and through that inform a certain institutional value, it is possible to forward both our practice-oriented and theoretical understanding of how documents work and what they do. The analysis carried out in this book has elaborated on a certain type of document with strict structural (hierarchic) conventions, but also with an unusually open semantic level in that subject divisions can, potentially, relate to any given contextual limitation—library collection, ideological position, national identity, or cultural distinction. Either way, this semantic openness provides insights into documents as reifications of social acts, in ways that allow for the arguably static "reification" to meet the needs of change elements that are always fundamental to sociocultural progress. It is here that we see a movement from the mimetically representational function of the document toward its isomorphic documentality. A document does not only mirror its institutional or cultural situation, or its practical use, but, through its inherent documentality, contributes to the formulation of change processes and new elements in its cultural or institutional environments. With knowledge of how such documentality plays out in practice with a given type of document, it is possible to look also at other kinds of documents and documentary environments, as all are different. With this, it is my hope that this book may be able to encourage more and better-informed scholarly debate on documents and documentality, both in historical and contemporary document environments. If that is the case, therein lies its isomorphic documentality.

NOTES

CHAPTER 1

1. While I, in this book, engage in an analysis of bibliographic classification systems, it is important to recognize that the wider role of classification in various social contexts has been studied by others. See, for instance, Geoffrey C. Bowker and Susan Leigh Star, *Sorting Things Out: Classification and Its Consequences* (Cambridge, MA: MIT Press, 1999), and Robert Montoya, *Power of Position: Classification and the Biodiversity Sciences* (Cambridge, MA: MIT Press, 2022).

2. For an overview of ancient libraries and their ways of organizing their holdings, see Lionel Casson, *Libraries in the Ancient World* (New Haven, CT: Yale University Press, 2001).

3. Harry Austryn Wolfson, "The Classification of Sciences in Medieval Jewish Philosophy," in *Hebrew Union College Jubilee Volume*, ed. David Philipson et al. (Cincinnati: Hebrew Union College, 1925, pp. 263–315).

4. B. Ogilvie, *The Science of Describing: Natural History in Renaissance Europe* (Chicago: University of Chicago Press, 2006).

5. Konrad Gesner, *Bibliotheca Universalis, sive Catalogus omnium Scriptoum locupletissimus, in tribus linguis, Latina, Græca, & Hebraica* (Zürich: Christophorum Froschouerum, 1545), and Konrad Gesner, *Bibliotheca universalis sive catalogus omnium scriptorum locupletissimus in tribus linguis Latina Graeca et Hebraica: Pandectarum sive Partitionum . . . Libri XXI*, Vol. 2. (Zürich: Christophorus Froschoverus, 1548). See also: B. H. Breslauer and R. Folter, *Bibliography: Its History and Development* (New York: The Grolier Club, 1984); Besterman, *The Beginning of Systematic Bibliography*, 2nd rev. ed. (London: Humphrey Milford/Oxford University Press, 1936).

6. Lorenz B., "Some Historical Remarks on Library Classification: A Short Introduction to the Science of Library Classification," in *Classification: The Ubiquitous Challenge*, ed. C. Weihs and G. Gaul (Berlin: Springer, 2005), pp. 506–512. Cf p.508.

7. A. Blair, *Too Much to Know: Managing Scholarly Information before the Modern Age* (New Haven, CT: Yale University Press 2010), pp. 164–166.

8. Naudé's reputation as a bibliographer was confirmed in the catalog of the prestigious exhibition *200 Years of Bibliography*, which opened at The Grolier Club in New York City in April 1981. Item 53 in the catalog is his *Bibliothecae Cordesianae Catalogus* published in Paris by Antoine Vitray in 1643. "This is the earliest catalogue of a private library which is strictly arranged according to subjects . . . its classification system remained the leading one throughout the seventeenth century" (Breslauer and Folter, 1984, p. 84).

9. G. Naudé, *Advis pour dresser une bibliothèque* (Paris: Klincksieck, 1644/1994), p. 131.

10. Naudé, *Advis pour dresser.*

11. *Manuel Abrégé du Répertoire Bibligraphique Universel* (FID, 1905).

12. Valfrid Palmgren, *Förslag angående de åtgärder som från statens sida böra vidtagas för främjandet af det allmänna biblioteksväsendet i Sverige, afgifvet den 28 september 1911* (Kungl. Eckesiastikdepartementet: Stockholm, 1911).

13. *Klassifikationssystem för svenska bibliotek* (Stockholm: Norstedt, 1921).

14. The Freidus system is commented on and reproduced in its original form in Joshua Bloch, "The Classification of Jewish Literature in the New York Public Library," in *Studies in Jewish Bibliography and Related Subjects in Memory of Abraham Solomon Freidus* (New York: Alexander Kohut Memorial Foundation/ New York Public Library, 1929), pp. L-LXXVII.

15. Ismar Schorsh, *From Text to Context: The Turn to History in Modern Judaism* (Hannover: Brandeis University Press, 1994).

16. Eric De Grolier, "Classifications as Cultural Artefacts," In *Universal Classification I: Subject Analysis and Ordering Systems*, ed. I. Dahlberg (Frankfurt: Indeks Verlag), p. 33.

17. Francis Bacon, *The Advancement of Learning and The New Atlantis* (Oxford: Benediction Classics, 2010).

18. Claire Beghtol, "Semantic Validity: Concepts of Warrant in Bibliographic Classification Systems," *Library Resources and Technical Services*, Vol. 30, No. 2, 1986, pp. 109–125.

19. For a detailed discussion of the concept of literary warrant, see Mario Barité, "Literary Warrant," *Knowledge Organization*, Vol. 45, No. 6, 2018, pp. 517–536.

20. Beghtol is not the only one who has touched upon the idea of cultural influence on knowledge organization in the context of information systems or information institutions. See an alternative approach based on the concept of social epistemology in Richard Smiraglia, *Cultural Synergy in Information Institutions* (New York: Springer, 2014). For more on social epistemology, see Jonathan Furner, "'A Brilliant Mind:

Margret Eagan and Social Epistemology," *Library Trends*, Vol. 52, No. 4, 2004, pp. 792–809, and Jesse Hauk Shera, *Libraries and the Organization of Knowledge* (London: Crosby and Lockwood, 1965).

21. Elaine Svenonius, *The Intellectual Foundation of Information Organization* (Cambridge, MA: MIT Press, 2000), p. 34.

22. Svenonius, *Foundation of Information Organization*, p. 35.

23. Svenonius provides an in-depth analysis of the first category of document sets, work, in relation to Wittgenstein picture theory of meaning in Elaine Svenonius, "The Epistemological Foundations of Knowledge Representations," *Library Trends*, Vol. 52 No. 3, 2004, pp. 571–587.

24. Formative discussions on the relation between classification and digital humanities can be found in Koraljka Golub and Ying-Hsang Liu, eds., *Information and Knowledge Organisation in Digital Humanities: Global Perspectives* (London: Routledge, 2022).

25. Claire Beghthol, "Relationships in Classificatory Structure and Meaning," in *Relationships in the Organization of Knowledge*, eds. Carol A. Bean and Rebecca Green (Dordrecht: Kluwer, 2001), pp. 104–105.

26. R. A. Fairthorne, "Temporal Structure in Bibliographical Classification," in *Theory of Subject Analysis: A Sourcebook*, ed. L. M. Chan, P. A. Richmond, and E. Svenonius (Littletown, CO: Libraries Unlimited, 1985), pp. 359–368.

27. A. Lloyd and J. Wilkinson, "Tapping into the Information Landscape: Refugee Youth Enactment of Information Literacy in Everyday Spaces," *Journal of Librarianship and Information Science*, Vol. 51, No. 1, 2017, pp. 252–259. Another example is S. Burnett and A. Lloyd, "The Road Not Taken: Locating Desire Lines across Information Landscapes," *Information Research*, Vol. 24, No. 4, 2019, paper colis1911.

28. Beghtol, "Classificatory Structure and Meaning," p. 109.

29. Jack Goody, *The Domestication of the Savage Mind* (Cambridge: Cambridge University Press, 1977).

30. Jacob Collins, "Parallel Structures: André Leroi-Gouhran, Claude Lévi-Strauss, and the Making of French Structural Anthropology," *History of the Human Sciences*, Vol. 34, No. 3–4, 2021, pp. 307–335.

31. Koraljka Golub, "Automated Subject Classification of Textual Web Documents," *Journal of Documentation*, Vol. 62, No. 3, 2006, pp. 350–371.

32. Goody, *Savage Mind*, p. 78.

33. H. Rosemont, "On Representing Abstractions in Archaic Chinese," *Philosophy East and West*, Vol. 24, 1974, pp. 71–88. A general overview of the historical development of Chinese bibliographic classification, is given in Tsuen-Hsuin Tsien, "A History of Bibliographic Classification in China," *The Library Quarterly*, Vol. 22, No. 4, 1952, pp. 307–324.

34. See for instance Richard Smiraglia, *Elements of Knowledge Organization* (New York: Springer, 2014).

CHAPTER 2

1. In her book *La science de l'information: Origine, théories et paradigmes* (Paris: Lavoisier, 2012), Fidelia Ibekwe-SanJuan defines five basic paradigms in information science: (1) rationalism and positivism, (2) empiricism, (3) cognitivism, (4) social constructivism, and (5) pragmatism. She sees classification, both scientific and bibliographic, as part of, primarily, the rationalist-positivist paradigm (pp. 161–168). This epistemological position is also used as a point of departure in R. Smiraglia, "The Progress of Theory in Knowledge Organization," *Library Trends*, Vol. 50, No. 3, 2002, pp. 330–349.

2. K. Golub, *Subject Access to Information: An Interdisiplinary Approach* (Santa Barbara, CA: Libraries Unlimited, 2014), p. 4.

3. Derek W. Langridge, *Classification and Indexing in the Humanities* (London: Butterworths, 1976). See also J. Andersen and J. Hansson (Eds), *Exploring Contemporary Classification practices: Organizing Information, Technological change and Ideological Contestation* (London: Routledge, 2025).

4. B. Hjørland, *Information Seeking and Subject Representation: An Activity-Theoretical Approach to Information Science* (Westport, CT: Greenwood Press, 1997), pp. 86–87.

5. See various entrances to this problem in: Hope Olson, "Patriarchal Structures of Subject Access and Subversive Techniques for Change," *Canadian Journal of Information and Library Science*, Vol. 26, No. 2–3, 2001, pp. 1–29, and Jens-Erik Mai, "Classification in a Social World: Bias and Trust," *Journal of Documentation*, Vol. 66, No. 5, 2010, pp. 627–642.

6. J. Furner, *Information Studies and Other Provocations: Selected Talks 200–2019* (Sacramento, CA: Library Juice Press, 2020), 97.

7. Ingwersen and Järvelin, *Information Seeking and Retrieval*, 2005.

8. A problematization of the aboutness concept is provided by Hauser and Tennis, 2019.

9. For an expanded discussion on relevance in information science, see Saracevic 1975; 2007a; 2007b.

10. Furner, *Information Studies and Other Provocations*, 82.

11. Paul Otlet, *Traité de Documentation: Le livre sur le livre* (Bruxelles: Mundaneum / Les Impressions Nouvelles, 1934/2015), p. 44.

12. Otlet, *Traité de Documentation*, p. 44.

13. Otlet, *Traité de Documentation*, p. 44.

14. Suzanne Briet, *What Is Documentation?* (Lanham, MD: Scarecrow Press, 2006), p. 10.

15. Briet, *What Is Documentation?*

16. Briet was head of the catalog department at Bibliothèque Nationale and oversaw its restoration and adaptation to modern cataloging convention, also including the implementation of the Universal Decimal Classification.

17. M. N. Maack, "The Lady and the Antelope: Suzanne Briet's Contribution to the French Documentation Movement," *Library Trends*, Vol. 52, No. 4, 2004, pp. 719–747.

18. Ronald E. Day, "'A Necessity of Our Time': Documentation as 'Cultural Technique' in What Is Documentation?" in *What Is Documentation?*, ed. Suzanne Briet (Lanham, MD: Scarecrow Press, 2006), pp 47–63, p. 53.

19. Michael Buckland, *Information and Information Systems* (Westport, CT: Praeger, 1991), p. 44.

20. Ronald Day uses indexicality as a core concept, in its current linguistic, ontological, and semiotic iterations, in his book *Documentarity: Evidence, Ontology, and Inscription* (Cambridge, MA: MIT Press, 2019).

21. For an in-depth analysis of the relation between bibliography and various definitions of documentation, see G. Woledge, "'Bibliography' and 'Documentation': Words and Ideas," *Journal of Documentation*, Vol. 39, No. 4, 1983, pp. 266–279. Recently, Wayne de Fremery has tried to reestablish the bibliographical foundation of information science in his book *Cats, Carpenters, and Accountants: Bibliographical Foundations of Information Science* (Cambridge, MA: MIT Press, 2024).

22. Bernd Frohmann, *Deflating Information: From Science Studies to Documentation* (Toronto: Toronto University Press, 2004), pp. 97–98; Ronald E. Day, *The Modern Invention of Information: Discourse, History, and Power* (Carbondale: Southern Illinois University Press, 2001), p. 59.

23. A particular iteration of the critique of the bibliographic paradigm has the concept *complementarity*, originally derived from Danish physicist Niels Bohr, at its center. It manages to take the discussion all the way into realms that do not intuitively appear documentary, such as art, performances, music, and other human expressions. See, for instance, Niels Windfeld Lund, *Introduction to Documentation Studies* (London: Facet, 2024); Roswitha Skare, "Complementarity: A Concept for Document Analysis?" *Journal of Documentation*, Vol. 65, No. 5, 2009, pp. 834–840, and Joacim Hansson, "Representativity and Complementarity in Tai Chi as Embodied Documentation," *Proceedings from the Document Academy*, Vol. 4, No. 2, 2017a, Article 11.

24. Ronald E. Day, *Indexing It All: The Subject in the Age of Documentation, Information, and Data* (Cambridge, MA: MIT Press, 2014), p. 9.

25. Briet, *What Is Documentation?*, 9.

26. Brend Frohmann, "The Documentality of Mme Briet's Antelope," in *Communication Matters: Materialist Approaches to Media, Mobility, and Networks*, ed. J. Packer and C. B. Crofts Wiley (London: Routledge, 2012), pp. 173–182. The concept of documentary agency is further developed in Bernd Frohmann, "Multiplicity, Materiality, and Autonomous Agency of Documentation," in *A Document (Re)turn: Contributions from a Field in Transition*, ed. Roswitha Skare, Niels Windfeld Lund, and Andreas Vårheim (Frankfurt am Main: Peter Lang, 2007), pp. 27–39.

27. Bruno Latour, "Ces reseaux que la raison ignore: Laboratoires, bibliothèques, collections," in *Le pouvoir des bibliothèques: La memoire des livres en Occident*, ed. Marc Baratin and Christian Jacob (Paris: Albin Michel, 1996), pp. 23–46.

28. Maurizio Ferraris, *Documentality: Why It Is Necessary to Leave Traces* (New York: Fordham University Press, 2013).

29. Ferraris, *Documentality*, 249.

30. Ferraris, *Documentality*, 250.

31. The example of the documentality of a passport is discussed in Michael Buckland, "Documentality beyond Documents," *The Monist*, Vol. 97, No. 2, 2014, pp. 179–186, and within an anthropological context as part of creating a wider documentation of biographical evidence in C. A. Heimer, "Conceiving Children: How Documents Support Case versus Biographical Analysis," in *Documents: Artifacts of Modern Knowledge*, ed. Annelise Riles (Ann Arbor: University of Michigan Press, 2006), pp. 95–126.

32. Ernest Cushing Richardson, *Classification: Theoretical and Practical* (New York: Charles Scribner's Sons, 1901).

33. Henry Evelyn Bliss, *The Organization of Knowledge in Libraries and the Subject Approach to Books* (New York: The H. W. Wilson Company, 1933).

34. Eric de Grolier, *Théorie et Pratique des Classifications Documentaires* (Paris: Union Française des Organismes de Documentation, 1956).

35. M. Dewey, *Decimal Classification and Relative Index for Libraries, Clippings, Notes etc.*, 8th ed. (Lake Placid, NY: Forest Press, 1913), p. 41.

36. This introduction was reprinted in several editions of the Dewey system, with minor addendi for each edition. The quote here is from the eighth edition of M. Dewey, *Decimal Classification and Relative Index for Libraries, Clippings, Notes etc.* (Lake Placid, NY: Forest Press, 1913).

37. Richardson, *Classification*, p. 4.

38. The classification system developed by Richardson at Princeton University Library was in use, albeit in an adjusted version, until the mid-1960s. His book can be seen as a way of legitimizing this system, also published in 1901. The outline of the system is presented in pages 224–232, as part of a useful and detailed appendix of historical classification systems, with references of where to find them, portraying the Princeton system a designated role of fulfilment in the development of bibliographic classifications from antiquity to the early twentieth century.

39. Richardson, *Classification*, pp. 47–48.

40. Richardson, *Classification*, p. 70.

41. Richardson, *Classification*, p. 74.

42. Henry Evelyn Bliss, *The Organization of Knowledge and the System of the Sciences* (New York: Henry Holt, 1929).

43. Bliss, *Organization of Knowledge in Libraries*, p. 8.

44. Bliss, *Organization of Knowledge in Libraries*, p. 305.

45. Bliss, *Organization of Knowledge in Libraries*, p. 305.

46. Bliss, *Organization of Knowledge in Libraries*, p. 309.

47. A parallel development is seen for instance in the development of professional ethics, where the code of ethics published by Charles Knowles Bolton in 1922 put the ethical foundation on the institution and the professional role of the librarian rather than on the individual person as had previously been the case, for instance in the ethical code proposed by Mary Wright Plummer in 1904. It was a clear shift from

virtue ethics to duty ethics. I have elsewhere analyzed this development in J. Hansson, "Professional Value and Ethical Self-Regulation in the Devlopment of Modern Librarianship: The Documentality of Library Ethics," *Journal of Documentation*, Vol. 73, No. 6, 2017b, pp. 1261–1280.

48. Bliss, *Organization of Knowledge in Libraries*, p. 3.

49. In a later review, from 1991, Brian Vickery called the *Théorie et Pratique des Classifications Documentaires* (The big book on classification).

50. Maack, "The Lady and the Antelope," p. 727.

51. Robert Pagès was introduced to an international audience by Michael Buckland in a 2021 special issue of the *Proceedings of the Document Academy* along with the translation of his important 1948 article "Documentary Transformations and Cultural Context," cf. *Proceedings of the Document Academy*, Vol. 8, No. 1 2021, https://ideaexchange.uakron.edu/docam/vol8/iss1/.

Robert Pagès is mentioned several times in de Grolier's treatise, not least by reference to the former's idea of "classologie" that, in de Grolier's words, concerns itself with the role of classification and documentation in future progress of society: "Viendra ensuite l'immense ensamble des techniques [documentaires] proprement dites, forces productives de la societé" (de Grolier, *Classifications Documentaires*, p. 321).

52. Eric de Grolier, "Classifications as Cultural Artefacts," in *Universal Classification I: Subject Analysis and Ordering Systems*, ed. Ingetraut Dahlberg (Franfurt: Indeks Verlag, 1982), pp 19–34.

53. De Grolier, *Classifications Documentaires*, p. 297ff.

54. Goody, *Savage Mind*.

CHAPTER 3

1. Blair, *Too Much to Know*, pp. 162–164.

2. A broad overview of different practices organizing information and knowledge in Roman antiquity is given in Andrew M. Riggsby, *Mosaics of Knowledge: Representing Information in the Roman World* (Oxford: Oxford University Press, 2019).

3. The Dewey Decimal Classification System appeared in twenty-three separate editions between 1876 and 2011, when digital technology allowed new editorial policies creating a structure for updates "on demand," not least allowing for national developments in the approximately 140 countries using the system today in their national bibliographies. For analyses on the various editions and editorial policies of the system, see John Philip Comaromi, *The Eighteen Editions of the Dewey Decimal Classification* (Albany, NY: Forest Press/Lake Placid Educational Foundation, 1976), and M. P. Satija and Alex Kyrios, *A Handbook of History, Theory, and Practice of the Dewey Decimal Classification System* (London: Facet, 2023).

4. Ronald E. Day, "'Living Document': From Documents to Documentality, from Mimesis to Performative Indexicality," *Proceedings from the Document Academy*, Vol. 8, No. 2, article 15, 2021, p.1.

5. Day, "'Living Document,'" p. 10.

6. See chapter 2, p. xx

7. Ian Cornelius, *Meaning and Method in Information Studies* (Norwood, NJ: Ablex, 1996), and Hope A. Olson, *The Power to Name: Locating the Limits of Subject Representation in Libraries* (Dordrecht: Kluwer, 2002). The discussion on hermeneutics that was initiated by Cornelius's book has continued as a relevant but somewhat overlooked perspective on classification analysis, and as such bears relevance also for the study of documents and documentary agency. A variety of entry points to this discussion can be found in Benediktsson, "Hermeneutics"; Day, "LIS, Method, and Postmodern Science"; Joacim Hansson, "In My Mind's Eye: In Search for the Mimetic Relation between a Library Classification System and Its Social Discourses," in *Information Science: Integration in Perspective*, ed. Peter Ingwersen and Nils-Ole Pors (Copenhagen: The Royal School of Librarianship, 1996), pp. 99–115; Joacim Hansson, "Hermeneutics as a Bridge between the Modern and the Post-Modern in Library and Information Science," *Journal of Documentation*, Vol. 61, No. 1, 2005, pp. 102–113; Trosow, "Standpoint Epistemology"; Suominen, *About and On Behalf of Scriptum Est*; and Matthew Kelly, "Hermeneutics and Information Science: The Ongoing Journey from Simple Objective Interpretation to Understanding Data as a Form of Disclosure," in *Information Cultures in the Digital Age: A Festschrift in Honor of Raphael Capurro*, ed. Matthew Kelly and Jared Bielby (Wiesbaden: Springer, 2016), pp. 83–110.

8. I have elsewhere provided an in-depth analysis of this intersection between classification and document studies in the French Documentation Movement: see Joacim Hansson, "The Informative Potential of Bibliographic Classification Systems: Reflections on a Discussion in the French Documentation Movement," *Journal of Documentation*, Vol. 80, No. 3, 2024, pp. 632–648.

9. Buckland (2017) mentions this engagement as a kind of adolescent rave, but le Deuff (2018) ascribes a more pervasive meaning to his revolutionary commitment and points out that it was still very relevant for him also during his studies in documentation, suggesting that Pagès in 1946 sought to formulate an anarchist position colored less by idealism and more by realism. CNAM later became the Institut National de Techniques de Documentation (INTD).

10. Michael Buckland, "Document Theory," *Knowledge Organization*, Vol. 45, No. 5, 2018, p. 426.

11. Robert Pagès, "Documentary Transformations and Cultural Context," *Proceedings from the Document Academy*, Vol. 8, No. 1, 2021b, Article 2, p. 17.

12. Robert Pagès, "Transformations Documentaires et Milieu Culturel (1948)," *Proceedings from the Document Academy*, Vol. 8, No. 1, 2021a, Article 3, p. 1.

13. Walter Benjamin, *The Work of Art in the Age of Mechanical Production* (London: Penguin, 2008).

14. Ronald E. Day, "Robert Pagès' Concept of the 'Auto-document' as a Fore-runner to Neo-documentation's Philosophy of Documentality," *Journal of Documentation*, Vol. 80, No. 4, 2024, pp. 813–823.

15. French original: "L'interrelation des sciences (et des techniques) n'est qu'un cas particulier, suggestif d'une allure du milieu culturel qu'il faut décrire plus généralement. Il ne s'étend pas seulement aux sciences et aux techniques, mais à l'ensemble des activités sociales qui s'experiment sur le terrain culturel et dont il est bien impossible de faire une énumération complete. Bliss dit que les sciences sont "pervasive" chacune individuellement. C'est le cas de tout point de vue culturel possible d'être envahissant et égocentrique" (Pagès, *Problèmes de classification*, 38).

16. Beghtol, "Classificatory Structure and Meaning."

17. De Grolier, "Classifications as Cultural Artefacts."

18. Comaromi, *Dewey Decimal Classification*, pp. 21–25.

19. French original: "L'isomorphisme classificatoire en BN défini entre des métaphysiques et des classifications documentaires ne se limite pas nécessairement à ces deux domaines. Il peut exister aussi entre toute espèce de domaines explicitement classes (schémas) ou non (champs d'expérience)" (Pagès, *Problèmes de classification*, p. 15).

20. De Grolier relates his theory of classification to linguistic models, distinguishing three levels of communication between a sender and a receiver: (1) direct (the speech act), (2) intermediation through documents (author—book—reader), and (3) intermediation through institutionally organized documentation [organisme de documentation], which is constituted by collection, synthesis [synèse], and diffusion. This third level uses bibliographical tools such as catalogs and classification systems that are defined not by the collections of documents they organize but by their document-specific logics and unique semantic-syntactic relations. This division of communication modes also explains the relation between bibliographic classification and the classification of scholarly disciplines as de Grolier pronounces communication level (2) as the *first degree of documentation* (that is fixating thoughts and processes), and (3) as the *second degree of documentation* (organizing these fixations and making them retrievable for users) (De Grolier, *Classifications Documentaires*, p. 6).

21. Paul J. DiMaggio and Walter W. Powell, "The Iron Cage Revisited: Institutional Isomorphism and Collective Rationality in Organizational Fields," in *The New Institutionalism in Organizational Analysis*, ed. Walter W. Powell and Paul J. DiMaggio (Chicago: The University of Chicago Press, 1991), p. 66.

22. DiMaggio and Powell, "Iron Cage Revisited," p. 64.

23. Briet, *What Is Documentation?*, p. 25, and Eric de Grolier, *A Study of General Categories Applicable to Classification and Coding in Documentation* (Deventer: UNESCO, 1962), p. 9–10.

24. DiMaggio and Powell, "Iron Cage Revisited," p. 68.

25. DiMaggio and Powell, "Iron Cage Revisited," p. 70.

26. Paul Ricoeur, *Time and Narrative, Vol. 1* (Chicago: The University of Chicago Press, 1984); *Time and Narrative, Vol. 2* (Chicago: The University of Chicago Press, 1985); *Time and Narrative, Vol. 3* (Chicago: The University of Chicago Press, 1988). For a both scholarly and clarifying introduction to *Time and Narrative*, see William C.

Dowling, *Ricoeur on Time and Narrative: An Introduction to Temps et Récit* (Notre Dame, IN: University of Notre Dame Press, 2011).

27. Ricoeur, *Time and Narrative*, vol. 1, p. xi.

28. Ricoeur, *Time and Narrative*, vol. 1, p. xi.

CHAPTER 4

1. Folino and Guarasci propose an argument, with departure in C. P. Snow's famous essay from 1959, *The Two Cultures*, that bibliographic classification can illustrate a strive for an overarching third culture, bringing together scientific positivism with more humanistic, hermeneutic epistemologies. Their argument makes use of the Universal Decimal Classification, developed by Paul Otlet and Henri La Fontaine, as the primary example. See: Antonietta Folino and Roberto Guarasci, "Paul Otlet e la classificazione delle scienze," *AIB Studi*, Vol. 59, No. 3, 2019, pp. 375–391.

2. Melvil Dewey, *A Classification and Subject Index for Cataloguing and Arranging the Books and Pamphlets of a Library* (Amherst, MA, 1876), n.p. Digitized by the Gutenberg project: https://www.gutenberg.org/cache/epub/12513/pg12513-images.html.

3. For an in-depth analysis of the influence of Battezzeti and Bacon on the Dewey Decimal Classification, see: John Philip Comaromi, *The Eighteen Editions of the Dewey Decimal Classification* (Albany, NY: Forest Press/Lake Placid Educational Foundation, 1976), pp. 7–29.

4. Satija and Kyrios, *Dewey Decimal Classification System*, p. XIX.

5. For general historical and genealogical analyses of Paul Otlet and his work in documentation and bibliography, see for instance Rayward, *Universe of Information*; Françoise Levie, *L'homme qui voulait classer le monde: Paul Otlet et le Mundaneum* (Bruxelles: Les Impressions Nouvelles, 2006); and Alex Wright, *Cataloging the World: Paul Otlet and the Birth of the Information Age* (Oxford: Oxford University Press, 2014). The role of Otlet in the context of Belgian internationalism has been analyzed by Daniel Laqua. See: Daniel Laqua, "Transnational Endeavours and the 'Totality of Knowledge': Paul Otlet and Henri LaFontaine as 'Integral Internationalists' in *Fin-de-Siècle* Europe," in *Internationalism and the Arts in Britain and Europe at the Fin de Siècle*, ed. Grace Brockington (Bern: Peter Lang, 2009), pp. 247–271; and Daniel Laqua, *The Age of Internationalism and Belgium, 1880–1930: Peace, Progress and Prestige* (Manchester: Manchester University Press, 2013).

6. Iriye, *Cultural Internationalism and World Order*. Iriye's work has been influential also on a more postcolonial, critical school of inquiry such as found in the edited volume *Internationalism, Imperialism and the Formation of the Contemporary World: The Pasts of the Present* by Miguel Bandeira Jerónimo and José Pedro Monteiro (2018).

7. Brockington, *Internationalism and the Arts*, p. 19.

8. Brockington, *Internationalism and the Arts*, p. 19.

9. A brief discussion of the differences between Bataille and Otlet is found in Riusset-Lemarié (1997). Ronald Day provides a colorful description of their differences in

the approach to the evidence-based definition of documents: "Whereas documents give evidence of atomic facts and rationality in Otlet's work, in Bataille's work they give evidence of the unreasonable and violent tendencies that led to—through subjugation and violence upon those within and outside—to the dominant states of Western Europe and the idea of European civilization. In short, whereas Otlet's documents give evidence of logos, documents for Bataille give evidence of the violence that culminates in logos" (Day, *Documentarity*, p. 46).

10. The complex relations between various forms of distributed use and centralism in cultural and communication technologies are discussed in depth in the contributions to *Information Beyond Borders: International Cultural and Intellectual Exchange in the Belle Époque*, edited by W. Boyd Rayward (2014).

11. The relation between Paul Otlet and Melvil Dewey, developed over several years of correspondence on classification, is discussed in Comaromi, 1976, pp. 225–234, and Levie, *Paul Otlet et le Mundaneum*, pp. 54–59.

12. How to arrange this overarching association of associations is the subject of several publications by Paul Otlet, two of which are the English original "The Union of International Associations: A World Centre" By Paul Otlet and Henri LaFontaine from 1914 (reprinted in an edited version in Rayward 1990, pp. 112–129), and Paul Otlet's own *L'organisation international et les associations internationals* (Bruxelles: Office Central des Institutions Internationales, 1910).

13. The relation between the idea of universal knowledge and architectural representations of internationalism is subject to discussion in the contributions of a volume edited by Paul Ghils, *Connaissance totale et cité mondial:La double utopie de Paul Otlet* (2017). The architectural representation of knowledge and the relation between Paul Otlet and Le Corbusier is analyzed in Siracusa (2016) and Tega (2014).

14. French original: "L'Institute international de Bibliographie a entrepris l'étude et l'organisation de la bibliographie et de la documentation générale, de la coordination de ce domain. Il est établi sur le principe de la coopération de les organismes nationeaux d'ordre général (Bibliothèques et associations nationales) et les organismes internationeaux d'ordre spécial (Association et congrès internationaux). L'institut élabore des collections et répertoires centreaux" (Otlet, *L'organisation international*, p. 77).

15. Laqua, "Transnational Endeavours," and *Age of Internationalism*, pp. 17–34. Connections between Belgian and Swiss representatives within the field of documentation were abundant, and Otlet even briefly considered his World City to be situated in Switzerland. In Zürich, a parallel organization, the *Concilium Bibliographicum*, was founded by American scholar Herbert Haviland Field in 1895. The *Concilium* became important as a sparring partner to Otlet and La Fontaine in their development of the International Institute of Bibliography, with both organizations eventually serving as founding bodies of the International Federation of Information and Documentation, FID. See: Colin B. Burke, *Information and Intrigue: From Index Cards to Dewey Decimals to Alger Hiss* (Cambridge, MA: MIT Press, 2014); Michael Buckland, and Colin B. Burke, "Precis Zoological Information: The Concilium Bibliographicum, 1895–1940," *Bulletin of the Association for Information Science and Technology*, Vol. 42, No. 6, pp. 15–19; and

Andrea Capaccioni and Elena Ranfa, "Alle origini del controllo bibliografico universale: Il contributo di Paul Otlet e Henri La Fontaine (1895)," *AIB Studi*, Vol. 61, No. 3, 2021, p. 559.

16. Otlet and La Fontaine, 1914. This text was originally published in English by the *Union des Associations Internationales Office Central* in 1914. It is included in a slightly edited form in a volume of selected essays by Paul Otlet, edited by Boyd Rayward (Otlet 1990, pp. 112–129).

17. Laqua, *Age of Internationalism*, p. 126.

18. Paul Otlet, *Monde: Essai d'universalisme* (Bruxelles: Editions de Mundaneum, 1935).

19. Ducheyne, "'To Treat the World.'"

20. French original: "Créer une classification synthétique avec notations concise des idées, c'est doter l'esprit d'une véritable langue écrite universelle capable d'agir puissamment sur la forme elle-même de la Pensée" (Otlet, *Traité de Documentation*, p. 431).

21. Svenonius, *Foundation of Information Organization*, Chapter 4, pp. 53–66.

22. Marcia Bates, "The Invisible Substrate of Information Science," *Journal of the American Society for Information Science*, Vol. 50, No. 12, 1999, pp. 1043–1050. The quote is from *Bates, Selected Works, Volume 1*, p. 118.

23. Paul Otlet, "On the Structure of Classification Numbers," in *International Organisation and Dissemination of Knowledge: Selected Essays of Paul Otlet*, ed. W. Boyd Rayward (Amsterdam: FID/Elevier, 1990), p. 51. Original from 1896.

24. Olivier Le Deuff speaks of this as "the 'dark side' of indexing." See: Olivier, Le Deuff, *Hyperdocumentation* (London/New York: ISTE/Wiley, 2021), pp. 97–102.

25. Le Deuff, *Hyperdocumentation*, p. 52.

26. Universal Decimal Classification summary: https://udcsummary.info/php/index.php. This web-based summary is produced by the UDC Consortium to work as a practical tool in for instance general libraries. This particular version contains approximately 2,600 classes out of the total 70,000.

27. Otlet, "Classification Numbers," p. 56.

28. Otlet, "Classification Numbers," p. 59.

29. Paul Otlet, *Manuel du répertoire bibliographique universel: Extraits limités aux parties plus spécialment applicables à la bibliographie de la langue auxilliarie international Esperanto* (Bruxelles: Institute International de Bibliographie, 1908).

30. Pierre Janton, *Esperanto: Language, Literature, and Community* (Albany, NY: State University of New York Press, 1993), pp. 2–3.

31. Erich Funke, "Translingua Script: A Code of Interlinguistic Communication," *The Modern Language Journal*, Vol. 40, No. 1, 1956, p. 23.

32. Funke, "Translingua Script," p. 23.

33. During the first decades of the twentieth century, numerous national associations of Esperanto appeared, among them Switzerland in 1902, Spain and Mexico in 1903, England in 1904, the US and Bolivia in 1905, and Germany in 1906. These and others

were gathered in a world federation in 1908. See: Markus Krajewski, "Organizing a Global Idiom: Esperanto, Ido and the World Auxiliary Language Movement before the First World War," in *Information Beyond Borders: International Cultural and Intellectual Exchange in the Belle Époque*, ed. Boyd Rayward (London: Routledge, 2014), pp. 102–104. Otlet states that in 1908 there were 1,029 associations for esperantists, whereof 817 in Europe and 158 in the US, with over 80 active Esperanto journals worldwide (*L'organisation international*, p. 73).

34. Janton, 1993, p. 25.

35. Otlet expressed the need for an international language in international congresses and assemblies that would be crucial for their success. After discussing the consequences of preferring English, French, or German, and even considering the revocation of Latin, he concludes that Esperanto is a liable solution: "On a conclu de là à la nécessité d'une langue seconde, auxiliaire, simplifiée, la même pour tous. [. . .] L'esperanto, du Dr Zamenhof, est le plus complet, le plus important, celui qui a obtenu le plusd'adhésions" (Otlet, *L'organisation international*, p. 73).

36. Otlet, *Manuel du répertoire*, p. 1.

37. Italics in original.

38. M. Dewey, *Decimal Classification and Relative Index for Libraries, Clippings, Notes etc.*, 8th ed. (Lake Placid, NY: Forest Press, 1913).

39. For the early development of Esperanto literature, see Janton, 1993, pp. 93–98.

40. Otlet, *Manuel du répertoire*, p. 45. Italics in original.

41. French original: "Dans le langage comme dans le documentation, il s'opère une différentiation entre: ce qui est spontané, familier et ordinaire: langage vulgaire; ce qui est cultivé, imagé, esthétique: langage littérarie; ce qui est rationnel et précis; langage scientifique. Les trois langages tels qu'ils sont actuellement constitués, se parlent, mais les deux derniers, les littéraire et scientifique, s'écrivent de plus en plus" (Otlet, *Traité de Documentation*, p. 91).

42. French original: "Une langue international est le complement indiqué d'une civilization universelle. Les hommes appartenant à une même unité auront à se comprendre les uns les autres. La langue international devrait être choisie par un corps qualifié et être enseignée obligatoirement dans les écoles" (Otlet, *Traité de Documentation*, p. 91).

43. (Otlet, *Traité de Documentation*, p. 91). For the pursuit of a universal scientific language, and the differences in approaches between Esperanto and Ido, de Kloe goes so far as to describe the plethora of artificial languages during La Belle Époque as "the return of Babel." See: Fabian de Kloe, "Beyond Babel: Esperanto, Ido and Louis Couturat's Pursuit of an International Scientific Language," In *Information Beyond Borders: International Cultural and Intellectual Exchange in the Belle Époque*, ed. W. Boyd Rayward (London: Routledge, 2014), pp. 109–122.

44. Wright, *Cataloging the World*, pp. 67–68. Françoise Levie laments the lack of documentation of the event: "Hélas, il n'y aura pas de photo de group!" (*Paul Otlet et le Mundaneum*, p. 66).

CHAPTER 5

1. SAB is short for Sveriges allmänna biblioteksförening, the Swedish Library Association, founded in 1915.

2. I have elsewhere analyzed the relation between political change, document environments, and the development of new library infrastructures. See: Joacim Hansson, *Libraries and Identity: The Role of Institutional Self-Image and Identity in the Emergence of New Types of Libraries* (Oxford: Chandos, 2010).

3. Wallace Koehler, *Ethics and Values in Librarianship: A History* (Lanham, MD: Rowman & Littlefield, 2015), p. 97.

4. Magnus Torstensson, "Framväxten av en statlig folkbibliotekspolitik i Sverige," in *Styra eller stödja: Svensk folkbibliotekspolitik under hundra år*, ed. A. Frenander and J. Lindberg, Borås: Högskolan i Borås, 2012, p. 94. The parish library in Kjula was immediately followed at the turn of the century 1800 by one in Skurup, a municipality built by the railway between Malmö and Ystad on the south coast of Sweden, and one in Lekaryd, in the southeast, about ten kilometers west of the city of Växjö. From these, parish library practice spread across the country.

5. There were parliamentary motions presented in 1828, 1850–1851, 1856, and 1858. They all focused on securing the provision of books, usually with a strong moral overtone defining the role of parish libraries as one to balance the common reading of daily newspapers.

6. Anders Frenander, "Statens förhållande till folkbiblioteken 1912–2012," in *Styra eller stödja: Svensk folkbibliotekspolitik under hundra år*, ed. A. Frenander and J. Lindberg (Borås: Högskolan i Borås, 2012), p. 27.

7. Frenander, "Statens förhållande till folkbiblioteken," p. 27. The interest from the social establishment to prioritize their own cultural values in the development of libraries for the working classes is similar to that in the US during this period as described in Dee Garrison, *Apostles of Culture: The Public Library and American Society, 1876–1920* (Madison: University of Wisconsin Press, 1979).

8. For more on Key's understanding of the concept of *Bildung*, see Ronny Ambjörnsson, "Ellen Key and the Concept of *Bildung*," *Confero*, Vol. 2, No. 1, 2014, pp. 133–160.

9. Martha Nussbaum, *Cultivating Humanity: A Classical Defense of Reform in Liberal Education* (Cambridge, MA: Harvard University Press, 1997), and Martha Nussbaum, *Not for Profit: Why Democracy Needs the Humanities* (Princeton, NJ: Princeton University Press, 2010).

10. Bernt Gustavsson, *Bildningens väg: Tre bildningsideal i svensk arbetarrörelse 1880–1930* (Stockholm: Wahlström & Widstrand, 1991), and Bernt Gustavsson, "The Idea of Democratic *Bildung*: Its Transformations in Time and Space," in *Popular Education, Power, and Democracy: Swedish Experiences and Contributions*, ed. Ann-Marie Laginder, Henrik Norvall, and Jim Crowther (Leicester: National Institute of Adult Continuing Education, 2013), pp. 35–49.

11. Magnus Torstensson analyzes the role of libraries in the self-educational efforts of the Swedish labor movement in Magnus Torstensson, "Expectations and a Worthy,

Respectable Position in Society: Means and Aims of Library Work within the Early Labour Movement in Sweden," *Swedish Library Research*, No. 1, 1995, 16–26. A version of this text is available as part of the proceedings from the 60th IFLA General Conference in 1994: https://origin-archive.ifla.org/IV/ifla60/60-torm.htm.

12. Immanuel Kant, *An Answer to the Question: 'What Is Enlightenment?'* (London: Penguin Books, 1784/2009). The English term *immaturity* is only partly covered by the meaning of the originally German *Unmündigkeit.* While the English term covers a physical and a mental aspect, the German term has less physical significance, instead being primarily socially defined, denoting the inability to make rational choices and decisions and foster altruism and compassion while adapting to general social norms and values. The German concept also entails a legal aspect, *Mündigheit,* that also means the process (and point) where a person becomes legally adult.

13. Valfrid Palmgren, *Förslag angående de åtgärder som från statens sida böra vidtagas för främjandet af det allmänna biblioteksväsendet i Sverige, afgifvet den 28 september 1911* (Stockholm: Kungl. Eclesiastikdepartementet, 1911.)

14. *Läsning för folket* was one of the first popular education publications in Sweden, founded in 1833 by *Sällskapet för spridandet av nyttiga kunskaper till allmogen och de arbetande klasserna* [The society of dissemination of useful knowledge among the peasantry and the working classes]. This was one of the earliest popular education societies in the country, inspired by similar initiatives and societies in the United Kingdom. *Läsning för folket* became extremely influential as Swedish parliament in 1851 decided to distribute all published volumes of the journal, along with current subscriptions, to every municipality in the country, to be used in public schools. Siljeström's catalog thus ended up literally in every parish library in the country.

15. In 1868 there were 1,437 parish libraries across Sweden, serving 2,500 parishes. See: Knut Tynell, *Folkbiblioteken i Sverige* (Stockholm: P. A. Norstedts & söners förlag, 1931), p. 57.

16. Per A. Siljeström, "Förslag till inrättandet af sockenbiblioteker och hwad derwid bör iakttagas jemte förteckning å dertill lämpliga böcker och skrifter," *Läsning för folket,* Vol. 25, No. 1, 1859, pp. 47–68.

17. Paulo Freire, *Pedagogy of the Oppressed* (London: Penguin. 1993); Henry A. Giroux, *On Critical Pedagogy,* 2nd ed. (London: Bloomsbury Academic, 2020).

18. *Studentföreningen Verdandis folkbiblioteks-katalog jämte upplysningar och råd angående bildandet, skötseln och förkofrandet af folkbibliotek,* 4th ed. (Uppsala: Studentföreningen Verdandi, 1908).

19. *Föreningen Heimdals bokförteckning för svenska folkbibliotek till vägledning för socken-, arbetare- och ungdomsbibliotek* (Uppsala: Föreningen Heimdal, 1905), p. III.

20. *Föreningen Heimdals bokförteckning,* p. IV.

21. Arnold Barton, *Sweden and Visions of Norway: Politics and Culture, 1814–1905* (Carbondale: Southern Illinois University Press, 2003).

22. Valfrid Palmgren, *Bibliotek och folkuppfostran: anteckningar från en studieresa i Amerikas förenta stater* (Stockholm: P. A. Norstedt & Söner, 1909), p. 2.

23. I have previously written about the discussions mentioned in this segment in Joacim Hansson, "Why Public Libraries in Sweden Did Not Choose Dewey," *Knowledge Organization*, Vol. 24, No. 3, 1997, pp. 145–153. It is also mentioned in Joacim Hansson, "Bringing Political Upheaval and Cultural Trauma into Order: A Document-Theoretical Approach to the Social Significance of Bibliographic Classification Systems," *Proceedings from the Document Academy*, Vol. 8, No. 2, 2021, Article 5. Readers of Swedish may also consult my book *Dewey och de Svenska biblioteken*, (Lund: BTJ Förlag, 2023).

24. *Studentföreningen Verdandis*, p. 119.

25. Library representatives from the Scandinavian countries made several journeys to the US, the UK, and continental Europe to find inspiration for the establishment of public library systems. From Norway, Haakon Nyhuus visited the US, working briefly as head of the Catalog Department at the Chicago Public Library before returning to Oslo in 1898, where he immediately molded the new Deichman Library after American ideals, not least bibliographically. See: Øivind Frisvold, *Kunskap er makt, Norsk biblioteksshistorie: Kultur, politikk og samfunn* (Oslo: ABM Media, 2021), pp. 54–60. From Denmark, Andreas Schack Steenberg visited England in 1895 and 1897, France in 1900, and the US in 1902. His travels resulted in the implementation of American public library ideals and practices in Denmark. See: Nan Dahlkild and Steen Bille Larsen, *Dansk bibliotekshistorie: Vol. 1: biblioteker for de få, Tiden før 1920* (Aarhus: Aahrhus universitetsforlag, 2021), pp. 299–302.

26. Schack Steenberg wrote in *Biblioteksbladet*, Swedish Library Journal, in 1916, prompting a comment in the same issue by Swedish Library Consultant Fredrik Hjelmqvist explaining the Dewey system and Charles Ammi Cutter's cataloging principles. See: Schack Andreas Steenberg, "De nordiske lands folkebiblioteker og amerikanske systemer," *Biblioteksbladet*, Vol. 1, 1916, pp. 115–119, and Fredrik Hjelmqvist, "Dewey's klassificeringssystem och Cutter's namntabeller," *Biblioteksbladet*, Vol. 1, 1916, pp. 112–114.

27. Alvida Sandberg, *Bibliotek och biblioteksskötsel: En hjälpreda för bibliotekarier i skolbibliotek och andra mindre boksamlingar* (Stockholm: Norstedts, 1915).

28. Hjelmqvist, "Dewey's klassificeringssystem," p. 113, and *Klassifikationssystem för svenska bibliotek*, 1921, p. 6.

29. Gustav Adde, "Bibliotek och biblioteksskötsel," *Nordisk tidskrift för bok- och biblioteksväsen*, Vol. 2, 1915, p. 39.

30. M. Dewey, *Decimal classification and relative index for libraries, clippings, notes etc.*, 8th ed. (Lake Placid, NY: Forest Press, 1913).

31. Benedict Anderson, *Imagined Communities: Reflections on the Origin and Spread of Nationalism*, rev. ed. (London: Verso, 2016), chap. 7, "The Last Wave," pp. 113–140.

32. Fredrik Hjelmqvist, "Något om tillkomsten av SAB:s klassifikations- och katalogiseringsregler," *Biblioteksbladet*, Vol. 35, 1950, pp. 350–351.

33. Kungl. Ecklesiastikdepartementet. *Katalog över böcker som folk- och skolbibliotek samt riksförbund som bedriva biblioteksverksamhet kunna erhålla i stadsbidrag: Grundkatalog 1915–1916* (Stockholm: Kungl. Ecklesiastikdepartementet, 1915).

34. Kungliga biblioteket. *Accessionskatalog 28: Sveriges offentliga bibliotek: Stockholm, Uppsala, Lund, Göteborg*. (Stockholm: Kungliga biblioteket, 1913).

35. "Klassifikationssystem (plan för uppdelningen i en systematisk katalog), *Biblioteksbladet*, Vol. 5, 1920, p. 162.

36. *Klassifikationssystem för svenska bibliotek*, 1921.

37. Maj Klasson, "Knowledge Organization as a Mirror of Society," *Social Change and Adult Education Research: Adult Education Research in The Nordic Countries 1994* (Linköping: Linköping University Adult Education research group, 1995), pp. 19–34.

38. Since 2009, both the Sámi people and the Tornedalians are defined as Indigenous peoples, with their languages and cultures protected by Swedish national minority legislation.

39. Dewey, *Decimal classification*.

40. A. S. Kalvemark, "Malthus and neo-Malthusianism in Sweden," *Statistical Review*, Vol. 18 No. 6, 1980, pp. 481–486.

41. Documentary practices of the Swedish eugenics program have been analyzed in Ulrika Kjellman, "A Whiter Shape of Pale: Visuality and Race in the Work of The Swedish Institute for Race Biology," *Scandinavian Journal of History*, Vol. 38, No. 2, 2013, 180–201, and Ulrika Kjellman, "How to Picture Race? The Use of Photography in the Scientific Practice of the Swedish State Institute for Race Biology," *Scandinavian Journal of History*, Vol, 39, No. 5, 2014, pp. 580–611.

CHAPTER 6

1. General accounts of Jewish bibliographic classification can be found in Shimeon Brisman, *A History and Guide to Judaica Bibliography* (Cincinnati: Hebrew Union College Press, 1977), and David. B. Levy, "Ancient to Modern Jewish Classification Systems: An Overview from Beit HaMikdash Temple Archive to H.a. Wolfson, G. Sholem, A. Freidus, D. Elazar & LC," *Proceedings of the 36th Annual Convention of the Association for Jewish Libraries, La Jolla, CA, June 24–27, 2001*, 2001, pp. 1–11. Levy's paper is also reprinted in self-published volume: David B. Levy, *The History of Judaica Libraries Vol. 1*, 2019, pp. 38–57. Readers of Swedish may consult the following for a popular overview: Joacim Hansson, *De ordnade böckernas folk: Om klassifikation I jusdiska bibliografier och bibliotek* (Stockholm: Hillelförlaget, 2023). More specialized historical accounts can be found in Bella Hass Weinberg, "The Earliest Hebrew Citation Indexes," *Journal of the American Society for Information Science*, Vol. 48, No. 4, 1997, pp. 318–330, and Bella Hass Weinberg, "Indexes and Religion: Reflections on Research in the History of Indexes," *The Indexer*, Vol. 21, No. 3, 1999, pp. 111–118.

2. I have previously discussed the specific relation between Jewish and non-Jewish bibliographic practice in Joacim Hansson, "Classification Systems for Jewish Libraries and Bibliographies: Philosophy, Warrants, and Relation to Non-Jewish Bibliographic Practice," *Journal of Religion and Theological Information*, Vol. 21, No. 3–4, 2022, pp. 99–121.

3. Anselm Strauss, "Social Worlds and Legitimation Processes," *Studies in Symbolic Interaction*, Vol. 4, 1982, pp. 171–190.

4. Gerald Izenberg, *Identity: The Necessity of a Modern Idea* (Philadelphia: Pennsylvania University Press, 2016), pp. 409–414.

5. Izenberg, *Identity*, p. 411.

6. Strauss, "Social Worlds and Legitimation Processes," p. 177.

7. Strauss, "Social Worlds and Legitimation Processes," p. 180.

8. In his biography over Melvil Dewey, Wayne Wiegand presents a cultural, straussian social-world explanation for Dewey's anti-semitism as rooted in the religious environment of his youth, and not least his elementary school. See Wayne A. Wiegand, *Irrepressible Reformer: A Biography of Melvil Dewey* (Chicago: American Library Association, 1996).

9. Vanessa Freedman, "The Maskil, the Kabbalist and the Political Scientist: Judaica Classification Systems in Their Historical Context," *Proceedings from The Association of Jewish Library Annual Convention 46, Montreal, Canada*, 2011, pp. 1–11.

10. Emile G. L. Schrijvers, "The Hebraic book," *A Companion to the History of the Book*, ed. Simon Eliot and Jonathan Rose (Malden, MA: Blackwell, 2009), pp. 153–164.

11. Joshua Teplitsky, *Prince of the Press: How One Collector Built History's Most Enduring and Remarkable Jewish Library* (New Haven, CT: Yale University Press, 2019), p. 94.

12. Teplitsky, *Prince of the Press*, p. 95.

13. David Allan, "'The Advantages of Literature': The Subscription Library in Georgian Britain," *The Meaning of the Library: A Cultural History*, ed. Alice Crawford (Princeton, NJ: Princeton University Press, 2015), pp. 117–118.

14. Lucien X. Polastron, *Books on Fire: The Tumultuous Story of the World's Great Libraries* (London: Thames & Hudson, 2007), p. 73.

15. Brian W. Ogilvie, *The Science of Describing: Natural History in Renaissance Europe* (Chicago: The University of Chicago Press, 2006); G. Thomas Tanselle, *Bibliographical Analysis: A Historical Introduction* (Cambridge: Cambridge University Press, 2009); Blair, *Too Much to Know*, pp. 117–172.

16. Levy, "Ancient to Modern Jewish Classification Systems."

17. Martin Goodman, *A History of Judaism* (Princeton, NJ: Princeton University Press, 2018), p. 163; Bella Hass Weinberg, "Hebraica Cataloging and Classification," in *Cataloging and Classification of Non-Western Material: Concerns, Issues and Practices*, ed. Mohammed M. Aman (Phoenix, AZ: Oryx Press, 1980), p. 339.

18. Levy, "Ancient to Modern Jewish Classification Systems," p. 51.

19. Harry Austryn Wolfson, "The Classification of Sciences in Medieval Jewish Philosophy," in *Hebrew Union College Jubilee Volume*, ed. David Philipson et al. (Cincinnati: Hebrew Union College, 1925), p. 266.

20. Wolfson, "Classification of Sciences," p. 285.

21. Brisman, *Judaica Bibliography*, p. 9.

22. Teplitsky, *Prince of the Press*, p. 39.

23. Avriel Bar-Levav, "The Religious Order of Jewish Books: Structuring Hebrew Knowledge in Amsterdam," *Studia Rosenthaliana*, Vol. 44, 2012, p. 7. Bar-Levav provides a historical account of *Siftei yeshenim*, along with a full English translation of its first pages and introduction, originally written in Hebrew.

24. Ismar Schorsh, *From Text to Context: The Turn to History in Modern Judaism* (Hannover: Brandeis University Press, 1994), pp. 177–204.

25. Bar-Levav, "Religious Order of Jewish Books," pp. 24f.

26. Hjørland, *Information Seeking and Subject Representation*, p. 86.

27. Blair, *Too Much to Know*, p. 39.

28. Seth Jerchower and Heidi G. Lerner, "Johann Heinrich Hottinger and the Systematic Organization of Jewish Literature," *Judaica Librarianship*, Vol. 13, 2007, pp. 1–25. Hottinger's classification system consists of the following main categories: I. Biblical Studies; II. On Talmudic Writings and Authors; III. Dogmatic Teachings; IV. Polemical Treatises; V. Liturgical Works; VI. Practical Religion; VII. Casuistic and Catechetic Treatises; VIII. Cabalistic Works; IX. On Jewish Law; X. Medicine; XI. Philosophy.

29. Jerchower and Lerner, "Johann Heinrich Hottinger," p. 6.

30. Richard Gottheil, "Libraries," *The Jewish Encyclopedia* (New York: Funk & Wagnalls, 1906), p. 6.

31. Joshua Bloch, "The Classification of Jewish Literature in the New York Public Library," *Studies in Jewish Bibliography and Related Subjects in Memory of Abraham Solomon Freidus* (New York: Alexander Kohut Memorial Foundation/ New York Public Library, 1929), L-LXXVII. Bloch not only publishes the entire Freidus system but also, for the first time outside the New York Public Library, Freidus's informative preface to his system in which he (Freidus) explains the basic structure and provides instructions for the use of the system.

32. Jack Andersen and Laura Skouvig, "Knowledge Organization: A Sociohistorical Analysis and Critique," *Library Quarterly*, Vol. 76, No. 3, 2006, p. 316.

33. Jeffrey C. Alexander, "On the Social Construction of Moral Universals: The 'Holocaust' from War Crime to Trauma Drama," in *Cultural Trauma and Collective Identity*, ed. J. C. Alexander, R. Eyerman, B. Giesen, N. J. Smelser, and P. Sztompka (Berkeley: University of California Press, 2004), pp. 196–263.

34. Alexander, "Social Construction of Moral Universals," p. 228

35. Alvin H. Rosenfeld, "The Americanization of the Holocaust," in *Thinking about the Holocaust after Half a Century*, ed. A. Rosenfeld (Bloomington/Indianapolis: Indiana University Press, 1997), p. 131. pp. 119–150.

36. Yehuda Bauer, *Out of the Ashes: The Impact of American Jews on post-Holocaust European Jewry* (Oxford: Pergamon Press, 1989), p. xiv.

37. Zygmunt Bauman, "Sociology after the Holocaust," *The British Journal of Sociology*, Vol. 39, No. 4. 1988, pp. 469–497.

38. See for instance: David Shavit, "Jewish Libraries in the Polish Ghettos during the Nazi era," *Library Quarterly*, Vol. 52, No. 2, 1982, pp. 103–121, and Marek Sroka, "The Destruction of Jewish Libraries and Archives during World War II," *Libraries & Culture*, Vol. 38, No. 2, 2003, pp. 147–165.

39. Bella Hass Weinberg, "Judaica Classification Schemes for Synagogue and School Libraries: A Structural Analysis," *Judaica Librarianship*, Vol. 1, No. 1, 1983, pp. 26–30.

40. Shavit, "Jewish Libraries in the Polish Ghettos," p. 108.

41. Hans Nordesjö, "The Jacobowsky Collection of Judaica at Uppsala University Library," in *Serving the Scholarly Community: Essays on Tradition and Change in Research Libraries*, ed. Sten Hedberg (Uppsala: Uppsala University Library, 1995), pp. 205–212.

42. The system is published in its entirety in Karin Almbladh, *C. Vilh. Jacobowskys Judaicasamling* (Borås: Högskolan I Borås, 1986). Specialarbete 1986:24.

43. See: Karin Almbladh, "C. Vilh. Jacobowskys Judaicasamling," *Scandinavian Jewish Studies*, Vol. 8, No. 2, 1987, pp. 158–166, and Nordesjö, "Jacobowsky Collection of Judaica," pp. 211–212.

44. The final and most developed version of Scholem's system is: Jewish National and University Library, *Classification for Judaica: As Used in the Judaica Department of the Jewish National and University Library* (Jerusalem: Jewish National and University Library, 1964).

45. The edition used for this book is: Mae Weine, *Weine Classification Scheme and Relative Index for Judaica Libraries*, 9th ed. Revised by the Weine Revision Committee and Joel Tuschman. Los Angeles: Association of Jewish Libraries, 2013.

46. Wiegand, *Irrepressible Reformer*, pp. 264–282.

47. Jewish National and University Library, *Classification for Judaica.*

48. Vanessa Freedman, "Making the Dewey Jewey: Gershom Scholem as a Librarian," in *Scholar and Kabbalist: The Life and Work of Gershom Scholem*, ed. Mirjam Zadoff and Noam Zadoff (Leiden: Brill, 2019), p. 265.

49. Weinberg, "Judaica Classification Schemes," p. 28.

50. Freedman, "The Maskil, the Kabbalist and the Political Scientist," p. 8.

51. Mae Weine, "Preface to the Seventh Edition," *Weine Classification Scheme and Relative Index for Judaica Libraries*, 9th ed. Revised by the Weine Revision Committee and Joel Tuschman. Los Angeles: Association of Jewish Libraries, 2013, p. 1.

52. P. Mendes-Flohr, "The Emancipation of European Jewry: Why Was It Not Self-Evident?," *Studia Rosenthaliana*, Vol. 30, No. 1, 1996, pp. 7–20.

53. Amy Schoppert, "A Review of the Literature on Elazar's Classification System for Libraries of Judaica," *Cataloging & Classification Quarterly*, Vol. 52, No. 4, 2014, p. 426.

54. Bella Hass Weinberg, "The Hidden Classification in Library of Congress Subject Headings for Judaica," *Library Resources & Technical Services*, Vol. 37, No. 4, 1993, p. 374.

55. David Elazar and Daniel Elazar, *A Classification System for Libraries of Judaica* (Lanham, MD: Rowman & Littlefield, 1997), p. 3.

56. Yehuda Bauer, *Out of the Ashes: The Impact of American Jews on Post-Holocaust European Jewry* (Oxford: Pergamon Press, 1989), pp. XI-XXV. See also: Michael L. Morgan, "To Seize Memory: History and Identity in Post-Holocaust Jewish Thought," in *Thinking about the Holocaust after Half a Century*, ed. Alvin H. Rosenfeld (Bloomington/Indianapolis: Indiana University Press, 1997), pp. 151–181.

57. Elazar and Elazar, *Libraries of Judaica*, p. 15.

58. David Elazar, "The Making of a Classification Scheme for Libraries of Judaica," *Judaica Librarianship*, Vol. 14, 2008, p. 16. See also Elazar and Elazar, *Libraries of Judaica*, p. 14.

59. Monica Sax, *Mosaiska församlingens bibliotek I Stockholm: Dess verksamhet och organisation* (Borås: Högskolan i Borås, 1980). Specialarbete 1980:19.

60. Malin Norrby, "Judiska biblioteket: En del av berättelsen om stora synagogan," in *Jag må bo mitt ibland dem: Stockholms stora synagoga 150 år*, ed. Marina Burstein (Stockholm: Hillelförlaget/ Judiska församlingen i Stockholm, 2020), pp. 137–143.

61. Abraham Hirsch and Harald Leipzinger, *Meddelande från Mosaiska församlingens bibliotek* (Stockholms Mosaiska Församling, 1899).

62. Carl Vilhelm Jacobowsky, "Något om Stockholms mosaiska församlings bibliotek," *Judisk Tidskrift*, no. 8, 1928, 263–266.

63. *Hyllsignum Judiska biblioteket*, (Stockholm: Stockholm Jewish Library, n.d).

64. Bauer, *Out of the Ashes*, p. XIV.

BIBLIOGRAPHY, INCLUDING ANALYZED CLASSIFICATION SYSTEMS

Adde, Gustav. "Bibliotek och biblioteksskötsel." *Nordisk tidskrift för bok- och biblioteksväsen* Vol. 2, 1915, pp. 392–394.

Adler, Melissa. *Cruising the Library: Perversities in the Organization of Knowledge*. New York: Fordham University Press, 2017.

Allan, David. "'The Advantages of Literature': The Subscription Library in Georgian Britain." In Alice Crawford (Ed.). *The Meaning of the Library: A Cultural History*. Princeton, NJ: Princeton University Press, 2015, pp. 103–123.

Alexander, Jeffrey C. "On the Social Construction of Moral Universals: The 'Holocaust' from War Crime to Trauma Drama." In J. C. Alexander, R. Eyerman, B. Giesen, N. J. Smelser, and P. Sztompka (Eds.), *Cultural Trauma and Collective Identity*. Berkeley: University of California Press, 2004, pp. 196–263.

Almbladh, Karin. *C. Vilh. Jacobowskys Judaicasamling*. Borås: Högskolan i Borås, 1986. Specialarbete 1986: 24.

Almbladh, Karin. "C. Vilh. Jacobowskys Judaicasamling." *Scandinavian Jewish Studies*, Vol. 8, No. 2, 1987, pp. 158–166.

Ambjörnsson, Ronny. "Ellen Key and the Concept of *Bildung*." *Confero*, Vol. 2, No. 1, 2014, pp. 133–160.

Andersen, Jack, and Hansson, Joacim (Eds). *Exploring Contemporary Classification Practice: Organizing Information, Technological Change and Ideological Contestation*. London: Routledge, 2025.

Andersen, Jack, and Skouvig Laura. "Knowledge Organization: A Sociohistorical Analysis and Critique." *Library Quarterly*, Vol. 76, No. 3, 2006, pp. 300–322.

Anderson, Benedict. *Imagined Communities: Reflections on the Origin and Spread of Nationalism*, rev. ed. London: Verso, 2016.

Bacon, Francis. *The Advancement of Learning and The New Atlantis*. Oxford: Benediction Classics, 2010.

Bar-Levav, Avriel. "The Religious Order of Jewish Books: Structuring Hebrew Knowledge in Amsterdam." *Studia Rosenthaliana*, Vol. 44, 2012, pp. 1–27.

Barité, Mario. "Literary Warrant." *Knowledge Organization*, Vol. 45, No. 6, 2018, pp. 517–536.

Barton, Arnold. *Sweden and Visions of Norway: Politics and Culture, 1814–1905*. Carbondale: Southern Illinois University Press, 2003.

Bates, Marcia. "The Invisible Substrate of Information Science." *Journal of the American Society for Information Science*, Vol. 50, No. 12, 1999, pp. 1043–1050.

Bates, Marcia. *Information and the Information Professions: Selected Works, Volume 1*. Berkeley, CA: Ketchikan Press, 2016.

Bauer, Yehuda. *Out of the Ashes: The Impact of American Jews on post-Holocaust European Jewry*. Oxford: Pergamon Press, 1989.

Bauman, Zygmunt. "Sociology after the Holocaust." *The British Journal of Sociology*, Vol. 39, No. 4, 1988, pp. 469–497.

Beghtol, Claire. "Semantic Validity: Concepts of Warrant in Bibliographic Classification Systems." *Library Resources and Technical Services*, Vol. 30, No. 2, 1986, pp. 109–125.

Beghthol, Claire. "Relationships in Classificatory Structure and Meaning." In Carol A. Bean and Rebecca Green (Eds.), *Relationships in the Organization of Knowledge*. Dordrecht: Kluwer, 2001, pp. 99–113.

Benediktsson, Daniel. "Hermeneutics: Dimensions towards LIS Thinking." *Library and Information Science Research*, Vol. 11, No. 3, 1989, pp. 201–234.

Benjamin, Walter. *The Work of Art in the Age of Mechanical Reproduction*. London: Penguin, 2008.

Besterman, Theodore. *The Beginning of Systematic Bibliography*, 2nd rev. ed. London: Humphrey Milford/Oxford University Press, 1936.

Blair, Ann. *Too Much to Know: Managing Scholarly Information Before the Modern Age*. New Haven, CT: Yale University Press, 2010.

Bliss, Henry Evelyn. *The Organization of Knowledge and the System of the Sciences*. New York: Henry Holt, 1929.

Bliss, Henry Evelyn. *The Organization of Knowledge in Libraries and the Subject Approach to Books*. New York: The H. W. Wilson Company, 1933.

Bloch, Joshua. "The Classification of Jewish Literature in the New York Public Library." *Studies in Jewish Bibliography and Related Subjects in Memory of Abraham*

Solomon Freidus. New York: Alexander Kohut Memorial Foundation/ New York Public Library, 1929, L-LXXVII.

Bowker, Geoffrey C., and Star, Susan Leigh. *Sorting Things Out: Classification and Its Consequences*. Cambridge, MA: MIT Press, 1999.

Breslauer, B. H., and Folter, R. *Bibliography: Its History and Development*. New York: The Grolier Club, 1984.

Briet, Suzanne. *What Is Documentation?* Translated and edited by Ronald E. Day and Laurent Martinet with Hermina G. B. Anghelescu. Lanham, MD: Scarecrow Press, 2006.

Brisman, Shimeon. *A History and Guide to Judaica Bibliography*. Cincinnati, OH: Hebrew Union College Press, 1977.

Brockington, Grace, ed. *Internationalism and the Arts in Britain and Europe at the Fin de Siècle*. Bern: Peter Lang, 2009.

Buckland, Michael. *Information and Information Systems*. Westport, CT: Praeger, 1991.

Buckland, Michael. "Documentality beyond Documents." *The Monist*, Vol. 97, No. 2, 2014, pp. 179–186.

Buckland, Michael. "Before the Antelope: Robert Pagès on Documents." *Proceedings from the Document Academy*, Vol. 4, No. 2, 2017, Article 6.

Buckland, Michael. "Document Theory." *Knowledge Organization*, Vol. 45, No. 5, 2018, pp. 425–436.

Buckland. Michael. "Introduction to Robert Pagès' 'Documentary Transformations and Cultural Context.'" *Proceedings from The Document Academy*, Vol. 8, No. 1, 2021, Article 1.

Buckland, Michael, and Burke, Colin B. "Precise Zoological Information: The Concilium Bibliographicum, 1895–1940." *Bulletin of the Association for Information Science and Technology*, Vol. 42, No. 6, 2016, pp. 15–19.

Burke, Colin B. *Information and Intrigue: From Index Cards to Dewey Decimals to Alger Hiss*. Cambridge, MA: MIT Press, 2014.

Burnett, Simon, and Lloyd, Annemaree. "The Road Not Taken: Locating Desire Lines across Information Landscapes." *Information Research*, Vol. 24, No. 4, 2019, paper colis1911.

Capaccioni, Andrea, and Ranfa, Elena. "Alle origini del controllo bibliografico universale: Il contributo di Paul Otlet e Henri La Fontaine (1895)." *AIB Studi*, Vol. 61, No. 3, 2021, pp. 555–561.

Casson, Lionel. *Libraries in the Ancient World*. New Haven, CT: Yale University Press, 2001.

Classification Decimal Universelle. Edition Abrégée, 7 ed. Liège: UDC Consortium/Editions du CÉFAL, 2001.

Collins, Jacob. "Parallel Structures: André Leroi-Gouhran, Claude Lévi-Strauss, and the Making of French Structural Anthropology." *History of the Human Sciences*, Vol. 34, No. 3–4, 2021, pp. 307–335.

Comaromi, John Philip. *The Eighteen Editions of the Dewey Decimal Classification*. Albany, NY: Forest Press/Lake Placid Educational Foundation, 1976.

Cornelius, Ian. *Meaning and Method in Information Studies*. Norwood, NJ: Ablex, 1996.

Dahlkild, Nan, and Larsen, Steen Bille. *Dansk bibliotekshistorie: Vol. 1: Biblioteker for de få, Tiden før 1920*. Aarhus: Aahrhus Universitetsforlag, 2021.

Day, Ronald E. "LIS, Method, and Postmodern Science." *Journal of Education for Library and Information Science*, Vol. 37, No. 4, 1996, pp. 317–324.

Day, Ronald E. *The Modern Invention of Information: Discourse, History, and Power*. Carbondale: Southern Illinois University Press, 2001.

Day, Ronald E. "'A Necessity of Our Time': Documentation as 'Cultural Technique' in What Is Documentation?" In Suzanne Briet, *What Is Documentation?* Lanham, MD: Scarecrow Press, 2006, pp 47–63.

Day, Ronald E. *Indexing It All: The Subject in the Age of Documentation, Information, and Data*. Cambridge, MA: MIT Press, 2014.

Day, Ronald E. *Documentarity: Evidence, Ontology, and Inscription*. Cambridge, MA: MIT Press, 2019.

Day, Ronald E. "'Living Document': From Documents to Documentality, from Mimesis to Performative Indexicality." *Proceedings from the Document Academy*, Vol. 8, No. 2, Article 15, 2021, pp. 1–11.

Day, Ronald E. "Robert Pagès' Concept of the 'Auto-Document' as a Fore-Runner to Neo-Documentation's Philosophy of Documentality." *Journal of Documentation*, Vol. 80, No. 4, 2024, pp. 813–823.

Deuff, Olivier Le. "Robert Pagès, une necéssaire redécouverte par les sciences l'information." *Savoir CDI*, April 2018.

Deuff, Olivier Le. *Hyperdocumentation*. London/New York: ISTE/Wiley, 2022.

Dewey, Melvil. *A Classification and Subject Index for Cataloguing and Arranging the Books and Pamphlets of a Library*. Amherst, MA, 1876.

Dewey, M. *Decimal Classification and Relative Index for Libraries, Clippings, Notes etc.*, 8th ed. Lake Placid, NY: Forest Press, 1913.

DiMaggio, Paul J., and Powell, Walter W. "The Iron Cage Revisited: Institutional Isomorphism and Collective Rationality in Organizational Fields." In Walter W. Powell and Paul J. DiMaggio (Eds.), *The New Institutionalism in Organizational Analysis*. Chicago: The University of Chicago Press, 1991, pp. 63–82.

Dowling, William C. *Ricoeur on Time and Narrative: An Introduction to Temps et Récit*. Notre Dame, IN: University of Notre Dame Press, 2011.

Ducheyne, Steffen. "'To Treat the World': Paul Otlet's Ontology and Epistemology and the Circle of Knowledge." *Journal of Documentation*, Vol. 65, No. 2, 2009, pp. 223–244.

Elazar, David. "The Making of a Classification Scheme for Libraries of Judaica." *Judaica Librarianship*, Vol. 14, 2008, pp. 15–25.

Elazar, David, and Elazar, Daniel. *A Classification System for Libraries of Judaica*. Lanham, MD: Rowman & Littlefield, 1997.

Fairthorne, Robert A. 1985. "Temporal Structure in Bibliographical Classification." In L. M. Chan, P. A. Richmond, and E. Svenonius (Eds.), *Theory of Subject Analysis: A Sourcebook*. Littletown, CO: Libraries Unlimited, 1985, pp. 359–368.

Feinberg, Melanie. "Two Kinds of Evidence: How Information Systems form Rhetorical Arguments." *Journal of Documentation*, Vol. 66, No. 4, 2010, pp. 491–512.

Feinberg, Melanie. "How Information Systems Communicate as Documents: The Concept of Authorial Voice." *Journal of Documentation*, Vol. 67, No. 6, 2011, pp. 1015–1037.

Feinberg, Melanie. "Synthetic Ethos: The Believability of Collections at the Intersection of Classification and Curation." *The Information Society*, Vol. 28, 2012, pp. 329–339.

Folino, Antonietta, and Guarasci, Roberto. "Paul Otlet e la classificazione delle scienze." *AIB Studi*, Vol. 59, No. 3, 2019, pp. 375–391.

Freedman, Vanessa. "The Maskil, the Kabbalist and the Political Scientist: Judaica Classification Systems in Their Historical Context." *Proceedings from The Association of Jewish Library Annual Convention 46, Montreal, Canada*, 2011, pp. 1–11.

Freedman, Vanessa. "Making the Dewey Jewey: Gershom Scholem as a Librarian." In Mirjam Zadoff and Noam Zadoff (Eds.), *Scholar and Kabbalist: The Life and Work of Gershom Scholem*. Leiden: Brill, 2019, pp. 253–271.

Freire, Paulo. *Pedagogy of the Oppressed*. London: Penguin. 1993.

Fremery, Wayne de. *Cats, Carpenters, and Accountants: Bibliographical Foundations of Information Science*. Cambridge, MA: MIT Press, 2024.

Frenander, Anders. "Statens förhållande till folkbiblioteken 1912–2012." In Anders Frenander and Jenny Lindberg (Eds.), *Styra eller stödja: Svensk folkbibliotekspolitik under hundra år*. Borås: Högskolan i Borås, 2012, pp. 15–88.

Frisvold, Øivind. *Kunskap er makt, Norsk bibliotekshistorie: kultur, politikk og samfunn*. Oslo: ABM Media, 2021.

Frohmann, Bernd. *Deflating Information: From Science Studies to Documentation*. Toronto: Toronto University Press, 2004.

Frohmann, Bernd. "Multiplicity, Materiality, and Autonomous Agency of Documentation." In Roswitha Skare, Niels Windfeld Lund, and Andreas Vårheim (Eds.), *A Document (Re)turn: Contributions from a Field in Transition*. Frankfurt am Main: Peter Lang, 2007, pp. 27–39.

Frohmann, Brend. "The Documentality of Mme Briet's Antelope." In J. Packer and C. B. Crofts Wiley (Eds.), *Communication Matters: Materialist Approaches to Media, Mobility, and Networks*. London: Routledge, 2012, pp. 173–182.

Funke, Erich. "Translingua Script: A Code of Interlinguistic Communication." *The Modern Language Journal*, Vol. 40, No. 1, 1956, pp. 22–24.

Furner, Jonathan. "'A Brilliant Mind': Margret Eagan and Social Epistemology." *Library Trends*, Vol. 52, No. 4, 2004, pp. 792–809.

Furner, Jonathan. *Information Studies and Other Provocations: Selected Talks 200–2019*. Sacramento, CA: Library Juice Press, 2020.

Föreningen Heimdals bokförteckning för svenska folkbibliotek till vägledning för socken-, arbetare- och ungdomsbibliotek. Uppsala: Föreningen Heimdal, 1905.

Garrison, Dee. *Apostles of Culture: The Public Library and American Society, 1876–1920*. Madison: University of Wisconsin Press, 1979.

Gesner, Konrad. *Bibliotheca Universalis, sive Catalogus omnium Scriptoum locupletissimus, in tribus linguis, Latina, Græca, & Hebraica*. Zürich: Christophorum Froschouerum, 1545.

Gesner, Konrad. *Bibliotheca universalis sive catalogus omnium scriptorum locupletissimus in tribus linguis Latina Graeca et Hebraica: Pandectarum sive Partitionum . . . Libri XXI*, Vol. 2. Zürich: Christophorus Froschoverus, 1548.

Ghils, Paul (Ed.). *Connaissance totale et Cité mondial: Le double utopie de Paul Otlet*. Louvain-la-Neuve: Academia-L'Harmattan, 2017.

Giroux, Henry A. *On Critical Pedagogy*, 2nd ed. London: Bloomsbury Academic, 2020.

Golub, Koraljka. "Automated Subject Classification of Textual Web Documents." *Journal of Documentation*, Vol. 62, No. 3, 2006, pp. 350–371.

Golub, Koraljka. *Subject Access to Information: An Interdisciplinary Approach*. Santa Barbara, CA: Libraries Unlimited, 2014.

Golub, Koraljka, and Liu, Ying-Hsang (Eds). *Information and Knowledge Organisation in Digital Humanities: Global Perspectives*. London: Routledge, 2022.

Goodman, Martin. *A History of Judaism*. Princeton, NJ: Princeton University Press, 2018.

Goody, Jack. *The Domestication of the Savage Mind*. Cambridge: Cambridge University Press, 1977.

Gottheil, Richard. "Libraries." *The Jewish Encyclopedia*. New York: Funk & Wagnalls, 1906.

Grolier, Eric de. *Théorie et Pratique des Classifications Documentaires*. Paris: Union Française des Organismes de Documentation, 1956.

Grolier, Eric de. *A Study of General Categories Applicable to Classification and Coding in Documentation*. Deventer: UNESCO, 1962.

Grolier, Eric de. "Classifications as Cultural Artefacts." In Ingetraut Dahlberg (Ed.), *Universal Classification I: Subject Analysis and Ordering Systems*. Franfurt: Indeks Verlag, 1982, pp. 19–34.

Gustavsson, Bernt. *Bildningens väg: Tre bildningsideal i svensk arbetarrörelse 1880–1930*. Stockholm: Wahlström & Widstrand, 1991.

Gustavsson, Bernt. "The Idea of Democratic *Bildung*: Its Transformations in Time and Space." In Ann-Marie Laginder, Henrik Norvall, and Jim Crowther (Eds.), *Popular Education, Power, and Democracy: Swedish Experiences and Contributions*. Leicester: National Institute of Adult Continuing Education, 2013, pp. 35–49.

Hansson, Joacim. "In My Mind's Eye: In Search for the Mimetic Relation between a Library Classification System and Its Social Discourses." In Peter Ingwersen and Nils-Ole Pors (Eds.), *Information Science: Integration in Perspective*. Copenhagen: The Royal School of Librarianship, 1996, pp. 99–115.

Hansson, Joacim. "Why Public Libraries in Sweden Did Not Choose Dewey." *Knowledge Organization*, Vol. 24, No. 3, 1997, pp. 145–153.

Hansson, Joacim. "Hermeneutics as a Bridge between the Modern and the Post-Modern in Library and Information Science." *Journal of Documentation*, vol. 61, No. 1, 2005, pp. 102–113.

Hansson, Joacim. *Libraries and Identity: The Role of Institutional Self-Image and Identity in the Emergence of New Types of Libraries*. Oxford: Chandos, 2010.

Hansson, Joacim. "Representativity and Complementarity in Tai Chi as Embodied Documentation." *Proceedings from the Document Academy*, Vol. 4, No. 2, 2017a, Article 11.

Hansson, Joacim. "Professional Value and Ethical Self-Regulation in the Development of Modern Librarianship: The Documentality of Library Ethics." *Journal of Documentation*, Vol. 73, No. 6, 2017b, pp. 1261–1280.

Hansson, Joacim. "Bringing Political Upheaval and Cultural Trauma into Order: A Document-Theoretical Approach to the Social Significance of Bibliographic Classification Systems." *Proceedings from the Document Academy*, Vol. 8, No. 2, 2021, Article 5.

Hansson, Joacim. "Classification Systems for Jewish Libraries and Bibliographies: Philosophy, Warrants, and Relation to Non-Jewish Bibliographic Practice." *Journal of Religious and Theological Information*, Vol. 21, No. 3–4, 2022, pp. 99–121.

Hansson, Joacim. *De ordnade böckernas folk: Om klassifikation i judiska bibliografier och bibliotek*. Stockholm: Hillelförlaget, 2022.

Hansson, Joacim. *Dewey och de svenska biblioteken*. Lund: BTJ Förlag, 2023.

Hansson, Joacim. "The Informative Potential of Bibliographic Classification Systems: Reflections on a Discussion in the French Documentation Movement." *Journal of Documentation*, Vol. 80, No. 3, 2024, pp. 632–648.

Hauser, Elliott, and Tennis, Joseph. "Episemantics: Aboutness as Aroundness." *Knowledge Organization*, Vol. 46, No. 8, 2019, pp. 590–595.

Heimer, C. A. "Conceiving Children: How Documents Support Case versus Biographical Analysis." In Annelise Riles (Ed.), *Documents: Artifacts of Modern Knowledge*. Ann Arbor: University of Michigan Press, 2006, pp. 95–126.

Hirsch, Abraham, and Leipzinger, Harald. *Meddelande från Mosaiska församlingens bibliotek*. Stockholms Mosaiska Församling, 1899.

Hjelmqvist, Fredrik. "Dewey's klassificeringssystem och Cutter's namntabeller." *Biblioteksbladet*, Vol. 1, 1916, pp. 112–114.

Hjelmqvist, Fredrik. "Något om tillkomsten av SAB:s klassifikations- och katalogiseringsregler." *Biblioteksbladet*, Vol. 35, 1950, pp. 350–352.

Hjørland, Birger. *Information Seeking and Subject Representation: An Activity-Theoretical Approach to Information Science*. Westport, CT: Greenwood Press, 1997.

Hyllsignum Judiska biblioteket. Stockholm: Stockholm Jewish Library, n.d.

Ibekwe-SanJuan, Fidelia. *La science de l'information: Origine, théories et paradigms*. Paris: Lavoisier, 2012.

Ingwersen, Peter, and Kalervo Järvelin. *The Turn: Integration of Information Seeking and Retrieval in Context*. Dordrecht: Springer, 2005.

Iriye, Akira. *Cultural Internationalism and World Order*. Baltimore: Johns Hopkins University Press, 1997.

Izenberg, Gerald. *Identity: The Necessity of a Modern Idea*. Philadelphia: Pennsylvania University Press, 2016.

Jacobowsky, Carl Vilhelm. "Något om Stockholms mosaiska församlings bibliotek." *Judisk Tidskrift*, Vol. 1, No. 8, 1928, pp. 263–266.

Janton, Pierre. *Esperanto: Language, Literature, and Community*. Albany, NY: State University of New York Press, 1993.

Jerchower, Seth, and Lerner, Heidi G. "Johann Heinrich Hottinger and the Systematic Organization of Jewish Literature." *Judaica Librarianship*, Vol. 13, 2007, pp. 1–25.

Jerónimo, Miguel Bandeira, and Monteiro, José Pedro (Eds.), *Internationalism, Imperialism and the Formation of the Contemporary World: The Pasts of the Present*. Cham: Palgrave Macmillan, 2017.

Jewish National and University Library. *Classification for Judaica: As Used in the Judaica Department of the Jewish National and University Library*. Jerusalem: Jewish National and University Library, 1964.

Kalvemark, A. S. "Malthus and Neo-Malthusianism in Sweden." *Statistical Review*, Vol. 18, No. 6, 1980, pp. 481–486.

Kant, Immanuel. *An Answer to the Question: 'What Is Enlightenment?'* London: Penguin Books, 1784/2009.

Kelly, Matthew. "Hermeneutics and Information Science: The Ongoing Journey from Simple Objective Interpretation to Understanding Data as a Form of Disclosure." In Matthew Kelly and Jared Bielby (Eds.), *Information Cultures in the Digital Age: A Festschrift in Honor of Raphael Capurro*. Wiesbaden: Springer, 2016, pp. 83–110.

Kjellman, Ulrika. "A Whiter Shape of Pale: Visuality and Race in the Work of The Swedish Institute for Race Biology." *Scandinavian Journal of History*, Vol. 38, No. 2, 2013, pp. 180–201.

Kjellman, Ulrika. "How to Picture Race? The Use of Photography in the Scientific Practice of the Swedish State Institute for Race Biology." *Scandinavian Journal of History*, Vol. 39, No. 5, 2014, pp. 580–611.

"Klassifikationssystem (plan för uppdelningen i en systematisk katalog)." *Biblioteksbladet*, Vol. 5, 1920, pp. 161–162.

Klassifikationssystem för svenska bibliotek. Stockholm: Norstedts, 1921.

Klasson, Maj. "Knowledge Organization as a Mirror of Society." *Social Change and Adult Education Research: Adult Education Research in The Nordic Countries 1994*. Linköping: Linköping University Adult Education Research Group, 1995, pp. 19–34.

Kloe, Fabian de. "Beyond Babel: Esperanto, Ido and Louis Couturat's Pursuit of an International Scientific Language." In W. Boyd Rayward (Ed.), *Information Beyond Borders: International Cultural and Intellectual Exchange in the Belle Époque*. London: Routledge, 2014, pp. 109–122.

Koehler, Wallace. *Ethics and Values in Librarianship: A History*. Lanham, MD: Rowman & Littlefield, 2015.

Krajewski, Markus. "Organizing a Global Idiom: Esperanto, Ido and the World Auxiliary Language Movement before the First World War." In Boyd Rayward (Ed.), *Information Beyond Borders: International Cultural and Intellectual Exchange in the Belle Époque*. London: Routledge, 2014, pp. 97–108.

Kungliga biblioteket. *Accessionskatalog 28: Sveriges offentliga bibliotek: Stockholm, Uppsala, Lund, Göteborg*. Stockholm: Kungliga biblioteket, 1913.

Kungl. Ecklesiastikdepartementet. *Katalog över böcker som folk- och skolbibliotek samt riksförbund som bedriva biblioteksverksamhet kunna erhålla i stadsbidrag: Grundkatalog 1915–1916*. Stockholm: Kungl. Ecklesiastikdepartementet, 1915.

Langridge, Derek W. *Classification and Indexing in the Humanities*. London: Butterworths, 1976.

Laqua, Daniel. "Transnational Endeavours and the 'Totality of Knowledge': Paul Otlet and Henri LaFontaine as 'Integral Internationalists' in *Fin-de-Siècle* Europe. In Grace Brockington (Ed.), *Internationalism and the Arts in Britain and Europe at the Fin de Siècle*. Bern: Peter Lang, 2009, pp. 247–271.

Laqua, Daniel. *The Age of Internationalism and Belgium, 1880–1930: Peace, Progress and Prestige*. Manchester: Manchester University Press, 2013.

Latour, Bruno. "Ces reseaux que la raison ignore: Laboratoires, bibliothèques, collections." In Marc Baratin and Christian Jacob (Eds.), *Le pouvoir des bibliothèques: La memoire des livres en Occident*. Paris: Albin Michel, 1996, pp. 23–46.

Levie, Françoise. *L'homme qui voulait classer le monde: Paul Otlet et le Mundaneum*. Bruxelles: Les Impressions Nouvelles, 2006.

Levy, David. B. "Ancient to Modern Jewish Classification Systems: An Overview from Beit HaMikdash Temple Archive to H.a. Wolfson, G. Sholem, A. Freidus, D.Elazar & LC." *Proceedings of the 36th Annual Convention of the Association for Jewish Libraries*, La Jolla, CA, June 24–27, 2001, pp. 1–11. Paper also reprinted in self-published volume: Levy, David B. *The History of Judaica Libraries: Vol. 1*, 2019, pp. 38–57.

Lloyd, A., and Wilkinson, J. "Tapping into the Information Landscape: Refugee Youth Enactment of Information Literacy in Everyday Spaces." *Journal of Librarianship and Information Science*, Vol. 51, No. 1, 2017, pp. 252–259.

Lorenz, B. "Some Historical Remarks on Library Classification: A Short Introduction to the Science of Library Classification." In C. Weihs and G. Gaul (Eds.), *Classification: The Ubiquitous Challenge*. Berlin: Springer, 2005, pp. 506–512.

Lund, Niels Windfeld. *Introduction to Documentation Studies*. London: Facet, 2024.

Maack, M. N. "The Lady and the Antelope: Suzanne Briet's Contribution to the French Documentation Movement." *Library Trends*, Vol. 52, No. 4, 2004, pp. 719–747.

Mai, Jens-Erik. "Classification in a Social World: Bias and Trust." *Journal of Documentation*, Vol. 66, No. 5, 2010, pp. 627–642.

Mai, Jens-Erik. "The Modernity of Classification." *Journal of Documentation*, Vol. 67, No. 4, 2011, pp. 710–730.

Mendes-Flohr, P. "The Emancipation of European Jewry: Why Was It Not Self-Evident?" *Studia Rosenthaliana*, Vol. 30, No. 1, 1996, pp. 7–20.

Morgan, Michael L. "To Seize Memory: History and Identity in Post-Holocaust Jewish Thought." In Alvin H. Rosenfeld (Ed.), *Thinking about the Holocaust after Half a Century*. Bloomington/Indianapolis: Indiana University Press, 1997, pp. 151–181.

Montoya, Robert. *Power of Position: Classification and the Biodiversity Sciences*. Cambridge, MA: MIT Press, 2022.

Moura, Amanda Pacini de. "Consideration on the Social Role of the Document According to Paul Otlet." *Proceedings of the 77th ASIS&T Annual Meeting*, Seattle, 2014.

Naudé, Gabriel. *Advis pour dresser une bibliothèque*. Paris: Klincksieck, 1644/1994.

Nordesjö, Hans. "The Jacobowsky Collection of Judaica at Uppsala University Library." In Sten Hedberg (Ed.), *Serving the Scholarly Community: Essays on Tradition and Change in Research Libraries*. Uppsala: Uppsala University Library, 1995, pp. 205–212.

Norrby, Malin. "Judiska biblioteket: En del av berättelsen om stora synagogan." In Marina Burstein (Ed.), *Jag må bo mitt ibland dem: Stockholms stora synagoga 150 år*. Stockholm: Hillelförlaget/ Judiska församlingen i Stockholm, 2020, pp. 137–143.

Nussbaum, Martha. *Cultivating Humanity: A Classical Defense of Reform in Liberal Education*. Cambridge, MA: Harvard University Press, 1997.

Nussbaum, Martha. *Not for Profit: Why Democracy Needs the Humanities*. Princeton, NJ: Princeton University Press, 2010.

Ogilvie, Brian W. *The Science of Describing: Natural History in Renaissance Europe*. Chicago: The University of Chicago Press, 2006.

Olson, Hope. "Patriarchal Structures of Subject Access and Subversive Techniques for Change." *The Canadian Journal of Information and Library Science*, Vol. 26, No. 2–3, 2001, pp. 1–29.

Olson, Hope A. *The Power to Name: Locating the Limits of Subject Representation in Libraries*. Dordrecht: Kluwer, 2002.

Otlet, Paul. *Manuel du répertoire bibliographique universel: extraits limités aux parties plus spécialment applicables à la bibliographie de la langue auxilliarie international Esperanto*. Bruxelles: Institute International de Bibliographie, 1908.

Otlet, Paul. *L'organisation international et les associations internationales*. Bruxelles: Office Central des Institutions Internationales, 1910.

Otlet, Paul. *La fin de la guerre: Traité de paix générale basé sur une charte mondiale declarant les droits de l'humanité et organisant la confédération des états*. Bruxelles: Oscar Lamberty, 1914.

Otlet, Paul. *Monde: Essai d'universalisme*. Bruxelles: Editions de Mundaneum, 1935.

Otlet, Paul. *Traité de Documentation: Le livre sur le livre*. Bruxelles: Mundaneum / Les Impressions Nouvelles, 2015 (Facsimile. Orig: Editions Mundaneum/Palais Mondial, 1934).

Otlet, Paul. "Creation of a Universal Bibliographic Repertory: A Preliminary Note." In W. Boyd Rayward (Ed.), *International Organisation and Dissemination of Knowledge: Selected Essays of Paul Otlet*. Amsterdam: FID/Elevier, 1990, pp. 25–50.

Otlet, Paul. "On the Structure of Classification Numbers." In W. Boyd Rayward (Ed.), *International Organisation and Dissemination of Knowledge: Selected Essays of Paul Otlet*. Amsterdam: FID/Elevier, 1990, pp. 51–62.

Otlet, Paul, and LaFontaine, Henri. "The Union of International Associations: A World Centre." In W. Boyd Rayward (Ed.), *International Organisation and Dissemination of Knowledge: Selected Essays of Paul Otlet*. Amsterdam: FID/Elevier, 1990, pp. 112–129.

Pagès, Robert. *Problèmes de classification culturelle et documentaire*. Paris: Union Française des Organismes de Documentation, 1955.

Pagès, Robert. "Transformations Documentaires et Milieu Culturel (1948)." *Proceedings from the Document Academy*, Vol. 8, No. 1, 2021a, Article 3.

Pagès, Robert. "Documentary Transformations and Cultural Context." *Proceedings from the Document Academy*, Vol. 8, No. 1, 2021b, Article 2.

Palmgren, Valfrid. *Bibliotek och folkuppfostran: Anteckningar från en studieresa i Amerikas förenta stater.* Stockholm: P. A. Norstedt & Söner, 1909.

Palmgren, Valfrid. *Förslag angående de åtgärder som från statens sida böra vidtagas för främjandet af det allmänna biblioteksväsendet i Sverige, afgifvet den 28 september 1911.* Stockholm: Ecklesiastikdepartementet, 1911.

Polastron, Lucien X. *Books on Fire: The Tumultuous Story of the World's Great Libraries.* London: Thames & Hudson, 2007.

Rayward, W. Boyd. *The Universe of Information: The Work of Paul Otlet for Documentation and International Organization.* Moscow: All-Union Institute for Scientific and Technical Information, 1975.

Rayward, W. Boyd (Ed.). *Information beyond Borders: International Cultural and Intellectual Exchange in the Belle Époque.* London: Routledge, 2014.

Richardson, Ernest Cushing. *Classification: Theoretical and Practical.* New York: Charles Scribner's Sons, 1901.

Ricoeur, Paul. *Time and Narrative*, vol. 1. Chicago: The University of Chicago Press, 1984.

Ricoeur, Paul. *Time and Narrative*, vol. 2. Chicago: The University of Chicago Press, 1985.

Ricoeur, Paul. *Time and Narrative*, vol. 3. Chicago: The University of Chicago Press, 1988.

Riggsby, Andrew M. *Mosaics of Knowledge: Representing Information in the Roman World.* Oxford: Oxford University Press, 2019.

Riusset-Lamariet, I. "P. Otlet's Mundaneum and the International Perspective in the History of Documentation and Information Science." *Journal of the American Society for Information Science*, Vol. 48, No. 4, 1997, pp. 301–309.

Rosemont, H. "On Representing Abstractions in Archaic Chinese." *Philosophy East and West*, Vol. 24, 1974, pp. 71–88.

Rosenfeld, Alvin H. "The Americanization of the Holocaust." In A. Rosenfeld (Ed.), *Thinking about the Holocaust after Half a Century.* Bloomington/Indianapolis: Indiana University Press, 1997, pp. 119–150.

Sandberg, Alvida. *Bibliotek och biblioteksskötsel: en hjälpreda för bibliotekarier i skolbibliotek och andra mindre boksamlingar.* Stockholm: Norstedts, 1915.

Saracevic, Tefko. "Relevance: A Review of and a Framework for the Thinking on the Notion in Information Science." *Journal of the American Society for Information Science*, Vol. 26, No. 6, 1975, pp. 321–343.

Saracevic, Tefko. "Relevance: A Review of the Literature and a Framework for Thinking on the Notion in Information Science. Part II: Nature and Manifestations of Relevance." *Journal of the American Society for Information Science and Technology*, Vol. 58, No. 13, 2007a, pp. 1915–1933.

Saracevic, Tefko. "Relevance: A Review of the Literature and a Framework for Thinking on the Notion in Information Science. Part III: Behavior and Effects of Relevance." *Journal of the American Society for Information Science and Technology*, Vol. 58, No. 13, 2007b, pp. 2126–2144.

Satija, M. P., and Kyrios, Alex. *A Handbook of History, Theory, and Practice of the Dewey Decimal Classification System*. London: Facet, 2023.

Sax, Monica. *Mosaiska församlingens bibliotek I Stockholm: Dess verksamhet och organisation*. Borås: Högskolan i Borås, 1980. Specialarbete 1980:19.

Schoppert, Amy. "A Review of the Literature on Elazar's Classification System for Libraries of Judaica." *Cataloging & Classification Quarterly*, Vol. 52, No. 4, 2014, pp. 422–430.

Schorsh, Ismar. *From Text to Context: The Turn to History in Modern Judaism*. Hanover: Brandeis University Press, 1994.

Schrijvers, Emile G. L. "The Hebraic Book." *A Companion to the History of the Book*. Eds. Simon Eliot and Jonathan Rose. Malden, MA: Blackwell, 2009, pp. 153–164.

Shavit, David. "Jewish Libraries in the Polish Ghettos during the Nazi Era." *Library Quarterly*, Vol. 52, no. 2, 1982, pp. 103–121.

Shera, Jesse Hauk. *Libraries and the Organization of Knowledge*. London: Crosby Lockwood, 1965.

Siljeström, Per A. "Förslag till inrättandet af sockenbiblioteker och hwad derwid bör iakttagas jemte förteckning å dertill lämpliga böcker och skrifter." *Läsning för folket*, Vol. 25, No. 1, 1859, 47–68.

Siracusa, Mariana. "Paul Otlet's Theory of Everything." *AA Files*, No. 73, 2016, pp. 48–57.

Skare, Roswitha. "Complementarity: A Concept for Document Analysis?" *Journal of Documentation*, Vol. 65, No. 5, 2009, pp. 834–840.

Smiraglia, Richard. "The Progress of Theory in Knowledge Organization." *Library Trends*, Vol. 50, No. 3, 2002, pp. 330–349.

Smiraglia, Richard. *Cultural Synergy in Information Institutions*. New York: Springer, 2014.

Smiraglia, Richard. *Elements of Knowledge Organization*. New York: Springer, 2014.

Strauss, Anselm. "Social Worlds and Legitimation Processes." *Studies in Symbolic Interaction*, Vol. 4, 1982, pp. 171–190.

Sroka, Marek. "The Destruction of Jewish Libraries and Archives during World War II." *Libraries & Culture*, Vol. 38, No. 2, 2003, pp. 147–165.

Steenberg, Andreas Schack. "De nordiske lands folkebiblioteker og amerikanske systemer." *Biblioteksbladet*, Vol. 1, 1916, pp. 115–119.

Studentföreningen Verdandis folkbiblioteks-katalog jämte upplysningar och råd angående bildandet, skötseln och förkofrandet af folkbibliotek, 4th ed. Uppsala: Studentföreningen Verdandi, 1908.

Suominen, Vesa. *About and On Behalf of Scriptum Est: The Literary, Bibliographic, and Educational Rationality Sui Generis of the Library and Librarianship on Top of What Literature Has Produced*. Oulu: University of Oulu, 2016. (Studia Humaniora Ouluensia, 15)

Svenonius, Elaine. *The Intellectual Foundation of Information Organization*. Cambridge, MA: MIT Press, 2000.

Svenonius, Elaine."The Epistemological Foundations of Knowledge Representations." *Library Trends*, Vol. 52, No. 3, 2004, pp. 571–587.

Tanselle, G. Thomas. *Bibliographical Analysis: A Historical Introduction*. Cambridge: Cambridge University Press, 2009.

Tega, Walter. "Paul Otlet, Otto Neurath, Le Corbusier: Un project pour la paix perpétuelle." *Revue de Métaphysique et de Morale*, No. 4, 2014, pp. 545–559.

Teplitsky, Joshua. *Prince of the Press: How One Collector Built History's Most Enduring and Remarkable Jewish Library*. New Haven, CT: Yale University Press, 2019.

Torstensson, Magnus. "Expectations and a Worthy, Respectable Position in Society: Means and Aims of Library Work within the Early Labour Movement in Sweden." *Swedish Library Research*, No. 1, 1995, 16–26.

Torstensson, Magnus. "Framväxten av en statlig folkbibliotekspolitik i Sverige." In Anders Frenander and Jenny Lindberg (Eds.), *Styra eller stödja: Svensk folkbibliotekspolitik under hundra år*. Borås: Högskolan i Borås, 2012, pp. 89–134.

Trosow, S. "Standpoint Epistemology as an Alternative Methodology for Library and Information Science." *Library Quarterly*, Vol. 71, No. 3, 2001, pp. 360–382.

Tsien, Tsuen-Hsuin. "A History of Bibliographic Classification in China." *The Library Quarterly*, Vol. 22, No. 4, 1952, pp. 307–324.

Tynell, Knut. *Folkbiblioteken i Sverige*. Stockholm: P. A. Norstedts & söners förlag, 1931.

Weinberg, Bella Hass. "Hebraica Cataloging and Classification." In Mohammed M. Aman (Ed.), *Cataloging and Classification of Non-Western Material: Concerns, Issues and Practices*. Phoenix, AZ: Oryx Press, 1980, pp. 321–357.

Weinberg, Bella Hass. "Judaica Classification Schemes for Synagogue and School Libraries: A Structural Analysis." *Judaica Librarianship*, Vol. 1, No. 1, 1983, pp. 26–30.

Weinberg, Bella Hass. "The Hidden Classification in Library of Congress Subject Headings for Judaica." *Library Resources & Technical Services*, Vol. 37, No. 4, 1993, pp. 369–380.

Weinberg, Bella Hass. "The Earliest Hebrew Citation Indexes." *Journal of the American Society for Information Science*, Vol. 48, No. 4, 1997, pp. 318–330.

Weinberg, Bella Hass. "Indexes and Religion: Reflections on Research in the History of Indexes." *The Indexer*, Vol. 21, No. 3, 1999, pp. 111–118.

Weine, Mae. "Preface to the Seventh Edition." *Weine Classification Scheme and Relative Index for Judaica Libraries*, 9th ed. Revised by the Weine Revision Committee and Joel Tuschman. Los Angeles: Association of Jewish Libraries, 2013, pp. 1–2.

Wiegand, Wayne A. *Irrepressible Reformer: A Biography of Melvil Dewey*. Chicago: American Library Association, 1996.

Wildemuth, Barabara M. *Applications of Social Research Methods to Questions in Information and Library Science*. Westport, CT: Libraries Unlimited, 2009.

Woledge, G. "'Bibliography' and 'Documentation': Words and Ideas." *Journal of Documentation*, Vol. 39, No. 4, 1983, pp. 266–279.

Wolfson, Harry Austryn. "The Classification of Sciences in Medieval Jewish Philosophy." In David Philipson (Ed.), *Hebrew Union College Jubilee Volume*. Cincinnati: Hebrew Union College, 1925, pp. 263–315.

Wright, Alex. *Cataloging the World: Paul Otlet and the Birth of the Information Age*. Oxford: Oxford University Press, 2014.

INDEX

Aboutness, 25, 30
Adde, Gustav, 107
Advis pour dresser une bibliothèque (book), 5
Age of bibliography, 128
Age of description, 128
Alexander, Jeffrey C., 135–137
American Jewry, 135–136, 144
Andersen, Benedict, 107
Andersen, Jack, 135
An Answer to the Question: "What Is Enlightenment?" (book), 93
Arabic organization of knowledge, 131
Aristotelian classification, 3, 6, 35, 126, 128–130, 150
Aristotelian philosophy of knowledge, 127–128, 130
Aristotelian understaning of Mimesis, 56–57, 153
Aristotle, 12, 57, 128
Artificial Language Movement, The, 46, 63
Arts and Crafts Movement, 63

Bacon, Francis (philosopher), 12, 35, 52, 62
Bar-Levav, Avriel, 133
Bass, Shabbethai, 131–133, 156
Bates, Marcia, 70, 73
Bauer, Yehuda, 136
Bauman, Zygmunt, 137
Beghtol, Claire, 13–18
Benjamin, Walter, 10, 50, 140
Bibliographic language, 70, 83
Bibliographic objects, 26
Bibliographic paradigm, 29–30
  critique of, 29
Bibliology, 61, 71
Bibliotheca Rabbinica Nova, 133
Bibliotek och biblioteksskötsel (book), 106
Bibliotek och folkuppfostran (book), 95
Biblioteksbladet (journal), 104, 106, 110
Bibliotheca Universalis, 4, 5, 35, 44
Bildung, 88, 91–93, 96, 112, 139
Blair, Ann, 44, 133
Bliss, Henry Evelyn, 34, 37–38, 51
Bloch, Joshua, 134
Briet, Suzanne, 19, 25–30, 38–39, 48, 49–50, 54
Brockington, Grace, 64

Buckland, Michael, 28–29, 34, 39
Buxtorf, Johannes, 133

Century of the Child, The (book), 94–95
Cité mondial. *See* World City
Classification, Theoretical and Practical (book), 34–36
Classification System for Libraries of Judaica. *See* Elazar System, The
Classification systems as autonomous documents, 2, 13, 51, 56, 152–153, 158
Classification systems as bibliographic language, 70
Classification systems as cultural artefacts, 11, 17–18
Classificatory landscape, 16
Coercive isomorphism, 54–55, 120, 157
Complementarity (concept), 167n23
Concilium Bibliographicum, 173n15
Configuration, methodological, 57–58, 124. *See also* Prefiguration, methodological; Refiguration, methodological
Conservatoire National des Arts et Métiers (CNAM), 50–51
Le Corbusier, 66
Cornelius, Ian, 49
Critical padagogy, 99
Cultural Internationalism and World Order (book), 64

Day, Ronald E., 27–30, 48–50
Dewey, Melvil, 7, 35, 45, 55, 61, 65, 73, 77, 84, 107, 140
Digital humanities, 15
DiMaggio, Paul, 53–55, 57–58, 86, 120, 156
Document (concept), 26–34, 40
Documentality (concept), 30–35
Documentality: Why it is Necessary to Leave Traces (book), 32
Documentary agency, 2, 8, 30–33, 63, 86, 151, 156
Documentation and information, Relation between, 29
Documentation as communication, 52, 171n20
Documentation as cultural technique, 38, 45, 49, 58
Documentation as practice, 27, 50, 64
Document theory, 19, 39, 48, 50, 152
Domestication of the Savage Mind, The (book), 17

Elazar, Daniel, 10, 144–145
Elazar, David, 10, 144–145, 146
Elazar System, The, 10, 144–150, 155, 160
Esperanto, 61, 63, 69, 75–86, 153–155, 159
Ethnorace (concept), 125
Eurocentric colonial values, 113
European bibliographic tradition, 62

Fairthorne, Robert, 16
Fédération de Information et Documentation, 75
Ferraris, Maurizio, 32, 39–40
Field, Herbert Haviland, 173n15
First-wave feminism, 63
La Fontaine, Henri, 46, 64–68, 71–75, 85, 87, 94
La Fontaine, Léonie, 68
Freedman, Vanessa, 126, 141
Freidus, Abraham Solomon, 9, 10, 134–135, 147
Freidus System, The, 134–135, 147
Frenander, Anders, 91
Frohmann, Bernd, 29–31, 34, 49
Funke, Erich, 77
Furner, Jonathan, 24–25

Gesner, Konrad, 4, 35, 44, 132–133
Golub, Koraljka, 22, 27, 31
Goody, Jack, 17–18, 39–40, 76, 157–158

Gottheil, Richard, 133–134
De Groliér, Eric, 11, 35, 38–40, 51, 54, 117
Gustavsson, Bernt, 92, 93

Harris, William, 52
Heidegger, Martin, 50
Heimdal, Student Association, 99–104, 110, 111, 117
Heimdal classification system, 101
Hermeneutics, 8, 18, 41, 49, 56, 149–150, 153, 158, 170n7
Hjørland, Birger, 23, 33, 133
Hobot ha-Lebavot (book), 130
Holocaust, 10, 47, 123–126, 135–137, 144, 150
  in Elazar system, 145
  in Stockholm system, 148
  in Weine system, 141–143
Hottinger, Johann Heinrich, 133, 157

Ibekwe-SanJuan, Fidelia, 166n1
Indexicality, 28, 30, 33, 51, 158–159
Indigenous languages, 76, 115, 116
Information landscape, 8, 16
Information organization, 30
Information retrieval, 2, 7–8, 10, 22, 24, 27, 31, 43, 49, 58, 75, 151–153, 157
Information science, paradigms, 166n1
Information systems, 152
Informative potential of documents, 23, 33, 40, 51–52, 133, 158–160
Ingwersen, Peter, 24
Institutional isomorphism, 44, 53, 155
International Institute of Bibliography, 63, 66–68, 75
Internationalism and the Art in Britain and Europe at the Fin de Siecle (book), 64
International Organization of Knowledge Organization (ISKO), 24, 38
International Peace Movement, 46, 64–65, 85, 116–117
Iriye, Akira, 64
Isomorphic change, 8, 41, 54–55, 124–126, 150–155
Isomorphic documentality, 56, 154, 157–159, 161
Isomorphic processes, 54, 56, 59, 154–155
Isomorphic properties, 69, 154
Isomorphism, 43, 44, 50, 52–53, 54–56, 120, 123, 155–156, 157
Izenberg, Gerald, 125

Jacobowsky, Carl Vilhelm, 138–139, 149
Jacobowsky Collection Classification, The, 138–139, 143, 146, 153, 160
Janton, Pierre, 76, 78
Järvelin, Kalervo, 24
Jewish identity, 9–10, 123, 131, 135, 150
Jewish librarianship, 123–124, 127, 134
Judaica classification, 128, 130, 134, 137, 140

Kabbalah, The, 134, 141
Kant, Immanuel, 89, 93
Key, Ellen, 92, 94, 95
Klassifikationssystem för svenska bibliotek. *See* SAB system, The
Klasson, Maj, 111
Knowledge organization (academic discipline), 25, 38, 44, 49, 58, 61, 72, 100
Kowledge organization systems, 2, 25

Laqua, David, 67
League of Nations, The, 117
Levy, David, 129–130
Librarianship, 7, 10, 31, 36, 38, 44, 55, 58, 61, 70, 72–73, 106–107, 109, 111, 123–125, 127–128, 134, 139–140, 146

Librarianship, professional ethics, 169n47
Library of Congress Classification, 113, 137–138, 141, 143, 146
Library of Congress Subject Headings, 143
Lloyd, Annemaree, 16
Lund, Niels Windfeld, 167n23

Malthusianism, 114, 119
Manuel abrégé du répertoire bibliographique, 8. *See also* Universal Decimal Classification, The
Manuel du repertoire bibliographique universel, 63. *See also* Universal Decimal Classification, The
Manuel du repertoire bibliographique universel applicable à la bibliographie de l'Esperanto, 63, 75, 78, 84. *See also* Universal Decimal Classification, The
Meaning and Method in Information Studies (book), 49
Meänkieli. *See* Indigenous languages
Medieval bibliographic practice, 5, 44, 129–131
Mimesis, definition, 56–57, 153
Mimetic process, 55, 86, 157
Mimetic representation, 8, 32, 118, 150, 152, 155
Mishnah, The, 127, 129, 132
Modernity, Critique of, 51–52
Monde (book), 69

National Union Catalog of Sweden, 96–97, 104–110, 111, 120
Naudé, Gabriel, 5–7, 35, 55
Nazism, 147–148
New Institutionalism in Organizational Analysis, The (book), 53
Nordisk tidskrift för bok- och biblioteksväsen (Journal), 107
Notation, 47, 51, 69–70, 72–73, 75, 83, 110, 139

Office central de documentation féminine, 68
Olson, Hope, 49
Oppenheim, David, 127, 128
Oral Torah, The, 132
Organization of Knowledge in Libraries, The (book), 34, 37
Otlet, Paul, 8, 19, 25, 28–29, 45–46, 48, 61–75, 77–78, 80–87, 94, 120, 153–154, 159

Pagès, Robert, 38, 41, 43, 49–50, 52–55, 85–86, 155
Palmgren, Valfrid, 8, 94–96, 103, 105–106, 108, 118
Pandectae, Addendum to Bibliotheca Universalis, 4
Parish libraries, 97, 98, 100, 102
People of the Book, 123,127
Polastron, Lucien, 128
Post-Holocaust classification, 135, 147
Powell, Walter, 53–55, 57–58, 86, 120, 156
Power to Name: Locating the Limits of Subject Representation, The (book), 49
Prefiguration, methodological, 58, 88, 124. *See also* Configuration, methodological; Refiguration, methodological
Problèmes de Classification culturelle et documentaire (book), 50–51
Professionalization of librarianship, 7, 31, 37, 58
Promtuarium, sive Biblioteca Orientalia (bibliography), 133
Public libraries, 7, 12, 37, 87–90, 94–97, 99, 100, 103–105, 107, 110–118, 121, 155–156, 159

Qu'est-ce que la documentation? (book). See *What Is Documentation?* (book)

Ranganathan, S. R., 31, 35
Refiguration, methodological, 57–58, 86, 124, 149–150. *See also* Configuration, methodological; Prefiguration, methodological
Relevance (concept), 25
Richardson, Ernest Cushing, 34, 36, 72
Ricoeur, Paul, 56–57, 153

SAB system, The, 9, 46–47, 86–87, 104, 106, 108, 110–119, 138–139, 143, 149, 155, 157, 159
Sámi languages. *See* Indigenous languages
Sandberg, Alvida, 106, 107, 108
Scandinavian bibliographic exchange, 105–106
Schleyer, Johan Martin, 77
Scholem, Gershom, 10, 139, 140–141, 143, 153–154
Scholem system, The, 10, 140–141
Seven Pillars of Wisdom, 130
Shavit, David, 138
Siftei yeshenim (bibliography), 128, 131–133, 150, 155–157, 160
Siljeström, P. A., 97, 98, 100
Skare, Roswitha, 167n23
Skouvig, Laura, 135
Smiraglia, Richard, 164n20
Social documentation, Theory of, 41, 50–52
Social epistemology, 164n20
Social question, The, 91
Social World (concept), 125
Social worlds, legitimizing strategies, 126–127
Steenberg, Andreas Schack, 105
Stockholm Jewish Library, 144, 146
Stockholm Jewish Library classification system, 147–148, 150, 160
Strauss, Anselm, 125–126, 129
Structural-semantic relations, 16, 112–113, 147, 151, 158
Study of General Categories Applicable to Classification and Coding in Documentation, A (book), 54
Subject Access to Information: An Interdisciplinary Approach (book), 22
Svenonius, Elaine, 14, 70
Swedish bibliographic tradition, 88, 106–110, 113, 155
Swedish Dewey debate, The, 104–110
Swedish Library Journal. See *Biblioteksbladet* (journal)
Swiss School of Bibliography, 132–133

Talmud, 127–129, 132, 134, 147, 160
Teplitsky, Joshua, 127, 131
Théorie et pratique des classifications documentaires (book), 34
Time and Narrative (book), 56–57, 153
Totality of knowledge, The, 68–69, 75
Traité de documentation (book), 69, 83–84
Translingua project, The, 77
Trivium et Quadrivium, 5, 35, 130
Turn: Integration of Information Seeking and Retrieval in Context, The (book), 24

UDC. *See* Universal Decimal Classification, The
Union Française des Organismes de Documentation (UFOD), 38
Union of International Associations, 65, 67
Universal bibliographic repertory, 65, 75
Universal Decimal Classification, The, 8, 45–46, 54, 61–63, 65, 69–87, 113, 138, 153–159. *See also* Manuel abrégé du répertoire bibliographique; Manuel du repertoire bibliographique universel; Manuel du repertoire bibliographique universel applicable à la bibliographie de l'speranto

Verdandi, Student Association, 99–105, 110–111, 117, 119

Verdandi classification system, 101
Volapük, 77–79, 81, 83

Warrants, classificatory, 10, 13–16, 23, 43, 45, 70, 118, 139, 152
  cultural, 13, 16, 45, 103, 118, 139, 141, 150, 152–153
  educational, 13
  institutional, 13, 15, 17, 18, 45, 118, 152
  literary, 11, 13–16, 45, 72, 118, 120, 132, 135
  scientific/philosophical, 13, 17, 45, 159
Weine, Mae, 140–143, 149, 160
Weine Classification System, 143–145, 149–150, 160
What Is documentation? (book), 26–27, 38
Wissenschaft des Judentums, 9, 132
Wolfson, Harry Austryn, 130
Women's Suffrage Movement, 46, 63, 68
Work of Art in the Age of Mechanical Reproduction, The (book), 50
World City, 8, 66, 75, 154
Written Torah, The, 132

Zamenhof, Lazar Ludwig, 77–78, 81, 83–84
Zionism, 139, 141–145, 147
Zohar, The (book), 141

Publisher contact:
The MIT Press
Massachusetts Institute of Technology
77 Massachusetts Avenue, Cambridge, MA 02139
mitpress.mit.edu

EU Authorised Representative:
Easy Access System Europe, Mustamäe tee 50,
10621 Tallinn, Estonia
gpsr.requests@easproject.com

Printed by Integrated Books International,
United States of America